CHOP WOOD
CARRY WATER

"Chop wood, carry water, every day."
Calligraphy courtesy of Al Huang

CHOP WOOD
CARRY WATER

A Guide to Finding Spiritual Fulfillment in Everyday Life

RICK FIELDS, WITH PEGGY TAYLOR, REX WEYLER, AND RICK INGRASCI
Editors of NEW AGE JOURNAL

Jeremy P. Tarcher/Perigee

Jeremy P. Tarcher/Perigee Books
are published by
The Putnam Publishing Group
200 Madison Avenue
New York, NY 10016

Library of Congress Cataloging in Publication Data

Main entry under title:
Chop wood, carry water.

　Bibliography
　1. Spiritual life—Addresses, essays, lectures.
I. Fields, Rick.
BL624.C476　　1984　　　　291.4′48　　　　84–23942
ISBN 0–87477–209–5

Design: MIKE YAZZOLINO

Manufactured in the United States of America
　12　13　14　15　16　17　18　19　20

For all of those, past, present, and future,
who make everyday life
an adventure of the spirit.

The authors would like to thank the following publishers and authors for permission to reprint material from their books:

Reprinted by permission from *The Caring Question* by Donald A. Tubesing and Nancy Loving Tubesing, copyright 1983 Augsburg Publishing House.

The Possible Human by Jean Houston, published by J. P. Tarcher, Inc. Copyright 1982 by Jean Houston.

Excerpt from *Person/Plant* by Theodore Roszak. Copyright © 1977, 1978 by Theodore Roszak. Reprinted by permission of Doubleday & Company, Inc.

The Briarpatch Book by Michael Phillips, reprinted by permission of the author.

From *The Three Boxes of Life* by Richard Nelson Bolles. Used with permission. Copyright 1981. Available from Ten Speed Press, Box 7123, Berkeley, CA 94707. $8.95 + $.75 for postage & handling.

Preprinted by permission of A & W Publishers, Inc. from *How to Help Your Child Have a Spiritual Life* by Annette Hollander, M.D. Copyright © 1980 by Annette Hollander.

Reprinted with permission from *Refining Your Life: From the Zen Kitchen to Enlightenment* by Dogen and Kosho Uchiyama, translated by Thomas Wright. Published by Waterhill, 1983.

The Psychology of Romantic Love by Nathaniel Branden. © 1980 by Nathaniel Branden, Ph.D. By permission of Bantam Books., Inc. All rights reserved.

The First Step by Zalman Schachter-Shalomi and Donald Gropman. © 1983 by Zalman Schachter-Shalomi and Donald Gropman. Reprinted by arrangement with Bantam Books, Inc. All rights reserved.

Be Here Now © 1972, Lama Foundation. Distributed by Crown Publishers, 1 Park Ave., New York NY 10016.

Lifeways: Working with Family Questions, edited by Gudrun Davy and Bons Voors. Published by Hawthorne Press, 1 Berkeley Villas, Lower Street, Stroud, Gloucestershire, GL5 2HU, England; U. S. distributor: St. George Books, P. O. Box 163, Nanuet, NY 10977.

Acknowledgments

A book like this is really the expression—and acknowledgment—of a whole community of people. In fact, hardly anyone in the "new age" community who crossed our path during the writing of *Chop Wood, Carry Water* escaped without revealing to us their favorite books, quotes, stories, leads, warnings, cautions, and recommendations of where to look further.

We would like, however, to especially acknowledge the following people for their contributions to the making of *Chop Wood, Carry Water*: Catherine Ingram was an invaluable editorial assistant and project coordinator during the first and last stages; Robert Hunter contributed writing and ideas to several chapters; Keith Thompson helped with discipline; Beverly Sky with photo research; Betsy Taylor with research on the Family chapter; Sandy MacDonald and Mary Goodell pitched in with editing expertise on various occasions; Dee Allen, then managing editor of *New Age*, kept us thinking positively; Dell Riddle, manager of Shambhala Booksellers in Cambridge, supplied books and advice with unfailing generosity; Millie Loeb, our first editor at Jeremy P. Tarcher, guided and occasionally pushed us along the path the book became; Hank Stine brought us through the final difficult birth, into the world. And finally, Jeremy P. Tarcher, that rare creature, a visionary publisher, brought the intensity and genuineness of his own search to the writing and publishing of this book.

Contents

Introduction

More than a thousand years ago a Chinese Zen master wrote a poem:

> Magical power,
>   marvelous action!
> Chopping wood,
>   carrying water . . .*

The message is just as true today as it was then: we can find the profoundest heights and depths of the spiritual life in our everyday life. We might think, however, that it is easier to find spirituality in an everyday life that consists of such simple, basic, down-to-earth tasks as "chopping wood and carrying water" than in the things we do in contemporary America—tasks such as working in an office or working out at a gym, balancing a checkbook or a relationship, attending to our family and our world. For those of us on a spiritual path, or just beginning a spiritual path, the question is how can we make all these things a part of the path? How can we apply the insights of the great spiritual traditions, and of our own experience, to the speedy, often bewildering confusion which is so much a part of everyday life in contemporary America?

In 1976—the year of America's bicentennial celebration—Tom Wolfe wrote that we are now "seeing the upward role (and not yet the crest, by any means) of the third great religious wave in American history, one that historians will very likely term the Third Great Awakening."

* From *Zen Forest*, translated by Soiku Sigematsu.

This Third Great Awakening has been called by many names: the consciousness movement, the New Age, the Aquarian Conspiracy—or, as we have come to think of it while working on this book—"the new spirituality."

This "new spirituality" is not really new, of course, but more of a form of something very old, of something that has always been present, if often hidden. Aldous Huxley called it "The Perennial Philosophy," and found it at the center of all the great mystical traditions. The most familiar formulation of The Perennial Philosophy in the West is perhaps the statement that "The kingdom of God is within you."

The sources of the new spirituality are wonderfully varied and diverse. For the first time in history we have access to the spiritual treasures of the whole earth. In libraries, bookstores, and on our own shelves we can have the benefit of the accumulated wisdom of Tibetan Buddhists, Persian Sufis, shamans from Mexico, Africa, and the Arctic, Christian hermits in Trappist monasteries in America, Hasidic rabbis from Brooklyn, and Hindu sadhus from Benares—to which we have added a few scientists, scholars, psychologists, artists, athletes, businesspeople, and poets. Seminars, conferences, audio and video tapes with teachers of common and exotic disciplines abound. The spiritual seeker of today is faced not with a lack of information, which seemed to be the case not so very long ago, but with a potential overload of advice and information. Truly our cup runneth over.

Certainly the task of making sense of all this and of integrating it into our lives is a formidable one. But whether the new spiritual seeker chooses to concentrate on one tradition in depth, or to follow a combination of paths or no path at all, the challenge, as for the Chinese Zen master a thousand years ago, is to live in such a way that there is no duality, no separation between the spiritual path and its manifestation in everyday life. The real challenge is, so to speak, to bring heaven down to earth, where we all live. It is a question of what Ram Dass has called "applied spirituality."

It is for the spiritual seeker, or would-be spiritual seeker (for we are all always beginners in matters of this kind) who is facing this challenge that we have written this book.

The authors, editors, and compilers of *Chop Wood, Carry Water* are a group of four people with a long association with *New Age Journal,* a magazine that has led, chronicled, and reported on the new spirituality for the last ten years. We are, in fact, as diverse and varied a lot as the new spirituality itself.

Rick Fields, whose grandparents were Russian Jewish immigrants, is a practicing Buddhist and author of *How the Swans Came to the Lake, A Narrative History of Buddhism in America.* He is a contributing editor of *New Age Journal* and is the editor of *The Vajradhatu Sun,* which he describes as the liveliest Buddhist newspaper in America. He lives in Boulder, Colorado.

Peggy Taylor, the editorial director of *New Age Journal,* was raised a Congregationalist, but grew up with a strong interest in healing, which she feels may have been inspired by a Christian Scientist grandfather who died soon after her birth. In addition to her work with *New Age Journal,* she teaches classes in self-healing and the Bates Method, a method for learning to see more clearly without glasses.

Rex Weyler, a contributing editor and former associate publisher of *New Age Journal,* was brought up Catholic, but now considers himself to be an "agrarian Buddhist." His own spiritual orientation has been strongly influenced by the American Indian view of life. He was a founder of the Greenpeace organization and is the author of *Blood of the Land,* a book about the American Indian Movement.

Rick Ingrasci, M.D., health editor of *New Age Journal,* is a physician who practices psychospiritual healing at Turning Point Family Wellness Center in Watertown, Massachusetts. He was brought up Catholic but his path as a healer has led him to focus on the role of consciousness expansion in self-healing and social transformation. He is a founder of Interface, one of the most successful holistic adult education centers in the country.

Chop Wood, Carry Water is thus a collaboration in the truest sense of the word. We have agreed to disagree more than once, and we have not worried about presenting diverse or even conflicting viewpoints on any given subject. We have scrutinized the areas of our everyday lives—sex, work, money, and play, for example—through the prism of our own experience, the experience of our friends and colleagues, and the experiences of the great sages of our time and of all time, and we have (we hope) let the fascinating facets of the resulting jewels speak for themselves.

The book that has resulted from this method is in a sense holographic, the part reflecting the whole, and the whole including all the parts. We have cut up the pie of our everyday lives into sixteen chapters somewhat arbitrarily perhaps, (wondering, for example, if it made any sense at all to talk about Sex and Relationships in two different chapters, or Money and Work), but we have tried not to forget one of the most important lessons we learned during the two years spent working on the book: that life is always one, at the moment we realize it.

This book, then, is a guide to the nearly limitless possibilities of the life of the spirit today. It is a handbook filled with advice and hints, stories, inspiration, encouragement, warnings and cautions, roadmaps and atlases for an inner journey as we live it everyday.

Some of our guides have been known to all of humanity for millenia: they are the world's great spiritual teachers—for example, Christ, the Buddha, Lao Tse, and Confucius. Others are our contemporaries, some well-known within the world of the new spirituality (many of these have appeared in the pages of *New Age Journal*), and others less so.

This is, finally, a guide for all those who want to live everyday life as part of the spiritual path, to get (and to give) the most from each moment of our life. We have focussed on the challenges we meet everyday: how to live more meaningfully with those we love, how to earn a living, how to find love and be loved, how to be a member of a family and community and planet, how to make play, health, art, sex, and business a reflection (and stimulus to growth) of our spiritual lives.

We have, in short, tried to bring heaven down to earth in these pages. We have gathered and culled the wisest and most practical books, advice, anecdotes, and stories—spiritual shop talk straight from the heart. This guide to spiritual fulfillment in everyday life contains the accumulated wisdom of the ages, as well as our own state-of-the-art collective wisdom, but the true guide, when we listen carefully to the silence between the words, turns out to be none other than ourselves.

—Rick Fields
July 1984

Beginnings

A Tibetan lama who crossed the Himalayas on foot during the Chinese occupation of his country was once asked how he had managed such a difficult journey. He replied: "One step at a time."

The *Tao Te Ching* of Lao Tzu says it another way:

"A tree as great as a man's embrace springs from a small shoot;

A terrace nine stories high begins with a pile of earth;

A journey of a thousand miles starts under one's feet."

Nearly anything can provide the opening or initial impetus for setting out on the spiritual journey. This "entry point," or first stage of the spiritual journey, says Marilyn Ferguson in *The Aquarian Conspiracy,* often has a quality of "happenstance" about it.

In most cases, the entry point can only be identified in retrospect. Entry can be triggered by anything that shakes up one's old understanding of the world, the old priorities. Sometimes it is a token investment, made out of boredom, curiosity or desperation—a ten-dollar book, a hundred-dollar mantra, a university extension course.

For a great many, the trigger has been a spontaneous mystical or psychic experience, as hard to explain as it is to deny. . . .

The entry point experience hints that there is a brighter, richer, more meaningful dimension to life. Some are haunted by that glimpse and drawn to see more. Others,

"That all things are possible to him who believes; that they are less difficult to him who hopes; that they are more easy to him who loves, and still more easy to him who perseveres in the practice of these three virtues."

BROTHER LAWRENCE

"Some people talk about finding God—as if He could get lost."

ANONYMOUS

less serious, stay near the entry point, playing with the occult, drugs, consciousness-altering games. Some are afraid to go on at all.

Peak Experiences

Frequently the experience that sets people on the spiritual path seems to come "out of the blue." It is an experience of intense happiness or joy, or unity or love that has much in common with the "mystical" visions described in traditional literature.

The psychologist Abraham Maslow called these experiences "peak-experiences." Maslow was the founder, in many ways, of what we now call Humanistic Psychology. He discovered the importance of peak-experiences when he took the unusual task of studying people who were healthy. "I picked out the finest, healthiest people, the best specimens of mankind I could find," he wrote in *The Journal of Humanistic Psychology* in 1962, "and studied them to see what they were like."

Maslow discovered that these people "tended to report having had something like mystic experiences, moments of great awe, moments of the most intense happiness or even rapture, ecstasy or bliss (because the word happiness can be too weak to describe this experience). . . .

"These moments," said Maslow, "were of pure, positive happiness when all doubts, all fears, all inhibitions, all tensions, all weaknesses, were left behind. Now self-consciousness was lost. All separateness and distance from the world disappeared as if they felt *one* with the world, fused with it, really belonging in it and to it, instead of being outside looking in. (One subject said, for instance, I felt like a member of a family not like an orphan.)"

Maslow noted that these peak-experiences "had mostly nothing to do with religion—at least in the ordinary supernaturalistic sense."

They came from the great moments of love and sex, from the great esthetic moments (particularly of music), from the bursts of creativeness and the creative furor (the great inspiration), from great moments of insight and of discovery, from women giving natural birth to babies—or just from loving them, from moments of fusion with nature (in

"What we call the beginning is often the end
And to make our end is to make a beginning.
The end is where we start from."

T. S. ELIOT

a forest, on a seashore, mountains, etc.), from certain athletic experiences, e.g. skindiving, from dancing, etc.

Maslow then found that these peak-experiences were "far more common than I had ever expected. As a matter of fact, I now suspect they occur in practically everybody although without being recognized or accepted for what they are."

The Ten Ox-Herding Drawings are classic Zen teaching tools. Here the boy, looking for his vanished ox, first sights the hoofprints that lead him to begin his journey.

The First Noble Truth

For some people, the spiritual journey begins with what may first seem to be a "negative" experience. The Buddha, for example, began his spiritual search in earnest when he realized that all beings were subject to old age, sickness, and death. The First Noble Truth of the Buddha is the truth of suffering or unsatisfactoriness. It was only after he had faced this truth in deep meditation that he was led to the discovery of the three other Noble Truths—the origin of suffering, the cessation of suffering, and the path leading to the cessation of suffering.

"Is it then not a mistake to precipitate the time of awakening? . . . Not the greatest master can go even one step for his disciple; in himself he must experience each stage of developing consciousness. Therefore he will know nothing for which he is not ripe."

DE LUBICZ

"As you walk, you cut open and create that riverbed into which the stream of your descendants shall enter and flow."

NIKOS KAZANTZAKIS

"I have always known
That at last I would
Take this road, but yesterday
I did not know that it would be today."

NARIHIRA (TRANSLATED
BY KENNETH REXROTH)

This sort of entry point may range from a nagging sense of discomfort and boredom—the feeling that *there must be something more*—to the feeling that St. John of the Cross described as "the dark night of the soul." In any case, the negative entry point results from a feeling that something is lacking, and though it may seem to be the opposite of the kind of positive peak-experiences described by Maslow, it can have the same effect—it propels us through the entry point of our spiritual journey.

Or our search may "begin with a restless feeling, as if one were being watched," Peter Matthiessen writes in *The Snow Leopard.* "One turns in all directions and sees nothing. Yet one senses that there is a source for this deep restlessness; and the path that leads there is not a path to a strange place, but a path home. . . ."

P. D. Ouspensky, a teacher of the G. I. Gurdjieff system and author of *In Search of the Miraculous,* reports receiving the following advice from Gurdjieff: "It can be said that there is one general rule for everybody. In order to approach this system seriously, people must be disappointed, first of all in themselves, that is to say in their powers, and secondly in all the old ways. . . ."

Chogyam Trungpa Rinpoche, a Tibetan Buddhist teacher, says in a similar vein: "Disappointment is the best chariot to use on the path of the Dharma."

Persevere

The wiser and more honest spiritual teachers warn that the first flush of enthusiasm so characteristic of the new spiritual seeker may be a kind of false dawn. At this stage the whole world is suddenly alight with new knowledge and it seems that all the problems of the world can be explained or understood and resolved according to a certain experience or system of belief.

Before too long, however, a certain disillusionment or uncertainty may appear. "Times of growth," the *I Ching* tells us in the hexagram called Difficulty at the Beginning, "are beset with difficulties. They resemble a first birth. But these difficulties arise from the very profusion of all that is struggling to attain form. Everything is in motion: therefore if one perseveres there is a prospect of great success."

Here it is important to follow the advice of the *I Ching:* persevere, again and again.

"If you must begin," Trungpa Rinpoche writes in *The Myth of Freedom,* "then go all the way, because if you begin and quit, the unfinished business you have left behind begins to haunt you all the time. The path, as Suzuki-roshi mentions in *Zen Mind, Beginner's Mind,* is like getting onto a train that you cannot get off; you ride it on and on."

How to Keep Your Perspective Along the Path

"Doing *sadhana* [spiritual practice] can be as much a trap as any other melodrama," says Ram Dass, author of *Be Here Now.* "It is useful to have some perspective about the path in order to keep yourself from getting too caught up in the stage in which you are working." These thirteen helpful pointers first appeared in *Be Here Now:*

1. Each stage that one can label must pass away. Even the labeling will ultimately pass. A person who says, "I'm enlightened" probably isn't.
2. The initial euphoria that comes through the first awakening into even a little consciousness, except in a very few cases, will pass away . . . leaving a sense of loss, or feeling of falling out of grace, or despair. *The Dark Night of the Soul,* by St. John of the Cross, deals with that state.
3. *Sadhana* is a bit like a roller coaster. Each new height is usually followed by a new low. Understanding this makes it a bit easier to ride with both phases.
4. As you further purify yourself, your impurities will seem grosser and larger. Understand that it's not that you are getting more caught in the illusion, it's just that you are seeing it more clearly. The lions guarding the gates of the temples get fiercer as you proceed toward each inner temple. But of course the light is brighter also. It all becomes more intense because of the additional energy involved at each stage of *sadhana.*
5. At first you will think of your *sadhana* as a limited part of your life. In time you will come to realize that everything you do is part of your *sadhana.*

6. One of the traps along the way is the *sattvic* trap—the trap of purity. You will be doing everything just as you should—and get caught in how pure you are. In India it's called the "golden chain." It's not a chain of iron, but it's still a chain. You'll have to finally give up even your idea of purity if you expect to do it all in this lifetime.

7. Early in the journey you wonder how long the journey will take and whether you will make it in this lifetime. Later you will see that where you are going is HERE and you will arrive NOW . . . so you stop asking.

8. At first you try. Later you just do your *sadhana* because, "What else is there to do?"

9. At certain stages you will take your *sadhana* very seriously. Later you will see the wisdom of the statement of Jesus that to seek the Lord, men need not disfigure their faces. Cosmic humor, especially about your own predicament, is an important part of your journey.

10. At some stages you will experience a plateau—as if everything had stopped. This is a hard point in the journey. Know that once the process has started it doesn't stop; it only appears to stop from where you are looking. Just keep going. It doesn't really matter whether you think "it's happening" or not. In fact, the thought "it's happening" is just another obstacle.

11. You may have expected that enlightenment would come ZAP! instantaneous and permanent. This is unlikely. After the first "ah ha" experience, the unfolding is gradual and almost indiscernible. It can be thought of as the thinning of a layer of clouds . . . until only the most transparent veil remains.

12. There is, in addition to the "up and down" cycles, an "in and out" cycle. That is, there are stages at which you feel pulled into inner work and all you seek is a quiet place to meditate and to get on with it. Then there are times when you turn outward and seek to be involved in the marketplace. Both of these parts of the cycle are a part of one's *sadhana*. For what happens to you in the marketplace helps in your meditation and what happens to you in meditation helps you to participate in the marketplace without attachment.

13. What is happening to you is nothing less than death and rebirth. What is dying is the entire way in which you understood "who you are" and "how it all is." What is being reborn is the child of the Spirit for whom things all are new. This process of attending an ego that is dying at the same time as you are going through a birth process is awesome. Be gentle and honor him (self) who is dying, as well as him (Self) who is being born.

Why Start

There are many reasons, then, to start the spiritual journey—possibly as many different reasons as there are people who undertake it. But the basic motivation is actually rather ordinary—the questioning intelligence and curiosity that is the birthright of every human being. We turn to the teachings and practices of the great spiritual traditions when the time is right, just as a flower blooms and rain falls when the time is right. The urge toward liberation is natural and, it often seems, inevitable. We simply want to help ourselves live more fully, and we want to help others do the same. But the turning inward that begins the spiritual search is perhaps most often the direct result of living our lives with others in the world: that in itself can serve as more than sufficient inspiration to begin the journey.

"There wouldn't be such a thing as counterfeit gold if there were no real gold somewhere."

OLD SUFI PROVERB

How to Begin

In the spiritual quest, as in any undertaking, we can only begin in the present, and we can only start from where we are. While this may seem obvious, it is often just this obvious fact that we tend to overlook. We want to begin at the "right" time and place—which usually turns out to be some time in the future and someplace else. Given this tendency, it is not surprising that so many of us never even begin.

Ouspensky met with his students when he knew he was dying. He refused to answer any of their questions about the system he had been teaching.

"In the landscape of the soul there is a desert, a wilderness, an emptiness, and all great singers must cross this desert to reach the beginning of their road. Jesus. Buddha. Moses. Mohammed. All wandered through the wasteland, speaking to demons, speaking to empty air, listening to the wind, before finding their dove, their bo tree, their stone tablets, before finding their true voice. I have hope for you exactly because I see you have entered this desert, following in the footsteps of those few who have been true teachers."

RAY FARADAY NELSON

"Genuine beginnings begin within us, even when they are brought to our attention by external opportunities."

WILLIAM BRIDGES

"Be simpler," he told them. "Start with what you know."

The necessary first step, then, is to acknowledge our present condition, even if it is (as it often is) one of confusion, hesitation, and doubt. This acknowledgement is the essence of spirituality. It is a simple act, but only by this simple act—seeing where we are rather than imagining where we would like to be—can we begin the process of transforming all those things we usually consider stumbling blocks into the stepping stones they really are.

Beginner's Mind

Many people feel that they cannot begin anything, especially anything spiritual in nature, unless they already are fairly well along on the path, or unless they know all the facts and details of one system or another. Others feel that they cannot begin until they have begun to live a more pure life—until, for instance, they have given up smoking, eating meat, or whatever.

But there is another way of looking at it. In his classic *Zen Mind, Beginner's Mind,* Shunryu Suzuki-roshi, the late founder of the San Francisco Zen Center, writes about the advantages of a mind that is open, uncluttered with preconceptions, flexible and curious. This attitude, says Suzuki-roshi, should be present during the whole journey, from beginning to end. "In the beginner's mind," he told his students, "there are many possibilities; in the expert's mind there are few."

It is in the beginning we are most acutely aware of what we don't know. This not-knowing can seem at first like simple ignorance, but if we stay with it—if we don't reject our "not-knowing"—we find that it is actually an important part of our intrinsic wisdom.

When Bodhidharma, the First Patriarch of Zen, traveled from India to China in the fifth century, the Chinese Emperor Wu asked him, "Who are you?"

"Don't know," he replied.

"Don't know mind" is the name for a method of meditation taught by the contemporary Korean Zen master Sahn Soen-Nim (whose talks are compiled in *Dropping*

Ashes on the Buddha.) "Don't know is clear mind," says Sahn Soen-Nim. "Practicing don't know you return to before thinking. Socrates used to go around Athens saying, 'You must know yourself.' Once a student of his asked him, 'Do *you* know yourself?' Socrates said, 'I don't know, but I understand this don't know.'"

The admission that we don't know is the first step on our journey toward knowledge.

At the beginning of the spiritual path, we are like children whose only real knowledge of themselves is a reflection cast in a mirror.

How to Give Birth to the Awakened Mind

"How to give birth to Bodhi, the awakened State of Mind?" writes Chogyam Trungpa Rinpoche, "There is always great uncertainty when you don't know how to begin and you seem to be perpetually caught up in the stream of life. A constant pressure of thoughts, of wandering thoughts and confusion and all kinds of desires continually arises. If you speak in terms of the man in the street he doesn't seem to have a chance, because he is never really able to look inwards; unless perhaps he reads some book on the subject and has the desire to enter into a disciplined way of life, and even then there seems to be no chance, no way to begin. People tend to make a very sharp distinction between spiritual life and everyday life. They will label a man as 'worldly' or 'spiritual' and they generally make a hard and fast division between the two.

"In fact, no one is excluded and all beings—anyone who possesses consciousness, anyone who possesses mind, or the unconscious mind—all are candidates for Bodhisattvahood, anyone can become an awakened person."

"Behold, I stand before the door and knock. And he who bids me enter, I will sup with him and he with me."

THE REVELATION OF ST. JOHN

Provisions for the Journey

Osel Tendzin (Thomas Rich), the American successor of Tibetan Buddhist meditation master Chogyam Trungpa Rinpoche, has written about the provisions for this journey in his book *Buddha in the Palm of Your Hand:*

Having a proper attitude towards journey is essential. If we make a journey properly, then everything we encounter is considered part of it. We are fully involved in the process of journeying rather than being fixated on our destination. We are not looking for quick solutions, but are willing to be open, precise, and thorough in relating with ourselves as well as all the facets of our environment—the weather, the scenery, the landmarks, and the obstacles or sidetracks along the way.

In entering the path to enlightenment, we are beginning the process of transforming confusion into wisdom. But in order to make this journey, we must first acknowledge that we are confused and that our environment is chaotic. Beyond that, we must understand that chaos and confusion are perpetuated because we do not have the training to see things as they are.

You Have to Be Somebody Before You Can Be Nobody

There is however a danger in forgetting the self that has ensnared many an unwary beginner on the path. At a recent conference on Buddhism and Mental Health sponsored by the Kuroda Institute in Los Angeles, clinical psychologist Steven Hendlin, Ph.D., discussed this danger in a paper on "Pernicious Oneness and Premature Disidentification."

Dr. Hendlin made the point that too often people try to lose their "ego," or sense of self, before they have actually worked through their own personal psychological material, and established a healthy sense of self—one which enables them to live effectively in the world. According to Dr. Hendlin this "trap" amounts to a "disrespect, discounting, or denigration" of the ego itself, and erroneously assumes that the normal concerns of the ego—such as being able to function well in the world—have nothing to do with the "quest for oneness." This amounts to what Dr. Hendlin calls "premature disidentification" with ego functions such as identity, security, and self-esteem.

"Put simply," says Dr. Hendlin, "you have to be somebody before you can be nobody."

Lessons to be Learned

All the spiritual traditions that find expression in the perennial philosophy agree that the central lesson to be learned from this journey is who you really are. This truth, as Aldous Huxley wrote, "is expressed most succinctly in the Sanskrit formula, *tat twam asi* (Thou art That)."

"When a man takes one step toward God, God takes more steps toward that man than there are sands in the worlds of time—this is called the Welcoming of God, or the Kaballah.

THE WORK OF THE CHARIOT

"In vain I have looked for a single man capable of seeing his faults and bringing the charge home against himself."

CONFUCIUS

Each of the major mystical systems has its own way of expressing this idea. The Hindus or Vedantists say that the Atman, or immanent eternal Self, is one with Brahman. Christians might say, "The kingdom of God is within you." Buddhists sometimes say, "You are the Buddha."

While this realization is actually at the heart of most spiritual traditions and journeys, in the culture at large it has been suppressed or ignored. "The most strongly enforced of all known taboos," writes Alan Watts in his basic primer, *The Book,* "is the taboo against knowing who or what you really are behind the mask of your apparently separate, independent, and isolated ego." This is the taboo that a person on the spiritual path must dare to break, a taboo created by society, authority and our own inner fear of knowing ourselves:

> As is so often the way, what we have suppressed and overlooked is something startlingly obvious. The difficulty is that it is *so* obvious and basic that one can hardly find the words for it. . . . The sensation of "I" as a lonely and isolated center of being is so powerful and commonsensical, and so fundamental to our modes of speech and thought, to our laws and social institutions, that we cannot experience selfhood except as something superficial in the scheme of the universe. I seem to be a brief light that flashes but once in all the aeons of time—a rare, complicated, and all-too-delicate organism on the fringe of biological evolution, where the wave of life bursts into individual, sparkling, and multicolored drops that gleam for a moment only to vanish forever.

Under conditions like these, Watts writes, "it seems impossible and even absurd to realize that myself does not reside in the drop alone, but in the whole surge of energy which ranges from the galaxies to the nuclear fields in my body. At this level of existence 'I' am immeasurably old; my forms are infinite and their comings and goings are simply the pulses or vibrations of a single and eternal flow of energy."

As Watts says, discovering who we really are may seem impossible or absurd, but it is the goal—if we can use that word—of all spiritual journeys.

The New Narcissism, the Me Decade, and You

Although many psychiatrists and therapists, like Nathaniel Branden, author of *Honoring the Self,* consider "self-knowledge" one of the most important goals of our time, during the seventies this aspect of the "consciousness movement" drew heavy fire from certain segments of the media. Peter Marin in *Harper's* and Tom Wolfe in *New York Magazine* described the new self-help and self-awareness techniques and programs as reflecting a retreat from social and political responsibility into a self-absorbed narcissism. In 1978, Marin and Wolfe were followed by social historian Christopher Lasch who documented the argument with academic thoroughness and jeremiad passion in his book-length study, *The Culture of Narcissism.*

In *New Rules,* a book that may be as on-target for the eighties as *The Lonely Crowd* was for the fifties, sociologist and pollster Daniel Yankelovich says that "the self-fulfillment search is a more complex, fateful, and irreversible phenomenon than simply the by-product of affluence or a shift in the national character toward narcissism."

"This is not to deny that many people *are* preoccupied with themselves," Yankelovich writes. "But the self-centeredness may yet prove to be an incidental feature of the search for fulfillment. . . . The Christian injunction that to find one's self one must first lose oneself contains an essential truth any seeker of self-fulfillment needs to grasp."

Or as the Japanese Zen master Dogen has said, "In Buddhism we study the self. To study the self is to forget the self. To forget the self is to be enlightened by all things."

The Path with a Heart

Learning and study—of the great scriptures, the lives of saints and realized men and women, the stories and instructions of famous teachers—are part of the great paths to self-realization. But these can seem dry as dust when read only for information. Study and words are dead only when they are undertaken without integrating them as personal experience. But when combined with actual practice, be it meditation, prayer, yoga, or dance, words have a way of igniting into flames of pure understanding.

That understanding is a sign that we are begun on our journey at last.

Having begun we are faced with many possibilities. So when in doubt we favor remembering Don Juan's advice in *The Teachings of Don Juan* by Carlos Casteneda:

> I warn you. Look at every path closely and deliberately. Try it as many times as you think necessary. Then ask yourself, and yourself alone, one question. This question is one that only a very old man asks. My benefactor told me about it once when I was young, and my blood was too vigorous for me to understand it. Now I do understand it. I will tell you what it is: Does this path have a heart?
>
> The trouble is nobody asks the question; and when a man finally realizes that he has taken a path without a heart, the path is ready to kill him. At that point very few men can stop to deliberate, and leave the path.
>
> For me there is only the travelling on paths that have heart, on any path that may have heart. There I travel, and the only worthwhile challenge is to traverse its full length.
>
> And there I travel looking, looking, breathlessly.

One More Zen Story

Zen master Dogen used to say "We should attain enlightenment before we attain enlightenment."

Shunryu Suzuki-roshi comments: "Which is more important: to attain enlightenment, or to attain enlightenment before you attain enlightenment; to make a million dollars or to enjoy your life in your effort, little by little, even though it is impossible to make that million; to be successful, or to find some meaning in your effort to be successful?

"If you do not know the answer," says Suzuki-roshi, "you will not even be able to practice *zazen* [meditation]; if you do know, you will have found the true treasure of life."

And then you will have begun.

"Eliminate something superfluous from your life.
Break a habit.
Do something that makes you feel insecure.
Carry out an action with complete attention and intensity,
as if it were your last."

PIERO FERRUCCI

"We cannot fully understand the beginning of anything until we understand the end."

G. SPENCER BROWN

Recommended Reading

"To read well, that is to read true books in a true spirit, is a noble exercise," Henry David Thoreau writes in *Walden*. "A written word is choicest of relics. It is something at once more intimate with us and more universal than any other work of art. It is the work of art nearest to life itself."

There are certain books that have proved themselves over the years as fit companions for the spiritual journey. Everyone will have personal favorites, no doubt, but here are seven of ours. Like all good companions, they travel well. They also have staying power. The more time we spend with them, the more they are willing to reveal. All but two are classics and are available in many editions. After each of these we have indicated our favorite edition, if any.

The Tao Te Ching, Lao Tzu. According to Dr. Lin Yutang, this is "the one book in the whole of Oriental literature which should be read above all others." Though Lao Tzu believed that "those who know don't say and those who say don't know," he left us a profound record of the Taoist Way in which (to sum up): "The way to do is to be."

The Tao Te Ching has been translated more times than any book besides the Bible. We like *The Tao Te Ching, A New Translation* by Gia-Fu Feng and Jane English (Viking, 1972), elegantly designed and superbly illustrated.

The I Ching. The *I Ching* or *Book of Changes* is more an oracle than a book per se. A toss of the coins or yarrow stalks leads you to one of sixty-four hexagrams. The *I Ching* never fails to give useful advice, and people have been consulting it for 3000 years. The originators obviously tapped into that collective primal wisdom that can be found deep inside each of us.

We recommend the *I Ching—Book of Changes*, translated by Richard Wilhelm and Cary Baynes, with an introduction by C. G. Jung (Princeton University Press, 1961).

The Bible. To some, the Bible is the literal word of God. To others, it is family history, a record of several thousand years of Judeo-Christian civilization and a rich storehouse of myths, parables, psalms, prayers, proverbs, tales, commandments, and good advice.

We are partial to the rolling cadences of the King James Version.

Walden, Henry David Thoreau. Thoreau is our own homegrown Yankee sage; *Walden* is the record of the year he spent in a little cabin on the banks of Walden pond. The book is built, like Thoreau's cabin, out of the simplest and sturdiest materials—a book fit to live in, especially for those who, like Thoreau, wish "to live deliberately, to confront only the essential facts of life."

There are many editions; the one that seems best matched to the book is the Modern Library edition.

Zen Mind, Beginner's Mind, Shunryu Suzuki-Roshi (Weatherhill, 1972). This is a book of informal Zen talks given to American students at the San Francisco Zen Center. It is about the practice rather than the theory of Zen, and about the fresh start that occurs every moment in the practice of meditation; it is about beginning, from beginning to end.

Journey to Ixtlan by Carlos Castaneda (Pocketbooks, 1976). This is the third, and many feel the best, of the incredible adventures of anthropology student Carlos with the Yaqui Indian sorcerer Don Juan. It is also the first of Castaneda's books to ignore the psychotropic drugs that figure so prominently in the two earlier books. Lately, there has been a fair amount of controversy about the reality of Don Juan, but whether he actually exists or not, most readers find him fully alive in the pages of Carlos Castaneda's imagination. The advice is also very much to the point. For example, "In a world where death is the hunter, my friend, there is no time for regrets or doubts. There is only time for decisions."

Instead of a First Book

When we asked Jean Houston, director of the Foundation for Mind Research, what first book she would recommend for beginners on the spiritual path, she said, "I wouldn't recommend a first book. I would recommend an extended period of quiet."

Resources

Possible Points of Departure

A Course in Miracles is a set of daily spiritual lessons transmitted through a New York psychologist some years ago. There is one "lesson" for each day of the year. Many people feel it is the most recent flowering of the perennial philosophy. The introduction to *A Course in Miracles* is true not only for the Course, but also for the course of all spiritual teachings. It begins:

> This is a course in miracles. It is a required course. Only the time you take it is voluntary. Free will does not mean that you can establish the curriculum. It means only that you can elect what you want to take at a given time. The course does not aim at teaching the meaning of love, for that is beyond what can be taught. It does aim, however, at removing the blocks to the awareness of love's presence, which is your natural inheritance. The opposite of love is fear, but what is all-encompassing can have no opposite.
>
> This course can therefore be summed up very simply in this way:
>
> > Nothing real can be threatened.
> > Nothing unreal exists.
>
> Herein lies the peace of God.

A Course in Miracles may be ordered from The Foundation for Inner Peace, P.O. Box 635, Tiburon, CA 94920.

Learning

2

There is a famous Zen story about a learned university professor of oriental studies who visited a master at a temple in Japan. The master received the professor in his private room, and an attendant served tea. As soon as he had seated himself, the professor began talking on and on about Zen philosophy. The master said nothing as he poured the tea into his guest's cup. The professor hardly noticed, and kept talking and talking—he felt, in fact, wonderfully inspired.

Suddenly he realized that the Zen master was still pouring tea even though the cup had long since overflowed, and the tea had spilled out onto the tatami mat. And still the master continued pouring.

"Stop, stop, what are you doing?" cried the professor. The master looked up. "Just as the cup cannot hold anymore tea when it is already filled," he said, "how can I give you anything when your mind is already filled?"

As the Zen master demonstrated, in order to learn anything at all, we must first empty our minds of our cherished notions and assumptions. An open mind is a necessary prerequisite to learning. To receive a cup of tea, we must hold an empty cup. However great our knowledge, there is still an infinite amount more to be learned. "In this world," as Margaret Mead says, "no one can complete an education."

"There is no end to education," agrees Krishnamurti. "It is not that you read a book, pass an examination and finish with education. The whole of life, from the moment

"The last and most important branch of non-verbal education is training in the art of spiritual insight. . . . To know the ultimate Not-Self, which transcends the other not-selves and the ego, but which is yet closer than breathing, nearer than hands and feet—this is the consummation of human life, the end and ultimate purpose of individual existence."

ALDOUS HUXLEY

"Even when walking in a party of no more than three I can always be certain of learning from those I am with. There will be good qualities that I can select for imitation and bad ones that will teach me what requires correction in myself."

CONFUCIUS

you are born to the moment you die, is a process of learning."

Our school system encourages the idea that learning has a beginning (grade school), a middle (high school), and an end (college or graduate school). Most people who step out of this progression find themselves locked out of our educational system—and, they might think, of learning itself—forever. "This now-or-never pressure," writes Theodore Roszack, "is one of the worst tyrannies of the system; it denies us the freedom to experiment, to fail, to turn back, to begin again—if necessary, to start a second career, to launch a new life."

For the person on the spiritual path, there is always more to learn. The journey is not finished or completed; it is endlessly deepened and broadened. We do not, for example, "learn" compassion, humility, or wisdom—or any of the other factors that make up the spiritual life—but we do continually deepen and broaden them as we live our lives.

"Even the Buddha," goes an old saying, "is still working on himself."

"He who by reanimating the Old can gain knowledge of the New is fit to be a teacher."

CONFUCIUS

Learning How to Unlearn

To begin this education, according to the nineteenth-century English explorer and Sufi mystic Richard Burton, "What we have to learn first is 'how to unlearn.'" This process of unlearning—a kind of reverse education—involves coming out of what the Sufis and others have called "the cultural trance." This state of being is made up of millions of assumptions and "truths" that are woven into the cloth of our culture. It is carried by our institutions and social forms, even by the structure of our language. At a still deeper (or more interior) level, we are all conditioned by the process of our own thoughts and feelings—by the linear workings of our rational mind, and by the ramblings of our "subconscious gossip."

Learning how to quiet or still this level of conditioning is one of the first steps in developing spiritual knowledge, intuition, or illumination. "Stop thinking and talking about it," said the third Chinese Zen Patriarch, "and there is nothing you will not be able to know." Easier said than done, as anyone who has tried meditation knows.

Finally, we come to unlearn the habits and ways of thinking that anchor us to our usual ego-centered ways of seeing the world and ourselves. We must unlearn and let go of our most cherished idea: our idea of ourselves.

Learning How to Learn

If learning how to unlearn is actually the first step to true learning, the next step is learning *how* to learn. This process, and not a collection of facts, is at the heart of what our better instructors are trying to communicate to us. As John Holt, the well-known educator and author of bestselling books such as *How Children Fail,* puts it: "What we can best learn from good teachers is *how* to teach ourselves better." The superiority of training one's ability to learn over merely exercising our capacity to remember is underlined by Doris Lessing, who quotes Sir Richard Burton in her introduction to *Learning How to Learn,* a collection of Sufi stories: "Abjure the why and seek the how."

> "On the subject of Esalen's unimpressive record in using the methods it helped to popularize for its own problems, Richard Price wryly cites what he calls Esalen's Law. The law, he says, is that you always teach others what you most need to learn yourself. Its corollary is that you are your own worst student."
>
> WALTER TRUETT ANDERSON

> "It is the function of God's teachers
> to bring true learning to the world.
> Properly speaking it is unlearning that they bring,
> for that is 'true learning' in the world."
>
> A COURSE IN MIRACLES

"To understand truth one must have a very sharp, precise, clear mind; not a cunning mind, but a mind that is capable of looking without any distortion, a mind innocent and vulnerable. Only such a mind can see what truth is. Nor can a mind that is filled with knowledge perceive what truth is; only a mind that is completely capable of learning can do that. Learning is not the accumulation of knowledge. Learning is movement from moment to moment."

J. KRISHNAMURTI

"Modern education is competitive, nationalistic and separative. It has trained the child to regard material values as of major importance, to believe that his nation is also of major importance and superior to other nations and peoples. The general level of world information is high but usually biased, influenced by national prejudices, serving to make us citizens of our nation but not of the world."

ALBERT EINSTEIN

Following are some suggestions drawn from a number of sources that can teach us (or more correctly help us teach ourselves) how to learn.

Don't Be Afraid to Be Afraid

In *The Teachings of Don Juan*, Carlos Castenada reminds us that for the man—or woman—of knowledge real learning engenders fear because it is a departure from the known. Overcoming this fear becomes the challenge. "What he learns is never what he pictured or imagined," Castenada writes, "and so he begins to be afraid. Learning is never what one expects. Every step of learning is a new task, and the fear the man is experiencing begins to mount mercilessly, unyieldingly. His purpose has become a battlefield. . . .

"He must not run away. He must defy his fear, and in spite of it he must take the next step in learning, and the next, and the next. He must be fully afraid, and he must not stop. That is the rule! And a moment will come when his first enemy retreats. Learning is no longer a terrifying task."

Learn By Doing, Learn Like a Baby

John Holt, the well-known educator and author of *How Children Fail,* and many other books, writes in a newsletter:

Not many years ago I began to play the cello. Most people would say that what I am doing is "learning to play" the cello. But these words carry into our minds the strange idea that there exist two very different processes: 1) learning to play the cello; and 2) playing the cello. They imply that I will do the first until I have completed it, at which point I will stop the first process and begin the second; in short, that I will go on "learning to play" until I have "learned to play" and that then I will begin to play. Of course, this is nonsense. There are not two processes, but one. We learn to do something by doing it. There is no other way.

Holt further described this process in an instructive book, *Never Too Late.* He says:

What I am slowly learning to do in my work with music is revive some of the resilience of the exploring and learning baby. I have to accept at each moment, as a fact of life, my present skill or lack of skill, and do the best I can, without blaming myself for not being able to do better. I have to be aware of my mistakes and shortcomings without being ashamed of them. I have to keep in view the distant goal, without worrying about how far away it is or reproaching myself for not being already there. This is very hard for most adults. It is the main reason why we old dogs so often do find it so hard to learn new tricks, whether sports or languages or crafts or music. But if as we work on our skills we work on this weakness in ourselves, we can slowly get better at both.

Another story that illustrates this point is told by Dennis Genpo Merzel, a young American Zen teacher from Los Angeles. Genpo was once invited into the cockpit of a 747 bound for Hawaii. There he saw a little black box. "This little black box," he says, "is a computer which the pilots call *Fred*. Every time the 747 goes off course, Fred,

"A sage of Chelm went bathing in the lake and almost drowned. When he raised an outcry other swimmers came to his rescue. As he was helped out of the water he took a solemn oath: 'I swear never to go into the water again until I learn how to swim!'"

A TREASURY OF JEWISH FOLKLORE

"To know that you do not know is the best. To pretend to know when you do not know is disease."

LAO TZU

"The Great Way is not difficult— Just cease to cherish opinions."

THE THIRD ZEN PATRIARCH

who serves as the navigator, can tell how many degrees the plane's off course. Fred then communicates this information to another computer called *George* who steers. Every time Fred communicates a necessary correction in course, George adjusts the plane's steering in the right direction.

The 747 is "off-course" about 90 percent of the time, during the 5½ hour flight to Hawaii. Every few seconds something like this conversation occurs: Fred says, "Hey, George, we're 10 degrees starboard off course. Correct." George responds, "Thank you, Fred, will do." George corrects. Then Fred says, "We're five degrees port off course. Correct." George responds, "Thank you, Fred, will do. . . ."

"Imagine," says Genpo Merzel, "how their conversation would go if Fred and George were human beings. It would not take long for George to say something like, 'Damn it, Fred, why don't you shut your big mouth and quit telling me what to do. Yap, yap, yap. Always correcting me. Always telling me what to do.'"

In learning something new, or in trying to transcend our habitual limits, we are always going to be a little off-course, just like the 747. Correction, either through feedback from the environment or another person, is a necessary part of the process of learning and living. And yet our formal training in schooling tends to ignore this obvious fact. We are rewarded for the "right" answers—for the time we are on course—but never for the corrections we must constantly make. Often we are in fact "punished" for those corrections; some people call them "mistakes." Perhaps it is better—as a Zen master once suggested—to see life as one big mistake. Then we can let Fred and George do their job and more often than not land on target." (In Hawaii—which isn't bad.)

Have Humility

Says Arthur Deikman in *The Observing Self:* "Humility is the acceptance of the possibility that someone else can teach you something else you do not know already, especially about yourself. Conversely, pride and arrogance close the door of the mind."

Be Sincere

Says Deikman: "Mystics define sincerity as honesty of intention. People may think they desire to learn when what they actually want is to receive attention. When the attention is taken away, they lose interest and leave to seek other sources of 'learning.' It can be observed in any educational system that if the dominant wish of a student is to be fed with praise or attention, the learning that takes place will be very limited, regardless of what the student may think is taking place. This is especially true if the learning requires self-initiated effort. After all, physiological and psychological survival require that we be efficient at obtaining what we actually want, not what we say we want, or even what we think we want."

Avoid Competition

Krishnamurti says: "Real learning comes about when the competitive spirit has ceased. The competitive spirit is merely an additive process which is not learning at all. This is true not only of competition with others, but competition with yourself as well."

Don't Be Afraid to Be a Fool

In *Laws of Form*, the mathematician G. Spencer Brown writes: "Discoveries of any great moment in mathematics and other disciplines once they are discovered, are seen to be extremely simple and obvious, and make everybody, including their discoverer, appear foolish for not having discovered them before. It is all too often forgotten that the ancient symbol for the prenascence of the world is a fool, and that foolishness, being a divine state, is not a condition to be either proud or ashamed of."

Find the Pattern Which Connects

Gregory Bateson subtitled his last book, *Mind and Nature: A Necessary Unity*. It is a universal and fundamental spiritual teaching (and increasingly, a scientific one) that we are all parts of a whole, that the individual isolated self or event, or nation, is but one level of reality. To see it as the only level is a fiction. But our educational system rewards the ability to separate, to categorize, to analyze. Rather than focus on these bits and pieces of the universe, Bateson suggests we find "the pattern which connects."

"Break the pattern which connects the items of learning and you necessarily destroy all quality," he says.

Bateson therefore advised the teacher and learner to focus on what connects the crab to the lobster and the orchid to the primrose and all four of them to you and me. His interest was in the pattern which connects all living creatures, and it was this issue to which he devoted his professional life. Bateson would have been among the first to admit that this quest was spiritual as well as scientific since to learn how we are all part of the pattern which connects is one of the great lessons of the spiritual life.

"Most of us," he wrote, "have lost that sense of unity of biosphere and humanity which would bind and reassure us all with an affirmation of beauty. Most of us do not today believe that whatever the ups and downs of detail within our limited experience, the larger whole is primarily beautiful."

By looking closely at the natural world, we may learn anew what the deepest spiritual traditions of humanity have always taught: namely, that there is an ultimate and

"He who knows others is wise. He who knows himself is enlightened."

LAO TZU

"To learn is to change. Education is a process that changes the learner."

GEORGE LEONARD

sacred unity. The new sciences of ecology and cybernetics, which take a holistic approach to life, gave Bateson at least a measure of hope. Writing of them he has said, "There is at least an impulse still in the human breast to unify and thereby sanctify the total natural world, of which we are a part."

Educating the Whole Person

Western education, unfortunately, does not emphasize this unity. Rather it violates and obscures the underlying pattern that connects the universe. Education, as nearly all of us have experienced it, addresses only one part of our nature, what Aldous Huxley calls, "the world of abstract, verbalized knowledge."

"Whether we like it or not," Huxley says, we are "living simultaneously in the world of experience and the world of notions, in the world of direct apprehension of Nature, God, and ourselves; and the world of abstract, verbalized knowledge about these primary facts. Our business as human beings is to make the best of both these worlds."

Looking back over his own years of schooling, Huxley says, "I can see the enormous deficiencies of a system which could do nothing better for my body than Swedish drill and compulsory football, nothing better for my character than prizes, punishments, sermons and pep talks, and nothing better for my soul than a hymn before bedtime, to the accompaniment of the harmonium." In most schools things have changed very little in this regard in the decades since.

The solution is to educate the whole person. This means paying special attention to what Huxley called the "non-verbal humanities." For him, the most fundamental missing element in this curriculum was the body. Huxley was, in particular, impressed by the work of F. M. Alexander, a pioneer of what might be called education to heal the mind-body connection. The nonverbal humanities would also include educating our emotions, and perhaps a grounding in contemplative and spiritual studies.

Today the idea of educating the whole human being has crystallized into a movement of people who often call themselves holistic educators. Since holistic education is

"Indeed we are running away all the time to avoid coming face to face with our real selves."

ANONYMOUS

still in its early stages, and since it aspires to nothing less than educating the whole person, there is naturally no single authoritative system. Most programs do, however, share certain features. They may draw freely from the spiritual teachings of such figures as Rudolf Steiner and G. I. Gurdjieff; from the more traditional spiritual teachings, particularly of the East; and from the "body work" of teachers such as F. M. Alexander and Moshe Feldenkrais. Many programs in holistic education also make use of the expressive psychologies of Wilhelm Reich, the gestalt work of Fritz Perls, and the transpersonal psychologies, especially Assagioli's Psychosynthesis.

While much of holistic education might seem new—or even trendy—it actually responds to a very old need. As Theodore Roszack says, "this interest mirrors a contemporary fascination with forms of psychic and spiritual instruction that may be as old as the most primitive rites of passage."

Holistic education in this sense is a heroic attempt to recover all that has been left out or banished as not "real learning" from the usual school curriculum. If at times it seems to suffer, as some critics have charged, from a lack of intellectual precision and rigor, that is perhaps to be expected—for in order to correct an imbalance, the pendulum often has to swing rather widely in the opposite direction.

"If it is possible for a multibillion-dollar education program to train people to see themselves as limited beings, it should also be possible for that program to encourage people to see themselves as embodiments of the capacity to transcend their present concepts of themselves and their powers."

SIDNEY T. JOURARD

Still, the promise of holistic education as a way of viewing learning and schooling remains great. For the person on the spiritual journey, the small number of schools that are part of this stream are well worth exploring along with the colleges that prepare people to be holistic educators—since they make it possible to integrate spirituality into the educational process. With this kind of learning, we find that education and the spiritual journey are one and the same thing. As Theodore Roszack writes in *Person/ Planet:* "We enter upon an educational prospect that seeks to take the whole of life into account, from prenatal experience to the moment of death, and which does not stop short of the premise of spiritual enlightenment. Wise silence takes its place as a sign of knowledge beside lots of clever-language-in-the-head; the sage comes to stand alongside the scientist and scholar as a pedagogical model."

Transcultural Learning

As our planet grows smaller, our learning naturally becomes more holistic because we are exposed to all the other cultures on the planet. Now, for the first time in history the spiritual seeker has access to the spiritual treasures of the whole earth—not only East and West, but Africa, South America, and the open spaces of the Arctic have added their knowledge and wisdom to the spiritual store of humanity.

Many people in the West have thought it necessary to travel great distances in search of spiritual instruction. It may not be necessary to travel to India or Japan these days—since Zen centers and ashrams abound right here at home—but there is still always much to learn by living in the midst of another culture.

"Education helps us to get soul and body and spirit together. The way we learn arithmetic affects our moral sense. The way we understand geography affects our judgement. The ordeals of earthly life are a school in which we may develop consciousness and self-knowledge and become transparent to our neighbors. The transmutations of this schooling through the ages will create new qualities of freedom and of love.

"Yet teaching nowadays is becoming technology. Teachers are cautious about substance. They are cautious about truth. We think of agreement as being a standard for truth. But truth is not a uniform static formulation. The spirit of truth lights up all the parts in relation to the whole. This is a new way of seeing. It means seeing the individual in both light and shadow. It means reading contemporary culture as part of a symptomatology of history. It means seeking to know the teacher. And the teacher is *in life.*"

M. C. RICHARDS

The Need for a Teacher

The spiritual journey is first of all a personal quest. Most Eastern spiritual traditions consider a teacher necessary for at least part of the journey. The reason is that we seem to need someone to jolt us out of our habitual sleep, out of what psychiatrist Arthur Deikman calls "the trance of everyday life." As G. I. Gurdjieff, the teacher who first brought many of the ancient teachings to the West, explains: "A man cannot awaken himself. But, if let us say, twenty people make an agreement that whoever of them awakens first shall wake the rest, they already have some chance. Even this, however, is insufficient because all twenty can go to sleep at the same time and dream that they are waking up. Therefore, more still is necessary. They must be looked after by a man who is not asleep or who does not fall asleep as easily as they do. . . ."

More on Teachers

There is hardly any subject in the spiritual world that causes so much controversy as that of teachers, masters, and gurus.

Some people feel very strongly that to have a teacher is to give up their own independence. They want to face their life directly, to meet it head-on, to trust in their own intuition and insight.

Others swear by their guru. Without their teacher, they will tell you, they would never have stepped on the spiritual path, let alone continued on it. The teacher's very touch, they say, is enough to bring realization.

There are people who have studied or trained under one master all their lives, and come to feel that with time they came to understand much that had seemed puzzling or contradictory. Others have given everything to a teacher, only to leave embittered and feeling "had."

Actually, there are many ways of being a teacher and of being a student. Some teachers function as "kalyanamitras"—which is the Sanskrit word for "spiritual friend." Others are more like stern taskmasters; and others like kindly grandmothers. Some gurus—which is a Sanskrit word meaning teacher—live pure and seemingly exemplary lives. Others are like fierce fires that burn their students' impurities away. It is said that when the student is ready, the teacher will appear. It also works the other way around. Ramakrishna said, "When the flower blooms, the bees come uninvited."

"Without an integrated understanding of life, our individual and collective problems will only deepen and extend. The purpose of education is not to produce mere scholars, technicians and job hunters, but integrated men and women who are free of fear; for only between such human beings can there be enduring peace."

J. KRISHNAMURTI

Buckminster Fuller demonstrates his geodesic design.

The most important point is not to wait until you find a teacher to begin, or to think that because you feel no need of a teacher you are not on the spiritual path. The real teacher, as every true teacher explains, is within. And once you experience this, you begin to realize that the entire world is your curriculum. There is a lesson—sometimes delightful and sometimes painful—in everything that happens to you.

As Krishnamurti, who disavows all teachers and gurus, while teaching tirelessly and selflessly himself, told some young students in India:

"This is your life, and nobody is going to teach you, no book, no guru. You have to learn from yourself, not from books. It is an endless thing, it is a fascinating thing, and when you learn about yourself from yourself, out of that learning wisdom comes. Then you can live a most extraordinary, happy, beautiful life. Right?"

"We may know a little or much, but the farther we push the more the horizon recedes. We are enveloped in a sea of forces which seems to defy our puny intelligence. Until we accept the fact that life itself is founded in mystery we shall learn nothing."

HENRY MILLER

Resources

Five Centers of Holistic Education

The Interface Training Program in Holistic Education

Interface, sometimes called "the Esalen of the East," offers a masters degree in counseling, education and holistic health in conjunction with Lesley College. The Interface program is based in part on Robert Assagioli's Psychosynthesis.
Write: Interface
       230 Central St., Box B
       Newton, MA 02166

Masters Program in Confluent Education

Located at the University of California in Santa Barbara, this is widely regarded as the foremost training center for teachers interested in the holistic approach as well as those from industry and other institutions.
Write: Dr. George Brown
       University of California
       Phelps Hall, Room 2212
       Santa Barbara, CA 93106

John F. Kennedy University

The Graduate School for the Study of Human Consciousness offers masters degrees in Interdisciplinary Consciousness Studies, Art and Consciousness, Transpersonal Psychology, Holistic Health Education, and Counseling Psychology with specializations in Holistic Health and Transpersonal Psychology. The University is designed for the working adult, and most classes are held in the afternoons, evenings, and weekends.
Write: John F. Kennedy University
       12 Altarinda Rd., Orinda, CA 94563

The Naropa Institute

Founded by Tibetan Buddhist, the Ven. Chogyam Trungpa, Rinpoche (1940–1986), Naropa Institute is the only accredited college in North America whose educational philosophy is rooted in the Buddhist contemplative tradition. Bachelor of Arts degree programs are offered in Contemplative Psychology, Buddhist Studies, Movement Studies, Music, Writing, and Visual Arts. Masters of Arts programs are currently offered in Contemplative Psychotherapy, Dance Therapy, Buddhist Studies, and a Master

of Fine Arts program in Writing and Poetics. Each summer, Naropa also hosts a four-week Summer Institute.
Write: Naropa Institute, 2130 Arapohoe, Boulder, CO 80302

Organizations:

Association for Humanistic Education, P.O. Box 13042, Gainesville, FL 32604. An association for humanistic educators. Sponsors educational events and publishes a newsletter.

American Montessori Society, 175 Fifth Ave., New York, NY 10010. Publishes a nationwide list of Montessori schools.

The National Coalition of Alternative Community Schools, 58 Schoolhouse Rd., Summertown, TN 38483. Publishes an annual directory of alternative schools, a newsletter, and a journal.

Waldorf Institute, 23399 Evergreen Rd., Southfield, MI 48075, (313)352-8990. Publishes a list of Waldorf Schools in North America.

Adult Education Centers:

There are many holistic adult education centers springing up. By writing for catalogues from any of the following centers, you can get an idea of what's available.

Chinook Learning Center, P.O. Box 57, Clinton, WA 98236, (206)321-1884. Offers residential retreats and workshops on a variety of subjects on Whidbey Island and in Seattle.

Esalen Institute, Big Sur, CA 93920, (408)667-3000. The first center of its kind. Runs weekend and weeklong workshops year round.

Naropa Institute, 2130 Arapahoe Ave., Boulder, CO 80302, (303)444-0202. A Buddhist University founded by Tibetan teacher Chogyam Trungpa, Rinpoche. Offers courses in Buddhist studies, psychology, the arts and poetics each summer and year-round.

New York Open Center, 83 Spring St., New York, NY 10012, (212)219-2527. The Center offers 800 workshops, ongoing courses, lectures, and performances a year exploring ancient traditions and emerging innovations in world culture and focusing on spiritual and social issues, psychology, healing, and the arts.

Newsletters and Directories:

Changing Schools (TC 1008, Ball State University, Muncie, IN 47306). One of the oldest journals on alternative education.

Growing Without Schooling (John Holt Associates, 729 Boylston St., Boston, MA 02116 $15/year, six issues). Founded by the late educator John Holt, this newsletter provides information on home schooling.

How to Get the Degree You Want, John Bear (Ten Speed Press, 1984). An excellent guide to nontraditional degree programs for adults. Includes information on how to fund your education.

Cross-cultural Learning:

The Experiment in International Living, Kipling Rd., Brattleboro, VT 05301. A private nonprofit organization and the inventor of the homestay concept of cross-cultural learning. Its School for International Training conducts Bachelor programs in international studies and Master programs in languages and intercultural management. Also offers a college semester abroad program and specialized nondegree professional training.

World College West, 101 S. San Antonio Rd., Petaluma, CA 94952, (707)765-4502. An undergraduate degree program that offers intercultural programs in China, Nepal, and Mexico.

3

Intimate Relationships

One afternoon, according to an old Sufi tale, Nasruddin and his friend were sitting in a cafe, drinking tea, and talking about life and love.

"How come you never got married, Nasruddin?" asked his friend at one point.

"Well," said Nasruddin, "to tell you the truth, I spent my youth looking for the perfect woman. In Cairo, I met a beautiful and intelligent woman, with eyes like dark olives, but she was unkind. Then in Baghdad, I met a woman who was a wonderful and generous soul, but we had no interests in common. One woman after another would seem just right, but there would always be something missing. Then one day, I met her. She was beautiful, intelligent, generous and kind. We had everything in common. In fact, she was perfect."

"Well," said Nasruddin's friend, "what happened? Why didn't you marry her?"

Nasruddin sipped his tea reflectively. "Well," he replied, "it's a sad thing. Seems she was looking for the perfect man."

Like Nasruddin, we are always trying to find perfection outside of ourselves. And yet it is not quite enough to say that we only have to look within, for all of us exist in relationship to something or someone else.

Bertrand Russell once wrote that "love is the source of the most intense delights that life has to offer." It is also

> "Jewels on Indra's net reflect each other endlessly."
>
> THE AVATAMSAKA SUTRA

"One moon shows in every pool;
in every pool, the one moon."

THE ZEN FOREST SAYINGS

the source of much of the unhappiness and frustration that life has to offer. Loving another person awakens the heart and lifts us beyond the narrow confines of our self-interest; but loving another person can also bring with it the pain of attachment, possessiveness, unrequited love, and all the rest of it. Love is a two-edged sword.

In the past, the dedicated spiritual seeker often chose to live a life apart from the distractions and temptations of worldly life. By living outside the entanglements of relationships, the spiritual seeker was left free to pursue a life of simplicity and non-attachment.

This may have worked well enough for the monk, nun, hermit, or wandering pilgrim, but for most of us today our relationships, as distracting as they may be, are very much a part of our spiritual path.

In fact, life is relationship, and we are all in a "perfect" relationship with everything that makes up our lives at this very moment. To feel this inter-connectedness with all things, and to know that we are a part of the universe, is one of the great joys of the spiritual life. And, it is our intimate relationships that provide the greatest opportunity to learn this lesson.

Dante's love for Beatrice, for example, led him to conclude *The Paradiso* with a paean to the love "that moves the sun and other stars." In India the love between the youthful, flute-playing Krishna and the maiden Radha symbolized the eternal attraction between the human world and the world of the gods. These relationships, though they may seem remote or mythological, remind us of the truth that there is a path of relationship—a path based on acknowledging and honoring the sacred essence and consciousness of our partners.

To begin with, the same qualities that go to make up a fulfilling relationship—qualities such as love, commitment, forgiveness, surrender, and honesty—are also the qualities that contribute to our spiritual growth.

Secondly, the nature of our spiritual lives is reflected very much in the quality of relationships we have. In this way they become an accurate mirror. The people we spend most of our time with, who know us best, can give us immediate and generally reliable feedback about our lives.

Relationships bring spirituality down to earth, and into the home. Finally, the care and love we give to others is actually at the heart of spirituality. Since there is, in fact, no separation between us, to give is to receive. As the Beatles sing, "The love you take is equal to the love you make."

Relationships: The Great Challenge

There are two cornerstone ideas that appear again and again in most spiritual writings on relationships.

On the one hand, there is the notion that we are all one. Not only are we all related to each other as travelers on planet earth, but in a spiritual sense our essences are inextricably intertwined. We come from the same source and we are all on a common journey.

On the other hand, there is the notion that each of us is whole, complete, and perfect—exactly as we are. All that we need is contained within us.

In *The Art of Loving*, one of the classics on the subject, Erich Fromm comments on this paradox.

"Erotic love, if it is love, has one premise," he writes. "That I love from the essence of my being—and experience the other person in the essence of his or her being. In essence, all human beings are identical. We are all part of One; we are One. This being so, it should not make any difference whom we love. Love should be essentially an act of will, or decision to commit my life completely to that of one other person."

This, in effect, might be called the spiritual view of love—the view from the highest vantage point. It is also, interestingly enough, the view behind the arranged marriages followed by many traditional societies.

But, as Fromm goes on to say, "This view seems to neglect the paradoxical character of human nature and of erotic love. We are all One—yet every one of us is a unique, unduplicable entity. In our relationships to others the same paradox is repeated. Inasmuch as we are all one, we can love everybody in the same way in the sense of brotherly love. But inasmuch as we are all different, erotic love requires specific, highly individual elements which exist between some people but not between all."

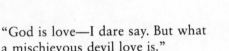

"God is love—I dare say. But what a mischievous devil love is."

SAMUEL BUTLER

The challenge of relationships, then, is to consciously make use of the double-edged sword of their paradoxical nature. The path of relationships leads us through the veil of separation to a realization of our ultimate oneness. Fromm calls this state "interpersonal fusion."

This desire for interpersonal fusion is, as he writes, "the most powerful striving in man. It is the most fundamental passion, it is the force which keeps the human race together, the clan, the family, the society."

Relationships as a Path

Through their own relationship and their therapy practice, Harrison and Olivia Hoblitzelle, two therapists from Cambridge, Massachusetts, have found that certain attitudes encourage a spiritual relationship. Longtime meditators who have been married for seventeen years, the Hoblitzelles make the following suggestions.

1. *Acknowledge that you have a sense of karmic destiny.* It's important that people accept that they are together for a purpose that goes beyond personal satisfactions. They are together to be teachers to each other and to recognize the divinity in one another.

2. *Respect the divine longing in one another* to know the greater meaning of life beyond our limited sense of ourselves.

3. *Accept the relationship as a central part of your spiritual path.* In India they speak of the *sadhana* or "practice" of relationship as being "hot like a chili pepper." Don't expect it to be easy.

4. *Look at difficulties as a training.* Relationships are a perfect learning experience to develop mindfulness and understanding of where we are caught in old models, attachments and identifications.

5. *Have faith in the process of growth and change in your partner as well as yourself.* You can specifically help your partner by providing support during difficult periods, giving space for developing a spiritual practice even though it may be different from your own, and creating a balance of time alone and time together—of solitude and society.

6. *Keep before you the vision of your partner's true self—especially when it is lost to view.* And also keep the faith that believing in your partner's true self will cause it to manifest.

The Couple's Journey

Even when couples set out without any spiritual goal in mind, they often find that the very dynamics of making a relationship work tend to promote or bring forth spiritual values, according to couples therapist Susan Campbell. After experiencing years of frustration in her own relationship, Ms. Campbell began to wonder if a fulfilling relationship were even possible. "There must be some people, some partners for whom the couple thing is working," she recalls telling herself, "where people love and fight and can still create and grow together." So she set out to find and study such couples.

What she discovered were several couples whose relationship had actually become their own path toward fulfillment. To her surprise, most of these couples had found themselves on a spiritual path quite unintentionally.

> They started out by trying to "make the best of a bad situation," and in the process learned that it's often more important to love what you've got than it is to get what you want. Couples trying to resolve their power struggles and differences often come to a realization that their individual egos are totally incapable of finding peace with another. It may be at this point that they face each other in helplessness, naked of defenses for the first time in a long time, and admit, "we don't want to be doing this to each other . . . we want to be loving each other . . . and we don't know how." With this act, which I call "letting go and letting God," space is created for an entirely new unifying force to enter the relationship—the force of God, the force of love.

By interviewing dozens of couples on the spiritual path together, Campbell found five stages in what she calls *The Couple's Journey:* Romance, Power Struggle, Stability, Commitment, and Co-Creation.

"Love does not consist in gazing at each other, but in looking outward together in the same direction."

ANTOINE DE SAINT-EXUPERY

The following material is drawn from her own summary of these stages:

Stage 1, the *Romance Stage:* an underlying assumption is held that positive feelings are the basis for the relationship. Partners often secretly feel that "the relationship exists for my pleasure and comfort, but I must keep her happy in order to reap those rewards." Thus a sort of "mutual admiration society" develops which accents the similarities and ignores or denies differences between the partners. The "good news" about this stage is that couples begin to develop an emotional bond (or trust) and a common vision that can sustain them later on when the going gets rough. The "bad news" is that they may become so attached to the apparent security of romance that they deny many of their real feelings in order to keep the peace.

In Stage 2, the *Power Struggle Stage,* differences begin to emerge, resulting in feelings of being less in control of the other and often, therefore, less in love. During this stage, partners often feel competitive with one another. The good news about this stage is that couples usually realize they can "survive" the recognition of their differences. The bad news is they may not like how it feels when they differ; thus, they may subtly punish the partner for causing disappointment, or try to dominate, overpower, or simply "change" each other—always a futile effort.

Couples often don't make it beyond this stage.

In Stage 3, the *Stability Stage,* the couple discovers that the power struggle is actually a reflection of unresolved conflicts within each of them. Thus they begin to get an idea that a relationship can be a source of learning about oneself. They also find that when they are able to communicate about their differences, they eventually come to see these differences from a new and expanded perspective—a perspective which includes her viewpoint as well as his. The Stability Stage thus provides the first glimpse that a relationship can foster spiritual growth and mutual discovery.

In Stage 4, the *Commitment Stage,* couples realize that not only do I need you to help me expand my perspective, but also my very being is in some ways interdependent with yours. We recognize ourselves as part of a vast interconnected network, wherein everything we do affects everything else. Thus, if we each act to foster the developing uniqueness of others, our own development will be likewise supported.

Couples who stay together through the Commitment Stage inevitably experience their mutual effects on one another. They find also with time that it is impossible to maintain an ideal image of "the perfect couple." They are forced to deal with disappointments and surprises, since these are inevitable. And, eventually they come to see these disappointments as painful but necessary lessons on one's own path to self-understanding.

In Stage 5, the *Co-Creative Stage,* partners not only value the other as he or she is, but also are able to apply this "unconditional love of other-ness" to the world beyond the couple. The "other" now becomes anyone or anything outside of oneself who causes one to stretch beyond one's accustomed limits toward the discovery of new potentials.

This Co-Creative Stage is also a time for shared creativity or work aimed toward the world beyond the couple. Here, couples who have learned to embrace uncertainty, ambiguity and change in their relationship can apply what they have learned in our equally uncertain, ambiguous and every-changing world.

Thus, increasingly through the five stages of the Couple's Journey, the opportunity to creatively interact with a real live *other* becomes increasingly valued over getting one's own way. The transition from the domain of Security and Control to the domain of Growth and Discovery is realized as we discover our capacity to affirm what is genuinely *other* and as we discover our capacity for love.

For most couples to survive the "power struggle" stage, however, requires sincere commitment.

> "A holy relationship is a means of saving time.
> One instant spent together restores the universe to both of you."
>
> A Course in Miracles

The Question of Commitment

It's not usually very long, in any serious relationship, before the question of commitment comes up. This is quite natural, says Scott Peck, who sees commitment as "the foundation, the bedrock of any genuinely loving relationship." Here's what he says about it in *The Road Less Traveled:*

> Commitment is inherent in any genuinely loving relationship. Anyone who is truly concerned for the spiritual growth of another knows, consciously or instinctively, that he or she can significantly foster growth only through a relationship of constancy. . . . Couples cannot resolve, in any healthy way, the universal issues of marriage—dependency and independency, dominance and submission, freedom and fidelity, for example—without the security of knowing that the act of struggling over these issues will not in itself destroy the relationship.

But commitment is not necessarily something that can be or should be entered into lightly or quickly, says John Welwood, a transpersonal psychologist and head of the East-West Psychology Department at San Francisco's Institute of Integral Studies. In his forthcoming book, *Passion and Surrender,* Welwood suggests entering into commitment in stages:

> Much of the pressure, ambivalence, and confusion surrounding commitment stem from trying to impose it on a relationship, as an all-or-nothing arrangement. A more conscious, realistic approach would be to see commitment as a gradual process with its own natural evolution, unfolding organically out of the ground of genuine resonance, passion, and communication. . . ."

Here are the stages of commitment as he sees them:

> *Stage One, Working With:* The first and perhaps most critical stage of developing commitment seems to be the *sincere intention to work with whatever comes up,* no matter how difficult or threatening it may be. Working with whatever comes along means: being present with it, letting it touch us, not withholding ourselves from it, meeting it with our full attention and energy. This involves a willingness and dedication to keep coming back to the present moment. It

"While I generally find that great myths are great precisely because they represent and embody great universal truths, the myth of romantic love is a dreadful lie. Perhaps it is a necessary lie in that it ensures the survival of the falling-in-love experience that traps us into marriage. But as a psychiatrist I weep in my heart almost daily for the ghastly confusion and suffering that this myth fosters. Millions of people waste vast amounts of energy desperately and futilely attempting to make the reality of their lives conform to the unreality of the myth."

M. SCOTT PECK

also means being there with the other person in any pain that your behavior might produce for him or her.

Stage Two: Going Beyond Me First: This second stage involves learning to go beyond allegiance to our own pleasure and needs. If the first stage is preparation for stepping out of a cocoon, this second stage is actually taking that step. Going beyound the "me first" attitude must evolve from a real insight into the stagnation that results when we hold back from giving ourselves more fully to the situations we are a part of.

Stage Three: Long Range Journey: Having evolved through these first two stages, a couple may be ready to make a more enduring commitment to share and to follow out the destiny of their journey together, no matter where it leads. Real marriage is the joining of heart, mind, and spirit that has already happened at a very deep level. If a couple lets their commitment evolve gradually and naturally, marriage vows do not represent trying to live up to some ideal, but are more of a conscious celebration of the connection they have already made and learned to be true to.

Creating Intimacy

There are, of course, many degrees of commitment in any relationship. For example, the commitment of friendship, which is different than the commitment of lovers, which is different again than the commitment of husband and wife. But whatever the degree of commitment we choose, and whatever form of relationship we are in, there is always the central question of intimacy.

From the spiritual point of view, the process of discovering intimacy with another person is very similar to the process of becoming "intimate with yourself"—which is how Zen master Maezumi Roshi describes the spiritual path. It follows that all the qualities that encourage intimacy with others are also qualities that help us along the spiritual path.

Intimacy is the much-sought-after experience in any relationship, whether with our lovers or our friends. Sexual intimacy, which is so often confused with real intimacy, in no way insures that intimacy will occur in a relationship, and can even get in the way. Often we are closer to our

"When a man and woman with significant spiritual and psychological affinities encounter each other and fall in love, if they have evolved beyond the level of problems and difficulties, if they are beyond the level of merely struggling to make their relationship 'work,' then romantic love becomes the pathway not only to sexual and emotional happiness but also to the higher reaches of human growth. It becomes the context for a continuing encounter with the self, through the process of interaction with another self. Two consciousnesses, each dedicated to personal evolution, can provide an extraordinary stimulus and challenge to the other. Then ecstasy can become a way of life.

"Romantic love is not a myth waiting to be discarded, but, for most of us, a discovery waiting to be born."

NATHANIEL BRANDEN

friends than our lovers, for example.

Intimacy, which comes from opening ourselves ever more deeply to the other, is something we all both crave and fear, but our fear tricks us into isolating ourselves. How do we break down the barriers? Here are some suggestions:

Surrender

The notion of surrender is a tricky one in our culture, bringing up images of defeat and weakness. True surrender, of course, is something very different from "giving up the ship." It is at the heart of the spiritual life—the great mystery—and it is only natural, somehow, that surrender is also at the heart of a loving relationship.

Stewart Emery, co-founder of the personal-growth training called Actualizations, sees surrender as the essential ingredient in a relationship. In his book, *Actualizations, You Don't Have to Rehearse to Be Yourself*, he says:

> If a relationship is ever going to work in terms of life, in terms of supporting each other's well-being, we must surrender to each other. If you look up *surrender* in Webster's you will find that the first definition says, "To give up possession of or power over." Thus, surrender in a relationship would mean to give up possession of the power over the other. "Wait a minute! Are you kidding?! That is a horrendous notion to think about. If I don't have possession of you and I don't have power over you, what's going to keep you around?"
>
> Well, we really can't have a joyful relationship until we have removed all of the reasons to stick around—all the reasons of need, and of form, and of living. We should only stick around if the value is there—if together we enjoy the adventure of life, if we joyfully support and acknowledge each other's process.

We err when we think of surrender as "a form of behavior," agrees Sondra Ray in her book *Loving Relationships*.

"It is an openness and a willingness to receive. Surrender is giving up control but not losing power. It does not mean giving up your power to another person; on the

"What can also come up in the guise of spiritual truth—because the ego will use words like openness and unconditional love—is the idea that you should go out and have a sexual relationship with every person of the opposite sex. The ego will say, it's not important if you have this relationship because love should be universal. That all sounds very good, but it simply isn't the way it works. It certainly isn't sinful, but it does stop the forming of holy relationships. I've seen people try to work this out in a thousand different ways. Open marriage is one of those wonderful concepts because it has the word *open* in it. It sounds like it must be very spiritual. Some couples have been amazing in their ability to accommodate each other, but you don't see this deep peace growing in those relationships as long as that's going on."

HUGH PRATHER

contrary, it is an act made to increase your own power. This is because when you are willing to receive, you are taking in more love, and when you are taking in more love, you are taking in more independence, more freedom, and more God."

Stella Resnick, a gestalt therapist, puts it this way. "Surrender is not a defeat, nor a loss of power, but rather a skill that can improve with practice. To surrender is to let go, to give up control and just let it happen. Surrender is a physical experience: the control that you're letting go of is in the muscles, felt as tightness and restraint. To surrender is to relax the muscle's grip and to simply let yourself be."

Stella advises practicing a daily discipline of surrender. "There is an obvious paradox here," she says. "You must practice discipline to give up control. Yet that seems to be the case."

During the course of each day, she advises,

> Stop for a few minutes: Close your eyes, inhale deeply, all the way to the top of your chest, and blow the air out in a complete exhale. Imagine that you are also blowing out any tension or unpleasant feelings you've picked up along the way. Then rotate your head a few times, stretch your neck, your arms and back. Yawn and relax your jaw, and reconnect to your senses—scanning your environment slowly with your eyes, smelling the air, hearing distant sounds, feeling the objects that touch your skin, the tastes in your mouth.
>
> Practicing little moments of surrender makes big surrenders easier. As resistance and angst diminish, softness and trust grow, as so too grow feelings of love and tenderness. When we surrender, we become more loving, and, in the process, we end up showing more of what there is in us to love.

The Challenge of Honesty

While few would quarrel with the idea that honesty is the basis for true intimacy, honesty has its own traps. In a *New Age* interview, George Leonard, author of *The End of Sex,* says, "A good relationship really requires that you be totally open with each other—that you reveal every-

"One result of the mysterious nature of love is that no one has ever, to my knowledge, arrived at a truly satisfactory definition of love. In an effort to explain it, therefore, love has been divided into various categories: eros, philia, agape; perfect love and imperfect love, and so on. I am presuming, however, to give a single definition of love, again with the awareness that it is likely to be in some way or ways inadequate. I define love thus: The will to extend one's self for the purpose of nurturing one's own or another's spiritual growth."

M. SCOTT PECK

"Love is not primarily a relationship to a specific person; it is an *attitude,* an *orientation of character* which determines the relatedness of a person to the world as a whole, not toward one "object" of love. . . . If I truly love one person I love all persons, I love the world, I love life. If I can say to somebody else, 'I love you,' I must be able to say, 'I love in you everybody, I love through you the world, I love in you also myself.'"

ERICH FROMM

thing; fantasies, feelings, behavior, whatever you do and whatever you feel."

But he is quick to qualify the statement: "I'm not talking about twenty-five-hour-a-day processing! I think the old encounter mode of having to process every damn thing you do in your life, every fleeting thought, is just madness, and a big waste of time; it doesn't leave you any time to do anything creative. No, what I'm talking about is what the wellness movement calls 'withholding': if there's something that you're thinking or that you've done that would threaten the relationship if you told your partner, that's what you'd better tell."

Fidelity

The effect of sexual fidelity or non-fidelity on the bond of intimacy between individuals has been hotly debated

"Great love can both take hold and let go."

O. R. ORAGE

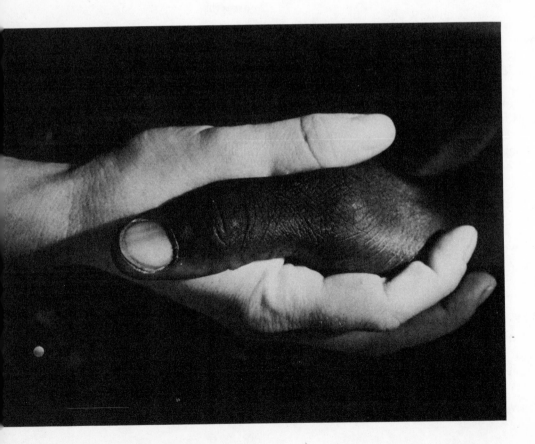

over the last two decades—and the positions on this issue couldn't be more polarized.

In *The End of Sex,* George Leonard decries the sexual revolution for depersonalizing the sexual experience and excising love and eroticism from our relationships. He suggests that we consider entering into what he calls "High Monogamy"—a relationship in which the partners are sexually faithful to each other out of choice rather than fear or religious or moral scruples (although you may have those). Leonard sees this as an adventure and a challenge:

> If you really stay in a High Monogamy relationship, where you are open to each other and committed to personal growth, eventually you are going to run up against some kind of barrier. What you are really going to run up against is this uncanny mirror in which you see yourself. And it is a wonderful mirror because it's like an x-ray; it goes right to the very heart of all your neuroses and your pettiness and your weakness and your phoniness, and you're going to get to see it all clearly. And you don't *want* to see it all. So the first thing that happens when you take one glimpse in this mirror of High Monogamy—the first response for a lot of us who were involved in the sexual revolution— is to just jump into somebody else's bed. Then you can run your games again. You can pull out your bag of tricks, tell your life story. The main purpose of that, of course, is to avoid change. If it's not working out with your partner— today or last week or next week—you figure, why not go try something else so you can keep staying the same; anything to avoid changing.

"For we are, actually, pioneers trying to find a new path through the maze of tradition, convention and dogma. Our efforts are part of the struggle to mature the conception of relationships between men and women—in fact all relationships. In such a light, every advance in understanding has value. Every step, even a tentative one, counts."

ANNE MORROW LINDBERGH

On the other hand, a number of people feel that rather than offering an escape from growth, "open" relationships can help promote it.

Filmmaker Dorothy Fadiman told us about her experiment in open marriage with her husband Jim:

"After eighteen years in a very loving, supportive relationship, which is also 'open,' all I can say is: the way we're living works for us. My husband Jim and I are both 43. We have two teenage daughters and we live as a nuclear family. Though it's not always been easy, having an open marriage has been for us the source of many more joys than problems."

"One of the things that goes on in most relationships is the attempt to control each other's behavior, especially when we are not together. We demand that our partner be a certain way. We usually demand fidelity, which is foolish and has never worked.

"I propose a new kind of agreement. It is this: *When I am not with you, I will conduct my life in a way that supports my ability to be with you when I am with you. When I am not with you, I will not do things that will interfere with my ability to be with you when I am with you.*

"In other words, when I am not with you, I will conduct myself in the adventure of life in such a way that when I am with you again, the time I was not with you will have become a foundation for a deeper experience of well-being and even more enjoyment when we are together.

"And if there are certain lessons that you have to learn, which I am not in a position to support you in learning, you need to be free to go to where you will get that support.

"A relationship should not suppress our adventure or suppress the speed with which we learn the lessons that are there for us to learn.

"Our experiences of being apart can totally support our experience of being together."

STEWART EMERY

Fadiman adds:

The real freedom for us has been an experience well beyond the sexual liberty. It's been in discovering the power of going past the arbitrary limits which marriage often sets: how much time you are free to spend with someone else; how deeply you are free to feel about someone other than your partner; to whom you are free to relate; and what you are actually free to do.

Some of our special times with others have included everything from a moment of fleeting, intense silent eye contact with a passing stranger to one of us taking a month-long trip with somebody else (as lovers) to bi-monthly lunches (totally non-sexual) with one of my old lovers and a favorite philosophical sparring partner! Jim and I both feel our own relationship keeps expanding as each of us individually expands our own sense of who we are.

Dorothy and Jim have arrived at a set of principles that make their open marriage work:

1. *Absolute honesty:* We don't want intimate details, but we do need clear information exchanges. We feel there should never be grounds for worry or suspicion about where somebody is.

2. *Consideration, sensitivity, unselfishness:* We've found that when we reach out more than halfway in our own and other relationships, there is a well-spring of love for everyone.

3. *A non-exploitive attitude:* As much as is humanly possible, we avoid any situation in which there are indications that someone will be hurt or in which someone else will have to lie.

4. *Discretion:* Although we've made no effort to hide our lifestyle, we tend to be low-keyed about how we conduct ourselves, and we don't draw attention or flaunt the "open" aspect in our day-to-day lives.

Fadiman says that the "key condition seems to be that the primary relationship must be solid. I definitely do not recommend this for partners who are struggling. I would only recommend opening a relationship if (1) both partners want to add this kind of freedom to their agreement, (2) both partners agreed that they want to be honest, and hear the truth as well, and (3) both partners feel their love for each other is greater than their need for each other."

The experts don't agree about much on the subject, except that both kinds of relationships involve risk and difficulty and that it takes exceptional love, honesty and commitment to make any kind of relationship work.

How to Argue in Peace

Contributed by Hugh Prather

1. *Sit down.* (Spiritual ears are strange birds. To open them you must first take a load off your feet.)

2. *Hear out the other person without interrupting.* (Interrupting tickles the underarms of the aura and causes a blinding glare—very much like being tickled pink. Therefore, if you interrupt, your spiritual eyes will not be able to look into the heart of the other person to see what he really wants. It will make you happy to see what he wants.)

3. *Begin and end your remarks by thinking, "I'd rather be happy than right."* (An ego clothed in righteousness stands upright and gazes arrogantly down on all. A nude ego always titters and runs. So by all means state your ego position. Get it out there where you can see it plainly. But remember: the only position that is right is peace. If your position is not extending peace, it must be wrong.)

4. *If at all possible state each opinion as a fear.* (Say what you are afraid of, because we are always more willing to give up fears than cherished opinions, even though inside every opinion that is causing a rift there is a fear. It lurks there like white sugar inside commercial granola. So read the labels on your opinions.)

5. *Close your eyes and remember your debt of gratitude to each other.* (Maybe you didn't mean to, but you have brought each other a very long way. Remembering love can never hurt you. But anger is mental constipation. The celestial laxative is one or two kind memories taken with every argument. Now remember several things the other person did that were gentle, or thoughtful, or made something happy. The first one or two will be hard to think of, but after that the rapture of divine diarrhea will overtake you.)

6. *Think of the gifts you wish to give the relationship, then open your eyes and share them.* (A relationship is more important than an issue. Being issue-oriented is as different from being people-oriented as leeches are from crystals. One sucks blood; the other carries light. Don't use this occasion to drain strength from the relationship. Let the outcome be a greater friendship. Therefore make your "gifts," your compromises, very specific so that they will have real value.

7. *Do not reconsider.* (You were more peaceful when you decided. Trust the state of mind you were in. Don't forget that Lot's wife was turned to a pillar of salt when she looked back. But now salt has been found out. Today if you look back you might end up as brown rice in somebody's stir fry. So don't be stirred up. Be at peace with this child of God.)

Mr. Prather is a poet and author of *Notes to Myself.*

Finding Help

"There is hardly any activity, any enterprise, which is started with such tremendous hopes and expectations, and yet which so regularly fails, as love," says Erich Fromm in *The Art of Loving.* Why, he wonders, are people so unwilling to examine their failures and get to the heart of the matter? Fromm views love as an art, and as such it requires the same sort of dedication and practice that one would expect to devote to any art or craft.

Most of us don't see it that way. We think we should just know how to be loving and that our relationships should somehow work out on their own accord. Getting help from the outside is seen as a failure or a sign of weakness in the relationship, when in fact it can mean quite the opposite. The willingness to get help is often the first and most important choice in improving a relationship.

John D. Buksbazen, former Zen monk, author of *To Forget the Self,* and a psychotherapist with extensive experience counseling couples involved in a spiritual discipline, says, "Often people who enter spiritual disciplines in this country have not yet themselves thoroughly attended to the more mundane issues connected with growing up,

handling their own emotional problems, and learning how to relate intimately with other people.

"When such a person announces to his or her secular spouse or lover his or her entry into The Path, that news frequently fails to justify the subsequent neglect, proselytizing, or spiritual chauvinism so often characteristic of new devotees."

As a therapist, Buksbazen counsels his clients to "make the relationship an explicit part of their spiritual practice. In practical terms, this means learning to identify and mutually solve problems as they arise rather than avoiding them or discounting their significance. This may also include the use of marital or family therapy. The need for such professional help shouldn't be viewed as failure or unworthiness on a spiritual level."

According to Buksbazen, those on a spiritual path "are more likely to benefit from some of the non-psychoanalytically oriented approaches such as strategic or structural family therapy." (See the work of Milton Erikson, Virginia Satir, Salvador Minuchin, and Jay Haley for examples.)

"These are therapies that could be said to work on the 'Sangha' principle, the interrelationships between people. They are based on the systemic ecology of families or couples. Instead of looking at one individual, they look at the totality of the entire system."

Relationships Seminars

Taking a weekend couples workshop or retreat can be a less threatening way to begin to work on your relationship than entering therapy. There are many relationships seminars that now take a spiritual approach. A number of these can be found by consulting one of the free Common Ground resource guides that are now available in most cities. As always, it is a matter of personal taste, but we advise trusting word-of-mouth more than self-promotion.

The safest relationships seminars—and by all accounts among the most successful—are the Marriage Encounters. Although they first started as a Catholic movement, there are now also Jewish and Protestant Marriage Encounter groups. These meet locally in many communities, and you can find out more about them through your church, temple, or parish house. Marriage Encounter provides a good basic course in what makes marriages work and how to enrich them.

Marriage Encounter was developed in the mid-1950s in Spain by a Catholic priest and "middle-class" working couples. It came to the United States in 1966. Forty-nine countries now have Marriage Encounter Weekends, including countries behind the Iron Curtain. Worldwide Marriage Encounter encompasses thirteen Christian faith expressions. Jewish Marriage Encounter, which is based upon similar guidelines, is a separate organization. Programs are staffed by volunteers comprised of both lay couples and religious leaders.

The Marriage Encounter Weekend is designed for married couples to examine their shared love and life through personal and private communication of feelings. Although couples meet in groups, they share their feelings about their marital relationship only with their spouse, not within the context of the group. The group environment

"As little as Bushido or the Order of Chivalry grew up accidentally does conscious love arise by nature. As these were works of art so must conscious love be a work of art. Such a lover enrolls himself, goes through his apprenticeship, and perhaps one day attains to mastery. He perfects himself in order that he may purely wish and aid the perfection of his beloved."

O. R. ORAGE

"The meeting of two personalities is like the contact of two chemical substances: if there is any reaction, both are transformed."

C. G. JUNG

provides an atmosphere in which lay couples and clerical staff present talks related to various aspects of marriage. Husband and wife then spend time, in the privacy of their room, sharing their reflections and, through dialogue, developing a greater understanding and a fuller knowledge of each other.

Marriage Encounter is for people who are essentially happy in their marriage but who wish to "recommit" to one another and strengthen their bond. The notion of "matrimonial spirituality" is an important part of the Marriage Encounter experience. It is felt that by being more open to one's spouse, one becomes more open to God. Couples experience the beauty of their married love relationship as a manifestation of God's love for them.

A high weekend experience can provide helpful insights, but caution should be exercised. As Sondra Ray says in her book, *Loving Relationships*, "A partner will bring up all your patterns. Don't avoid relationships; they are the best seminar in town. The truth is that *your partner is your guru.*"

The Twelve Hour, Do-it-Yourself Relationships Seminar

Therapy and workshops cost money. Here's a way to improve your relationships at home all by yourselves. Although Nathaniel Branden, in his book *The Psychology of Romantic Love,* proposes this specifically for couples in trouble, several of us who are quite happy with our relationships have tried it on a more limited basis—two hours a week. It works wonders!

Sometimes, when working with a man and a woman who have become estranged from each other or whose relationship appears to have become lifeless and mechanical, I will propose a certain "homework assignment." They are asked to spend a day together, entirely alone. No books, no television, no telephone calls. If they have children they make arrangements for someone to take care of them. No distractions of any kind are allowed. They are committed to remaining in the same room with each other for twelve hours. They further agree that no matter what the other might say, neither will leave the room refusing to talk. And, of course, there must, under no circumstances, be any physical violence. They can sit for several hours in total and absolute silence if they like, but they must remain together.

They are free during this twelve-hour session to talk about anything, providing it is personal, as opposed to discussions of business, problems concerning the children's schoolwork, domestic details, and so forth. They must talk about themselves or each other or the relationship. Having placed themselves in a situation where all other sources of stimulation are absent, they have only their own selves and each other, and then they begin to learn the meaning of intimacy. There is almost always a gradual deepening feeling, a deepening emotional involvement, an expanding experience of aliveness. More often than not, the day ends happily, but sometimes it ends with the realization that the relationship may no longer serve the needs of either and that they may not wish to remain together. This is not a failure of the experiment, but a success. It is a success because the waste of two lives in an empty marriage or relationship is a tragedy. I have found that for two people who love each other but who do not know how to make their relationship work, or do not seem to know how to communicate effectively, a twelve-hour session of this kind, participated in at least once a month, can produce the most radical changes in the quality of the relationship. One of the changes is the unexpected discovery of communications skills they did not even dream they could possess.

The Best Advice on Relationships

The overall best advice we could find on relationships was summed up by the Dalai Lama of Tibet during his visit to the Harvard Divinity School. As Randy Ring reported in *New Age Journal*:

"Over and over [the Dalai Lama] emphasized the practice of altruism. 'The purpose of life,' he said simply, 'is to increase the warm heart. Think of other people. Serve other people sincerely. No cheating. . . .'"

Despite the intricacies of Buddhist metaphysics, he said that all the teachings can be distilled into two sentences: "If you can, help others; if you cannot do that, at least do not harm them."

"Love is the pursuit of the whole."

PLATO

Recommended Reading

On Love, A. R. Orage (Samuel Weiser, 1974). This quaint little book shares Orage's philosophy on love and religion. A student of Gurdjieff and his chief representative in America in the 1930s, Orage is both a sensible and inspiring man.

Loving Relationships, Sondra Ray (Celestial Arts, 1980). This is a zany little handbook on how to get your relationships in order. Ray draws on affirmations, visualizations, and her own specialty, rebirthing. We can have it just the way we want, she says; we just have to think we can.

Relationship & Identity, David Spangler (Findhorn, 1977). This book is a series of lectures that Spangler gave at the Findhorn Foundation in the late seventies, in an attempt to make sense of the confusion surrounding relationships and sexuality. His interpretation of the role of sexuality and relationship in the evolution of the species is both practical and thought-provoking.

Gift From the Sea, Anne Morrow Lindbergh (Pantheon, 1967). A classic written in the 1950s about the relationship between spiritual growth and the various stages in any long-term healthy relationship. Poetic, inspiring, and way ahead of its time.

Resources

Organizations that provide training on improving relationships:

Actualizations, 1610 Tiburon Blvd., Tiburon, CA 94920, (415)-435-5122. Ongoing workshops nationwide with a strong focus on communications in relationships.

Marriage Encounter, 1925 West 3rd Ave., Columbus, OH 43212, (614)294-3774. A volunteer Catholic organization that provides weekend workshops for couples.

Relationships, 39 Harvard St., Brookline, MA 02146, (617)739-3300. Provides weekend workshops on improving relationships in several locations in North America and Europe.

Local Workshops: Many local holistic education centers hold workshops for couples or for improving relationships. Look for them in local or regional new age directories.

4

SEX

Bobo roshi was a perfect monk as a young man. He got up earlier than everyone, and sat in the garden long after everyone else had gone to bed. He never climbed over the monastery walls to visit the geisha houses, as the other monks did occasionally. He lived this way for fourteen years, working on his koan without a break. He did everything just as it was supposed to be done, and more. But he still couldn't find the answer to his koan, no matter what he did.

Suddenly, late one night, when he had been sitting on a rock in the garden, he decided to leave the monastery. He stopped concentrating on his koan, stood up abruptly, and climbed over the monastery walls. For the first time in years, he walked through the streets of Kyoto aimlessly, until he found himself in the floating world of the pleasure district.

A woman gestured to him through drawn shades. He went into her room, she served tea and then saki, and then embraced him. Everything fell away as they made love, and when the monk exploded into her at the height of his pleasure, he found that the universe fell away too, and the answer to his koan, which he had stopped thinking about for the first time in fourteen years, suddenly flashed into consciousness. He wept and laughed with joy, gave the lady of the night his rosary beads, and went back to the monastery, where his *satori* was confirmed by his astonished abbot.

"What is sex, after all, but the symbol of the relation of man to woman, woman to man? And the relation of man to woman is wide as all life. It consists in infinite different flows between the two beings, different, even apparently contrary. Chastity is part of the flow between man and woman, as is physical passion. And beyond these, an infinite range of subtle communication which we know nothing about."

D. H. LAWRENCE

Sex, as the young monk discovered, is not only one of the most powerful forces in our lives, it is also potentially one of the most liberating.

In many ways, sex is identical with the life-force itself. It brings us together, serves as an expression of love, creates life, and fulfills our longing for unity and wholeness. It is no wonder, then, that mystics of all traditions have often expressed their deepest spiritual ecstasy in images of sexual love. From the spiritual point of view, we engage in sex not only for physical release, but to merge with the beloved in a state of ecstatic spiritual union.

"For what is the beloved?" asks D. H. Lawrence. "She is that which I myself am not. In the act of love, I am pure male, and she is pure female. She is she, and I am I, and, clasped together with her, I know how perfectly she is not me, how perfectly I am not her, how utterly we are two, the light and the darkness, and how infinitely and eternally not-to-be-comprehended by either of us is the surpassing One we make."

"The height of sexual love," writes Alan Watts, in his classic *Nature, Man, and Woman,*

> coming upon us of itself, is one of the most total experiences of relationship to the other of which we are capable, but prejudice and insensitivity have prevented us from seeing that in any other circumstances such delight would be called mystical ecstasy. For what lovers feel for each other in this moment is no other than adoration in its full religious sense, and its climax is almost literally the pouring of their lives into each other. Such adoration, which is due only to God, would indeed be idolatrous, were it not that in that moment love takes away illusion and shows the beloved for what he or she in truth is—not the socially pretended person but the naturally divine.

Sex Is Not Separate From Life

When visionary culture-watcher George Leonard proclaims in *The End of Sex* that "sex is an idea whose time has passed," he is talking about the notion of sex as "an activity, a field of study, an entity that somehow seems to exist almost entirely separated from the rest of life." Leonard read "scores of current sex books" for his research,

"Only the united beat of sex and heart together can create ecstasy."

ANAïS NIN

and found that few of them ever mentioned "love" or creation. He said that the modern notion of sex ignores the close relationship that ancient and traditional cultures recognized "between the act of love and the process of creation—not just of babies, but of matter, earth, sky, water, islands, monsters and gods."

"This disconnection," Leonard points out, "makes us think that our erotic behavior actually has little to do with anything else that we believe, feel, or do and is, thus, essentially trivial."

What we need to do, Leonard reminds us, is "reconnect the bedroom with the rest of our lives, with society, and nature, and perhaps with the stars. We need to realize that the way we make love influences the way we make our world, and vice versa. We need to appreciate the connection between the erotic and the creative. We need, more than anything else to reawaken to the almost-endless, half-forgotten, life-transforming powers of full-bodied, fully committed erotic love."

"Sex is just the beginning,
not the end.
But if you miss the beginning,
you will miss the end also."

BHAGWAN SHREE RAJNEESH

In *The World of Sex*, Henry Miller echoes this theme:

For some, sex leads to sainthood; for others it is the road to hell. In this respect it is like everything else in life—a person, a thing, an event, a relationship. All depends on one's point of view. To make life more beautiful, more wonderful, more deep and satisfying, we must gaze with fresh, clear vision upon every contributing element of life. If there is something wrong about our attitude toward sex, then there is something wrong about our attitude toward bread, toward money, toward work, toward play, toward everything. How can one enjoy a good sex life if he has a distorted, unhealthy attitude toward the other aspects of life?

Unoriginal Sin

As most of us know all too well, conventional religion teaches that sex and spirituality are somehow mutually exclusive, if not antagonistic. There are many rationales for finding sexuality and spirituality incompatible: Saints Paul and Augustine equate desire with Original Sin; Hindus see sex as illusion or *maya*. Western esotericists teach that sexual energy is either wasted in the pursuit of pleasure *or* transmuted into a "higher" spiritual energy. In any case, it all comes down to what Alan Watts aptly characterizes as "the ancient and widely prevalent conflict between spirituality and sexuality—the belief, found in East and West alike—that sexual abstinence and freedom from lust are essential prerequisites for man's proper and ultimate development."

But, as Rajneesh pointedly observes: "Sex has been called the original sin. It is neither original nor sin."

It is not surprising that, because of the way our culture has tended to view sex, few of us have been taught to see sex as a spiritual path. In fact, many of the attitudes and qualities that make up the spiritual life can be developed and refined through sex. Seen from the spiritual point of view, sex becomes a path of great subtlety and beauty.

Exploring the Path of Sex: Five Guideposts

Here are five aspects that illuminate the spiritual side of sexuality for us:

1. Sex as Communication

Sex is our most intimate form of communication. At its most intense, communication becomes communion—a mutual opening and meeting beyond words and concepts from our deepest and most vulnerable parts. Such communication is only possible when there is openness, honesty, and regard for your partner as an equal. This may seem obvious, but it is the most fundamental aspect of sex, and one that is too often forgotten. Sex reminds us of our interdependence and oneness.

2. Sex as Surrender

Communication in its deepest sense leads to surrender, to openness to your partner. Stella Resnick, writing in *New Age,* says, "In sexual surrender, the emphasis is not so much on action as it is on receptivity, on becoming more and more sensitive to the waves of excitement that wash over the body. Giving up technique and fixed notions about what one is supposed to do to have good sex opens up the element of surprise and makes sex more like a dance choreographed not by the mind but by the natural rhythms of the body."

"The greatest resistance to sexual surrender is in the mind," continues Resnick. "When people have trouble letting themselves go sexually, often it has to do with interference from mental instructions that result in holding the breath and tensing. The mind keeps you distracted from what you're feeling and works against your full physical and emotional participation."

As Resnick points out, "surrender takes place primarily in the breath, and even more specifically, on the exhale, since we take in on the inhale and let go on the exhale. . . . Conscious breathing focuses you in the present. As the breath releases tension, you begin to feel yourself floating and you can let your body take over. You can synchronize your breath with your lover's, matching inhales and exhales—breathing the one breath."

3. Sex As Delight

"Bhoga is Yoga," goes an old Indian saying, or roughly translated, "delight is religion." Sexual pleasure and ecstasy provide a foretaste and preparation for the experience of "mahasukha," The Great Bliss of Liberation. "Orgasm is an explosion which clears my mind," one woman reported in *The Hite Report,* "a force collected from my entire body, revitalizing and inspiring—like waves of fire, like becoming one with the rhythms that run the universe,

"In this technique it is common for the individual to experience as many as a dozen or twenty peaks of response which, while closely approaching the sexual climax, deliberately avoid what we should interpret as actual orgasm. Persons who practice such techniques commonly insist that they experience orgasm at each and every peak even though each is held to something below full response and . . . ejaculation is avoided."

ALFRED KINSEY

like receiving a personal message that life is good and beautiful. . . ."

4. The Union of Opposites

According to a myth that Plato retells in the *Symposium,* human beings were originally joined to each other. In the distant past they were separated and ever since then they have been trying in the act of sex to reunite with their lost halves. According to this Platonic myth, then, in sex we are trying to regain our wholeness and completion.

In the East the Tantras—ancient Hindu and Buddhist scriptures—use sexual symbolism to express the union of opposites necessary for enlightenment. In the Hindu Tantras the Shakti, or goddess, is considered the primal energy of the world, and the male deity (often Siva) symbolizes meditative stillness. In Buddhist Tantra, the female deity symbolizes emptiness or wisdom (stillness), while the male deity symbolizes compassion or skillful means (activity). (Scholars have written volumes on the significance of this difference, but for us it only goes to show that it is the union of opposites, not the identification of them as male or female, that is the important point.)

In Taoism, union is expressed through the familiar yin and yang symbols. The female is symbolized by the yin—dark, passive, soft, yielding energy—and the male by the yang: active, hard, light energy. The universe is made up of the union of both. Light cannot exist without dark, active without passive, hard without soft.

"The Taoists," Jolan Chang writes in *The Tao of Loving,* "held that sexual harmony put one in communion with the infinite force of nature, which they believe had sexual overtones too. Earth for instance was the female, or Yin element, and Heaven the male, or Yang. It was the interaction between these two that constituted the whole. By extension the union of men and women also created a unity. And one was as important as the other."

There is, of course, no reason to simplify the polarities of love as unambiguously "male" and "female"; in fact, it is probably closer to the truth (and more enjoyable) to realize that we all include both male and female qualities, both positive and negative poles, and that in our love-

"Our sexuality is the deepest and most primal impulse we possess. Repressed, it drains our vital energies and weakens all our faculties of mind and body. Fulfilled, it becomes a great creative and regenerative force. Sexual liberation does not lie in mastering techniques which see our bodies as pleasure mechanisms, but in the realization that our bodies are holy and that sexual relationships are sharing of the divine energy that animates the universe."

LAYNA VERIN

making we can each manifest different qualities at different times.

5. Sex As Cosmos: As Above, So Below

In *The Way of Splendor,* Edwin Hoffman tells us that according to the ancient Jewish mystical tradition of the Kabbalah, "the celestial 'King' and 'Queen' unite in sexual ecstasy to sustain the cosmos each day. . . . Whenever marital partners engage in lovemaking with intense concentration, they help to harmonize all the realms of the universe. That is, just as the full sexual embrace—if performed with the proper attitude and desire—is seen to bring the human couple together on many levels of their being, so too does this act cause peace and love to reign more thoroughly everywhere. 'As above, so below.'"

Contemplative Love

The path that recognizes the inseparability of sex and spirituality is most fully described in the ancient Tantric and Taoist traditions. Alan Watts calls this the tradition of contemplative sex.

The key to spiritual lovemaking or contemplative sex is to not make orgasm the goal. "The pleasure in sex," writes Rollo May in *Love and Will,* "is described by Freud and others as the reduction of tension; in eros, on the contrary, we wish not to be released from the excitement but rather to hang onto it, to bask in it, and even to increase it."

The secret of this kind of goalless lovemaking is actually quite simple and natural. As excitement builds, we usually increase our movements to increase tension and force release. But in contemplative sex, you simply relax. You slow down, and breathe deeply and slowly. If your eyes are closed, open them; open your mind and senses too. Notice your breathing, and the radiance of your partner.

"Sexual love in this spirit is a revelation," writes Alan Watts. "Long before the male orgasm begins, the sexual impulse manifests itself as what can only be described, psychologically, as a melting warmth between the partners, so that they seem veritably to flow into each other. To put it another way, 'physical lust' transforms itself into the most considerate and tender form imaginable."

"One has to be beyond sex one day, but the way beyond goes through it, and if you never go into it rightly, it is very difficult to go beyond it. So going through it is part of going beyond."

BHAGWAN SHREE RAJNEESH

They came to a stream. There stood a girl unable to cross for fear of ruining her dress. The first monk picked her up and carried her across. The monks continued their journey in silence. After a few hours the second monk turned and asked, "How could you pick her up when we have made vows not to even look at a woman?" The first monk replied, "I left her back at the stream but you seem to be still carrying her."

ZEN STORY

Shiva and Shakti, the personifications of male and female energy in the tantric system. The lotus symbolizes the ascent of kundalini energy up the spine, the sword our need to surrender the personal self to higher self, the wheel the cycles of Karma and rebirth, and the jewel the ideal of attainment, liberation, and enlightenment.

Beyond Orgasm

While nearly all traditions of contemplative love agree that it is a mistake to make orgasm the goal of lovemaking, it is also a mistake to make *not* having an orgasm the goal of lovemaking. Certain Tantric and Taoist texts give elaborate instructions on how to channel the sexual energy ordinarily discharged during orgasm. We do not recommend that you try to use sexual energy to open *chakras* (psychic energy points) or to awaken the Kundalini, the so-called "serpent power" said to lie dormant at the base of the spine. Practices like that need a great deal of spiritual and yogic preparation and personal guidance. Without the proper prerequisites, they may be dangerous.

"The entire social and cultural game of antisexual, 'spirit against flesh' education is so monstrous, so opposed to incarnate human happiness and human responsibility, as well as the ultimate transcendental sacrifice of the individual body-mind through moral and spiritual processes, that it must be considered the primary social and even philosophical issue of our time."

DA FREE JOHN

Alan Watts reminds us:

The point is so important that it can bear repetition: contemplative love—like contemplative meditation—is only quite secondarily a matter of technique. For it has no specific aim; there is nothing particular that has to be made to happen. It is simply that a man and a woman are together exploring their spontaneous feeling—without any preconceived idea of what it ought to be, since the sphere of contemplation is not what should be, but what is.

Most people who experiment with contemplative sex find that the attitude is most important, not the final result. Nothing is wrong with making love in a contemplative way, enjoying the moment, your partner, and the slow meditative dance for as long as you like—and then, if it feels right, going on to climax. Contemplative sex is meant to allow you to explore the dimensions of your own sexuality, not to add more rules. Since contemplative sex is goalless, let your lovemaking assume whatever form it takes.

Karezza

In the latter part of the nineteenth century, a remarkable woman named Dr. Alice Stockham discovered a way of spiritual lovemaking that had a striking similarity to Taoist and Tantric techniques. Dr. Stockham, who practiced medicine in Cincinnati towards the end of the nineteenth century, was one of the first women doctors in America. She had traveled to India (where she apparently found the inspiration for her method), and was an early advocate of women's rights.

Dr. Stockham's method, called *karezza* (from the Italian for "caress") is set forth in her book, *The Ethics of Marriage* (Health Research, Box 70, Mokelumme, CA 95245). Though Dr. Stockham's method enjoyed a fair amount of popularity during her lifetime, Victorian prudery kept the practice from spreading widely. Recently, however, there has been a renewed interest in karezza, which bears a remarkable resemblance to Masters and Johnson's technique for curing frigidity and impotence.

The following reappraisal first appeared in *New Age* magazine:

In essence karezza is just conscious, slow, gentle sex without orgasm for either man or woman.

Couples who practiced karezza on Stockham's suggestion began to report intense spiritual experiences, such as holy love for their partners (after years of boredom), feelings of total union, the presence of spirit beings, a glow of blue or golden lights, and pure bliss lasting for hours, both during and after amazingly long periods of lovemaking.

Wilhelm Reich and the Function of the Orgasm

"Love, work, and knowledge" wrote Wilhelm Reich, "are the well-springs of our life. They should also govern it."

Reich was a close student and colleague of Freud's until the two had a parting of the ways—mostly (according to Reich) because he followed up the implications of Freud's theories of sexuality, not only psychoanalytically but also biologically.

It was Reich's belief that a healthy, life-affirming person was a person with a healthy, life-affirming sex life. This belief led Reich to a close investigation of the function of the orgasm—and his discovery that many people, even if they seemed to have "normal" sexual relations, were actually crippled by their "character armor."

Reich found evidence of this "armor" not only in the psyche, but also in the characteristic way people held their bodies and breathed. Reichian therapy, as it developed, thus included exercises, massage, and deep breathing. Reich's approach is now recognized as having paved the way for many of the body therapies made popular by the human potential movement—bio-energetics, gestalt therapy, rolfing, primal scream therapy, et al. owe much to Reich's pioneering work.

For Reich, Ken Dychtwald writes in *Bodymind*, "Sexual energy was the most sublime of all energies, and sexual freedom the highest of all aspirations. . . . The healthy person, according to Reich, is one who regularly engages in lovingly uninhibited sexual exchange leading to a thoroughly satisfying orgasm."

In *The Function of the Orgasm,* Reich writes:

Psychic health depends upon orgastic potency, i.e., upon the degree to which one can surrender to and experience the climax of excitation in the natural sexual act. It is founded upon the healthy character attitude of the individual's capacity for love. Psychic illnesses are the result of a disturbance of the natural ability to love. In the case of orgastic impotence, from which the overwhelming majority of people suffer, damming-up of biological energy occurs and becomes the source of irrational actions. The essential requirement to cure psychic disturbances is the reestablishment of the natural capacity for love.

Gay Sex

Nearly all traditional descriptions of contemplative lovemaking make use of images arising from the male-female polarity. The possibility of contemplative lovemaking, however, is open to everyone, whether heterosexual, bisexual, or homosexual.

Allen Ginsberg tells us that he once asked a Tibetan tantric master if there were any "special" teachings or sexual rituals for homosexuals. "It's not so important if you make love with a man or woman," he was told. "The important thing is the communication—whoever it is with."

J. G. Bennett, a close disciple of Gurdjieff, makes an interesting statement about Gurdjieff's attitude towards homosexuals in spiritual work.

"A homosexual who thinks himself special or superior to others cannot even enter the deeper aspects of self-worth," he writes. "It is equally necessary here to put aside any sense of guilt or inferiority. I have myself observed the way that Gurdjieff dealt with homosexuals. He was at pains to give them confidence that they could work on themselves, and he never allowed them to feel that they were special."

In *My Guru and His Disciple,* Christopher Isherwood, author of *I The Camera* and *The Berlin Stories* (together filmed as *Cabaret*), recalls how he first met Swami Prahbavananda of the Hollywood Vedanta Society, and then studied with him, more or less, for thirty years. That Isherwood was gay did not faze the Swami at all. When Isherwood finally confessed to his guru that he had a male lover, the Swami told him to treat his lover, Vernon, as "the young Lord Krishna."

Writes Isherwood, "I understood the Swami to mean that I should try to see Vernon's beauty—the very aspect of him which attracted me to him sexually—as the beauty of Krishna, which attracts devotees to him spiritually."

The more traditional religions, of course, have often condemned homosexuality, thus excluding gay men and women from meaningful participation in the spiritual life of the community. With the rise of the gay liberation movement, a new phenomenon has occurred. There are churches, such as the Metropolitan Church in New York City, that address themselves primarily to the gay community. There are also groups within the established churches that address gay Catholics or gay Jews. In San Francisco a group of gay Zen Buddhists have started a group called the Maitri (a Sanskrit word meaning "friendliness") Association, and have also started a zendo for the gay community in the Castro District. *The Advocate,* a national gay newspaper, also runs an est-type seminar, called The Advocate Experience, for gay men and woman.

From a spiritual point of view, it is important that men and women learn to develop and appreciate both the "male" and "female" qualities of their psyche, though how each person does this is very much an individual matter.

Sexual Rituals: Seeing Your Lover as Divine

In ancient India, contemplative love often took the form of a ritual, which emphasized the sacred nature of the sexual encounter. Such ritual might include a period of meditation, the repetition of mantras, mudras (symbolic gestures), visualization, and advanced yogic breathing practices. Incense, wine, and ritual foods were also included.

While it would not make much sense for a contemporary Westerner to duplicate such rituals, certain basic elements and attitudes taken from these ancient rituals can help enhance the contemporary experience of contemplative love. The basic idea behind ritual is that it enables us to see the universe as sacred. According to the Tantric view,

"Sexual liberation implies the liberation of the whole being: body, mind and spirit. This holistic viewpoint is an essential ingredient to the understanding of the Sexual Secrets."

NIK DOUGLAS

we forget to see our partners as divine—as the gods or goddesses they (and we) truly are. Ritual slows us down, lifts us out of our habitual way of seeing the world, and reminds us of who we can be.

"Ritual can be many things and take many forms. Ritual should be what works for you," says Lewis Durham. Durham, Dean of the Institute for the Study of Human Sexuality in San Francisco, has adapted Tantric and Taoist rituals for Westerners. He suggests meditating at least thirty minutes or more before you begin.

"Sexual union is an auspicious Yoga which, through involving enjoyment of all the sensual pleasures, gives release. It is a Path to Liberation."

KAULARAHASYA

Think about your partner and begin to focus your energy on the moment—erase all the rest of your concerns from the day and let your mind be at rest.

Let whatever happens happen. The Taoists have an expression for this—*Wu Wei*—which means non-doing. It may sound a bit contradictory, but Wu Wei does not mean you do not believe things can happen—you know that there is female and male energy that can unite. Wu Wei will let it happen or not happen, if that is the nature of things at the moment. You participate in the natural flow of life and energy and do not expect that anything has to happen. It is a continuous letting-go of expectations in successive moments of now.

"Vishnu and Lakshmi are ever in love-dalliance together; for this purpose they assume various forms. Their changing manifestations tell of their inner communication with each other. They are the Eternal Lovers."

VISHNU PURANA

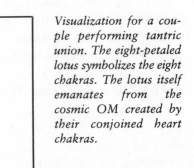

Visualization for a couple performing tantric union. The eight-petaled lotus symbolizes the eight chakras. The lotus itself emanates from the cosmic OM created by their conjoined heart chakras.

A Taoist Ritual

Here is an example of such a ritual from the book *Sexual Secrets*.

The authors tell of a Taoist text called *The Yellow Book for Passing Over to the Other Side*. In it is described an ancient sexual ritual in which the partners act out a cosmic drama. This ritual was created to "help couples to unify their Yin and Yang essences," which would "enable them to enter the timeless realm of Immortality." The couple first undergoes a retreat and purification for several days:

> Then the couples stand, face to face and holding hands, the man's index finger between the index and middle finger of the woman. Standing thus, the couples meditate on the gods and goddesses of the body, the spirits of the season and the purpose of the ritual. Then each couple separates and singly meditates on the gestures and postures of the rite.
>
> The master instructs the participants to undress, pair off, and begin a slow mystic dance. First standing, then seated, and finally reclining, the couples perform a series of mystic movements and gestures, imitating animals, birds, natural forces and celestial bodies. Every move that the man makes is mirrored exactly by his partner. If he lifts his left arm or leg, she must raise her right arm or leg. This is called *Cosmic Harmonization*. Gradually the movements accelerate and spontaneity prevails. Intoning a prayer that expresses their desire to move both Heaven and Earth, the couples lie down and touch each other on the head, the heart and the sexual region, all the while controlling their breathing and holding in mind the concept of Cosmic Harmonization.

"This ancient sexual ritual," the authors write, "has many elements that can be incorporated into modern love-rites. The linking of fingers helps channel energy. Meditation on the *beings* within the body, seasonal spirits and the purpose of the ritual all help to direct sexual energy along the path to fulfillment. Mystic dance, made up of natural movements and gestures, mirrored in each partner and increasing in tempo, greatly aids the harmonization of mood; personality limitations are quickly overcome by

"The lotus-flower, the sex organ of the partner is an ocean filled with Bliss. . . . When it is united with the Scepter, the male organ, their mixture is compared to the Elixir produced from the combination of myrrh and nutmeg. From their union a pure knowledge arises, which explains the nature of all things."

KALACHAKRA TANTRA

this joyous opening. Breath and mind control are essential to any concept of *Cosmic Harmonization*."

Celibacy

In many spiritual traditions celibacy or abstaining from sex is considered an important part of the spiritual path.

In the East, and in certain Western esoteric traditions, celibacy is practiced as a means to store and transmute sexual energy into spiritual energy. Dio Neff, who has written extensively on the subject for *Yoga Journal* and other publications, calls this approach "positive celibacy."

"Positive celibacy is where sexual energy is considered an honorable, even sacred force, as distinct from those teachings which view sexuality with distaste and suspicion, where it's thought to be the antithesis of spirit," she writes in an article in the *Yoga Journal*. "Positive celibacy adherents believe in abstinence not to avoid something 'lowly' but to retain that powerful energy within the body—not letting it out through orgasm—so that it can, by virtue of its accumulated pressure, help transform, transmute, and *spiritualize* the body."

Some people practice celibacy for more practical reasons. Sexual desire, as we all know, often leads to attachment, and attachment often leads to suffering. In Asia, monks and renunciates viewed celibacy as an aid to leading a life of non-attachment, simplicity, and tranquillity. Such a way of life, free from the distractions of the flesh, is considered conducive to pursuing the spiritual path.

The word celibacy comes from the Latin for single, and a celibate person is singular—traditionally a monk or nun or hermit. True celibacy does not come from fear or aversion, but, we are told, from a passionate love of the life of the spirit. Nuns wear rings signifying their marriage to Christ, and Saint Theresa of Avila wrote passionate love poems filled with mystical ecstasy.

In the past people often took vows of celibacy for a lifetime. But temporary celibacy can also be a valuable and insight-provoking experiment. By abstaining and stepping back from sex, many people gain new insights into their relationship with their own sexuality. In a book called *The New Celibacy,* Dr. Barbara Brown writes that celibacy "is beginning to emerge in our society as a useful and positive vehicle to further personal growth."

When we learn the "rules" of sex, she says, "we need to learn not only what is socially acceptable and what might not be, but also that sex has an extended value that goes well beyond both its pleasure and procreative functions. The way to learn everything we ever wanted to know about sex is in the context of *full* knowledge of its range of expression—which must include celibacy. If we all have the potential to be celibate, then it is really a matter of finding out about and accepting this aspect of being sexual along with the active aspect of sex."

We should ignore sexual thoughts when they come to us, Dr. Brown advises. "There's no sense being celibate if you make it a big strain for yourself. Thinking about sex constantly can be just as sexual as having sex. And not as rewarding."

"When you stop being celibate sex will have something new to offer you," Dr. Brown concludes. "Not only because you've been away, but because you are more settled within yourself. Or you can continue being on vacation if

The Sacrament of Sexual Intimacy

"In the loving cosmogeny of Reb Hayim Haikel, an eighteenth-century Hasidic master, 'Creation was for the purpose of lovemaking. As long as there was only one-ness, there was no delight. But when division occurred and afterwards they [man and woman] were connected with one another, this brought about great delight.' For the wisest and most elevated among us, every carnal thought leads to God. The rest of us must strive toward this goal."

RABBI ZALMAN-SCHACTER

you're enjoying it. In either case, you can count on some very profound personal benefits to have occurred."

Afterglow

Contemplative lovemaking does not end as the act of love ends. In the afterglow, we open our eyes to see our partner in a new way: without agenda or preconceptions.

As Alan Watts writes:

Mystical vision, as has always been recognized, does not remain at the peak of ecstasy. As in love, its ecstasy leads into clarity and peace. The aftermath of love is an anticlimax only when the climax has been taken and not received. But when the whole experience was received the aftermath finds one in a marvelously changed and yet unchanged world, and here we are speaking of spirituality and sexuality in the same breath. For the mind and senses do not now have to open themselves; they find themselves naturally opened, and it appears that the divine world is no other than the everyday world.

Recommended Reading

My Favorite Books on Sex and Spirit

In addition to her work for *Yoga Journal* and an upcoming book on sex and spirituality, Dio Neff conducts a radio interview show in Nevada City, California. Here are some of her recommended readings:

Sexual Energy and Yoga, Elizabeth Haich (ASI Publishers, 1975). One of the most direct statements about the spiritual nature of sexual energy available, it explains the mechanics of how one's level of consciousness dictates the use of this energy. Although Haich argues for abstinence as part of one's *sadhana,* she claims an aspirant on any path must develop increasingly strong and resistant nerves to tolerate accelerating frequencies of sexual/vital energy generated by a spiritual practice.

Esoteric Philosophy of Love and Marriage, Dion Fortune (Samuel Weiser, Inc., 1974). Another very lucid treatment of esoteric cosmology, which focuses particularly on the nature of sexual energy, exactly how it functions, and the metaphysics of energy level that makes relationships succeed or fail. Very highly recommended.

Tantra: The Yoga of Sex, Omar Garrison (Crown Books, 1983). Garrison is a reporter rather than a Tantra expert; nevertheless he provides an unusually clear explanation of Tantric theory and offers a step-by-step Tantra technique developed especially for Westerners by a Bengali guru.

The Tao of Love and Sex, Jolan Chang (E. P. Dutton, 1977). A delightful how-to book on Taoist orgasm-conserving methods for men. It argues that conservation of semen is vital to a man's health, and that orgasm ideally should occur only once in so many occasions of lovemaking. This practice is said to enhance, rather than decrease, a man's enjoyment, for it increases his tolerance to sexual pleasure and recirculates the "vital forces" within his body. And Taoist sex is supposedly wonderful for women, who, according to the ancient Chinese, are "inexhaustible." *The Tao of Love and Sex* offers very specific techniques for prolonging intercourse, and many erotic, but tasteful, illustrations.

Sexual Secrets, Nik Douglas and Penny Slinger (Destiny Books, 1979). At first glance, one notices the *pictures:* literally hundreds of erotic drawings of what must be every Hindu deity, Tantric ritual, and sexual position known to men and women. A massive tome, and expensive even in paperback, *Sexual Secrets* covers Indian, Tibetan, Chinese, and Arabic practices, and is packed with fascinating Eastern sexual lore. It seems intended more for fun than for scholarship, however. Although Douglas lived in the Orient for eight years and translated excerpts of Sanskrit and Tibetan texts, the book contains no references to original sources for either artwork or scripture, and has been called, by one scholar at least, a "travesty." A Chinese academician has pointed out, however, that the Taoist translations are absolutely correct. Slinger's drawings are sensitive and charming, and the book, on the whole, is very entertaining.

Sex, compiled and edited by Ma Amrit Chinmay. (This "little black book" of Rajneesh's sayings on sex is available from Lear Enterprises, PO Box 649, Woodland Hills, CA 91365.)

On Gay Spiritualities

Embracing the Exile: Healing Journeys of Gay Christians (Seabury, 1982), by John Fortunato. News of change: gay christians come home.

Visionary Love: A Spirit Book of Gay Mythology (Treeroots, 1980), by Mitch Walker. A personal account of Gay Spirit Power, Gay Shamanism, and Transmutational Faeries.

Dio Neff

Resources

Newsletters on Gay Spirituality:

Franklin's Insight, 711 Atlantic Avenue, Box 1, Boston, MA 02111. An affiliate of Franklin Research & Development. A monthly investment advisory newsletter and quarterly industry reports with information on socially responsible investing. An introductory copy is available free of charge.

Integrity Forum, Integrity Inc, P.O. Box 891, Oak Park, IL 60303, $12/year, monthly. A newsletter for gay Episcopalians.

Sisters United, Woman Prints Enterprises, 118 W. Sparks St., Golena, KS 66739. $5/year, six issues. A newsletter on lesbianism and spiritual development.

5

The Family

Maureen Freedgood, a mother and roshi of the Cambridge Buddhist Association, tells the following story:

Once she was at a *sesshin*, an intensive meditation retreat, and someone asked her, "Does your family engage in this sort of thing?" She answered, she says, somewhat shamefacedly, "I'm sorry, but I have to say they do not." At which point, her teacher, the Zen master Soen-roshi, jumped up and said, "One in the family is enough!"

This story is worth keeping in mind, for it reminds us that we cannot force or cajole another person into setting out on what is after all an individual and personal journey—even if that other person is your husband, wife, or child. All members of a family have their own *karma* to work out, their own timing, and their own way of going.

This does not mean, however, that we can ignore or neglect the central place of the family in our spiritual life, for the family is itself the matrix of life and the source of love. It is no accident that so many of the metaphors for love and compassion in the spiritual life are drawn from the universal experience of family life. Christians and Jews speak of God the Father and teach that we are all brothers and sisters within the human family. Tibetan Buddhists say that we should treat all sentient beings as our mother. As the poet Gary Synder says, "The Family is the Practice Hall."

"All the arts we practice are apprenticeship. The big art is our life."

M. C. RICHARDS

Much of the time, of course, the family seems to be a stumbling block for the person setting out on the spiritual journey. This is especially true today, when many people have sought spiritual guidance outside the traditions they were born and raised in. But unless we become monks or nuns or hermits, most of us must find a way to take the solitary steps of our spiritual journey within a family—and, finally, find a way to create or join a family that is a living and growing expression of our own spiritual path.

In many ways the family is the most demanding training ground that life has to offer. We are born into our families. We do not choose them the way we choose our friends, and often parents, siblings, or children don't share our values or outlook on life. In fact, they may—and often do—radically disagree with us. They may prove difficult to get along with, and they may let us down in unimaginable ways. And yet we share a bond of common experience, and in most families, a kind of love that is unique in its strength and depth.

When we asked our friends what connection they made between the spiritual life and family, it was this aspect of family that they most often talked about. "A spiritual family is a loving family, and by definition a loving family is spiritual," said one friend. "A spiritual family is one which loves, supports and nourishes all of its members of whatever age to unfold as loving and caring individuals," said another.

Besides serving as a loving support system from which we can live our lives, the family also serves as a mini-society where we can test and put into practice all of our ideas about spiritual life. If we're interested in world peace, we have the opportunity to create peace within our families. If we're interested in living a loving life, we have the daily challenge of building loving family relationships. Our families almost never fail to mirror the quality of our own energy back at us quite clearly.

Life Before Conception

It is almost impossible to overestimate the influence our families have on us. Some people believe that the psychological imprint of our families begins well before birth. In *The Secret Life of the Unborn Child,* Dr. Thomas Verney cites a growing body of scientific evidence that suggests that "the unborn child is a feeling, remembering, aware being." Verney theorizes that soon after conception, the embryo begins to imbibe the physical and emotional experiences of the mother, so that by the time we are born our basic attitude or stance on life is already significantly influenced:

> The mother's love or rejection, or ambivalence begin defining and shaping [the child's] emotional life. What she creates are not specific traits such as extroversion or optimism or aggressiveness. . . . What is forming are broader, more deeply rooted tendencies—such as a sense of security or self-esteem.

Verney is careful to point out that this awareness should be seen as a challenge rather than a cause for engendering guilt. Knowing the difference it makes, he says, we can consciously choose to nurture our children in the

"Hui-Neng said 'If you come for the faith, stop all thy hankerings. Think not of good, think not of evil, but see what at this moment thy own original face doth look like, which thou hast even prior to thy own birth.'"

D. T. SUZUKI

"Birth is from the mystery of night into the greater mystery of day."

TAGORE

"Nothing has a stronger influence psychologically on their environment, and especially on their children, than the unlived life of the parents."

C. G. JUNG

womb. "By creating a warm, emotionally enriching environment in utero, a woman can make a decisive difference in everything her child feels, hopes, dreams, thinks and accomplishes throughout life."

Some people go even further and postulate that awareness begins long before conception—that, in fact, the soul of the child, as a conscious being swimming around in the spiritual realms, chooses its parents and time of birth. Dr. Norbert Glass, an English physician and follower of Rudolf Steiner, writes in his book *Conception, Birth and Early Childhood:* "The human being is not created merely by father and mother, but exists already before birth and conception. He exists as an individual, in a spiritual form, in a world that is not physically visible. Man, striving for incarnation, chooses his parents, the human beings with whose help it becomes possible for him to live on earth."

Conception, according to Glass, is a process of attunement with the new spirit that wants to be born. "Parents should listen inwardly," he says, "in order to discover when their child should come to them." He warns against basing pregnancy on purely practical considerations. Children want "to come to [their] parents at a special time from the spiritual world," he says. "[They] have no understanding, of course, of earthly reasoning, but will feel any resistance or opposition to [their] coming."

The Influence of the Family

Once born, we gain our first conscious experiences of love and support from our parents, we learn our first lessons about the meaning of existence in the context of the family. The influence of the family becomes most clear when we leave home and create a family of our own. Most family therapists have found that we tend to unconsciously recreate the unresolved problems and conflicts from the family in which we were raised. As Harold Bloomfield, M.D. points out in *How to Make Peace with Your Parents:* "Many of the here-and-now conflicts people have with their spouses, lovers, ex-lovers, bosses, partners or children are in part emotional reenactments of suppressed feelings stored from incidents that happened when they were children. The same unresolved conflicts they had with their parents always seem to 'mysteriously' reappear to affect their adult relationships."

Harvey White, M.D., suggests in *Your Family is Good For You* that the family is therefore the richest source of self-discovery. "In dealing with people with physical or emotional problems," he reports ". . . I discovered that the family out of which the individual emerged was always like the sea, the milieu that could explain and restore him. When thinking about someone's problems, I almost automatically referred to the family around him. It remains everyone's best hope for safe passage."

Carl Whitaker, a pioneer in the family therapy movement, is so convinced of the indelible effect our families have on us that he generally won't work with individuals or even couples and insists on seeing as many family members as possible for each session. After he began doing intergenerational work in 1945 he said, "I decided I didn't believe in individuals. They seemed more like fragments of a family." He does marathon sessions with sometimes as many as thirty or forty members of an extended family, believing that when the family faces itself, the unspoken patterns become clear and movement toward wholeness can begin.

The Importance of the Family

Besides the obvious opportunity the family offers for personal change, Elise Boulding, a noted sociologist, peace activist, and Quaker, suggests that strong families may be the most important ingredient for creating a positive future for the world. In a pamphlet called *Friends Testimonies in the Home,* she advises Quaker families to devote more time and assign more importance to family life:

> If we have a real concern for the spiritual welfare of the world we live in, we need to reexamine our calls. We spend so little time in our homes even at best because of the way modern life is organized, that any additional demands on our time may mean a further weakening of the kind of personal relationships that only common domestic activity can build. In a world which is crying for a new approach

"What the mother sings to the cradle goes all the way down to the coffin."

HENRY WARD BEECHER

"If the family were a container, it would be a nest, an enduring nest, loosely woven, expansive, and open.

"If the family were a fruit, it would be an orange, a circle of sections, held together but separable—each segment distinct.

"If the family were a boat, it would be a canoe that makes no progress unless everyone paddles.

"If the family were a sport, it would be baseball: a long, slow, nonviolent game that is never over until the last out.

"If the family were a building, it would be an old but solid structure that contains human history, and appeals to those who see the carved moldings under all the plaster, the wide plank floors under the linoleum, the possibilities."

LETTY COTTIN POGREBIN

to the rapidly multiplying social conflicts which seriously threaten to overwhelm our civilization, Friends ought earnestly to consider the role of the family in untangling our social confusion. . . . The truth is that the home is the training ground where people first learn to live with one another, where they learn to love, to hate, to get angry, to fear, to forgive. Unless they can learn in their homes how to love and work with other people, how to handle hate, anger and fear so that it does not destroy themselves or others, and unless they can experience the full depth of forgiveness in the give and take of family life, they are not going to be able to go into the world and help. . . .

Envisioning the Loving Family

If in fact a loving family is a spiritual family, it's worth stopping to reflect on the quality of one's family life as it now stands. In her book *Peoplemaking,* Virginia Satir suggests there is "what I call a *nurturing* family."

Here's how Virginia envisions the nurturing family:

Immediately, I can sense the aliveness, the genuineness, honesty and love. I feel the heart and soul present as well as the head.

I feel that if I lived in such a family, I would be listened to and would be interested in listening to others; I could openly show my affection as well as my pain and disapproval; I wouldn't be afraid to take risks because everyone in my family would realize that some mistakes are bound to come with my risk-taking—that my mistakes are a sign that I am growing. I would feel like a person in my own right—noticed, valued, loved, and clearly asked to notice, value and love others.

One can actually see and hear the vitality in such a family. The bodies are graceful, the facial expressions relaxed. People look *at* one another, not *through* one another or at the floor, and they speak in rich, clear voices. There is a flow and harmony in their relations with one another. The children, even as infants, seem open and friendly, and the rest of the family treats them very much as persons.

If Satir's description sounds hopelessly idealistic, she encourages us to take heart: "I am convinced that any troubled family can become a nurturing one. Most of the

"Allow children to be happy in their own way, for what better way will they ever find?"

DR. JOHNSON

"Don't limit a child to your own learning, for he was born in another time."

RABBINIC SAYING

things that cause families to be troubled are learned after birth. Since they are learned, they can be unlearned; and new things can be learned in their place."

But it does take work and attention. One of the biggest mistakes we can make, Elise Boulding warns, is to assume that it is harder today to create nurturing families than it was in the "good old days." "It is easy," she writes, "to assume that families of an earlier day just didn't have conflicts and problems as we do today and that therefore harmonious family life was much easier for them to achieve. The devils of two and three hundred years ago wore different costumes from the ones we meet today, but they were just as real. The 'domestic bliss' of which Clarkson, recorder of the eighteenth century Quaker life, writes was the chief source of enjoyment to Friends, was achieved through the same constant effort, devotion, and prayer that we need to put into our own family lives."

"In the Indian way, everything is for the children. They learn respect because we show respect for them; we let them be free, but at the same time, there is always someone there to teach them how to act, the right way to treat people. When we get our land back, the first thing we will do is to make places for spiritual things and for the children, places where the children can learn the right way to live, to be generous, to be respectful, and to love all the living things. We believe in the Great Hoop: the Great Circle of Life; everything comes back to where it started. We believe this. That is the Indian way."

MATTHEW KING

Creating the Tie that Binds

In their book, *The Caring Question,* Donald and Nancy Tubesing, a Lutheran minister and educator, offer the following six ways to create and sustain a loving family:

1. *Reach out in your family:* Each time we choose to care for our family, even when we don't really feel like it, we forfeit immediate rewards in favor of long-term gains. . . . as we give ourselves to others we grow in caring, tolerance and understanding.

2. *Make the family top priority:* The healthiest families we've encountered have one characteristic in common. They make deliberate decisions to invest time and energy in their relationships. They make family a number one priority.

3. *Expand the family memory bank:* Every family has a storehouse of collective memories. . . . Recalling peak experiences, reliving familiar rituals and traditions, and re-telling family stories keeps the family connected and its spirit alive.

4. *Deal with family problems:* Our commitment to one another in the family provides the context for working out, rather than walking away from, the problems.

All families have problems—some more than others. Part of our commitment to family is the resolution to keep looking for alternative solutions when the current approach isn't working.

5. *Finding the forgiveness factor:* Families need some way to reach out to one another with love and forgiveness. Most of us haven't had much experience with true forgiveness. We need to learn how to ask for, grant and accept forgiveness. . . .

The starting point is to acknowledge that forgiveness is not a feeling, it's a choice. It's actually two choices—the decision made by one person to repent and the decision made by the other to forgive. When you've done something for which you need forgiveness, admit it. Swallow your pride, take the risk, and make your request directly to the injured person: "Will you forgive me? I really hurt you, and I'm sorry." This kind of direct request gives the other person the chance to say, "Yes, I forgive you," rather than retaliate. It also provides a wonderful model for others in the family to imitate. . . .

Forgiveness is not forgetting: it's refusing to hold grudges. Forgiveness doesn't demand that the other change first. Forgiveness is an attitude freely given that accepts hurts and drops the charges. . . . Seek out and practice a variety of rituals for asking and offering forgiveness in your family.

6. *Accentuate the positive:* The most wonderful gift we can give to one another is affirmation. . . .

Say I love you. . . . Don't delegate this powerful gift. Don't assume that others know you care. Don't be stingy with your love. Tell your family you love them with your words, with your looks, with your touch, with your attitude, with your thoughtfulness—several times a day!

Affirm one another. Focus on each individual in your family and identify several qualities that make that person unique. Tell each what you appreciate as special about him or her. . . . One wise mother we know shared her secret of success. "I've never said this out loud before," she told us, "but one of my guiding principles in raising a family has been to treat each member with as much courtesy, respect and interest as I would a guest." Judging by the obvious love, the positive spirit, and the vibrant health of her family, her strategy has worked wonders.

The Hearth As the Center of the Universe

In the seventies first many women left the home in an attempt to escape from the boredom and isolation of parenting. But after a good ten years of rebalancing family relationships, women and men alike are returning home, so to speak—trying to redefine the role of family in their lives. In a book of essays called *Lifeways, Working with Family Questions,* one group of parents associated with Emerson College in England, a school founded on the teachings of Christian mystic Rudolf Steiner, wrestled with the question of how we can have a vital family life in the midst of our fast-moving culture. In "The Meaning of Being a Mother Today," Margli Matthews suggests two ways for using home life to bring an awareness of spirit into the world. The first is to attend to the small details of home life with the same mindfulness we might apply to tasks we consider more important:

"When the father is in truth a father, and the son a son, when the elder brother is an elder brother, and the younger brother a younger brother, a husband a husband and a wife a wife, then the house is in the right way. When the house is set in order, the world is set in order, the world is established on a firm course."

I CHING

A real attention to detail can be a process of transformation, creating spaces for the spirit to enter. In cleaning a room, if we are present in what we are doing, we soon realize that we are not only clearing a physical space for physical bodies but also for the human soul and spirit, for the human imagination.

When I am very busy with the work that draws me outside the home, I often forget this. I ignore all the details and tear through my household in full gear with my focused consciousness, ticking off the "jobs" on my list as soon as they are done, caught in my busyness. This works for a while, but if it goes on too long I am aware that the house begins to feel empty and hollow.

Secondly, Matthews suggests that in order to create vital families we need to renew our sense of natural rhythms. In the past, she says, out of necessity people lived according to the rhythms of nature: "All human activities took place in relation to the activities of the natural world and the cosmos. People experienced a connection between the changing seasons and their own alternating states of consciousness." But today, as we have lost that connection, our lives have become arhythmic, a situation resulting "in stress and tension—cutting us off from each other and any sense of wholeness of our days, weeks, and years."

To bring a sense of rhythm into our lives, Matthews suggests practicing daily rituals, particularly during the times of transition from one activity to another: awakening in the morning, meal times, returning home from school or work and bedtimes. Matthew reports that for her fmaily, evening rituals are a favorite:

> First, after supper, I tell or read the children a story before taking them to bed; then we say prayers and, when they were younger, we would sing a song or two. Now, as they are older, I find that we have some of our deepest talks at this time, in the quiet of the evenings, when the bustle of the day is over. Both girls have also had particular rituals, regular "things" to be said before I turn out the light and they cross the threshold into sleep.

For Bons Voors, a co-editor of the book, breakfastime has become the favorite time for family sharing:

After many years of hectic breakfasts, which everybody took at different times, according to duties in the outside world, we decided it would probably make a great difference to start the day together, before everyone took off. So we looked for a song or a melody. After trying several melodies, which disappeared because they did not work, we found a simple Alleluia which is very short and can be sung in a round. It starts at a high pitch, so not only do you have to arrive at breakfast at the same time, you even have to reach up to that high note to greet the day! It does make a difference! It shapes a conscious moment in the on-goingness of time to say hello to the day.

Clearly, for daily rituals to work for your family, they have to be created with a great deal of fun and understanding. They can take the form of something that "looks" spiritual or they can be some kind of simple daily encounter. Leo Buscaglia, in his book *Love*, recalls how his father asked each child in the family at dinner each night to tell one thing they had learned that day. Buscaglia says that that ritual has had an indelible impact on his life, reminding him that learning is a daily challenge in life.

Celebrations and Festivals

Celebrating rituals on the traditional days as well as on the equinoxes and solstices allows the family to reconnect with the natural rhythms of life. Celebrations to mark seasonal change have been practiced by most cultures since ancient times, says Paula Klimek, a specialist in holistic education who uses myth and ritual in her work. These celebrations, she says, "acknowledge not only the outward seasonal changes but also the symbolic/subjective rhythms of our lives. In taking the time to honor these festivals, we honor our own symbolic process of unfoldment. In this way we cooperate with the natural life progression and live with a true consciousness." There is a rich tradition of seasonal celebrations in most cultures to draw upon or, if you feel the need, you can create your own.

Most religious celebration days come complete with a traditional set of rituals, but again the trick is to take the time to do it together and make the rituals a personal expression of your own family. Seasonal celebrations can be very simple—digging the first shovelful of dirt in the garden for the year together, or taking time to appreciate the moment when you put your baskets of plants on the porch in the spring sun, or when you open the house up for the first time after winter. They are a pause—a moment to take an in-breath together.

The Life Cycle: Birth, Death, and In Between

Seasonal celebrations also serve to remind us that life, like nature, has its own individual cycles, and what the significance of those cycles can be. Our very language tacitly admits this connection, when we speak of people being in the "autumn of their years" or having a "May-December" romance. Everything has its season, and the words from Ecclesiastes—"a time to be born and a time to die"—hold true for the course of our individual lives as well. "The life cycle" is the name given to the pattern or shape of our lives from birth to death. It is unique for each of us, of course, but it is also universal.

According to Daniel J. Levinsen, the author of *The Seasons of a Man's Life* (a ten-year study that was the basis for the popular *Passages*), the idea of the life cycle has two main components.

First, there is the idea of the *process* or *journey* from a starting point (birth, origin) to a termination point (death, conclusion). To speak of a general, human life cycle is to propose that the journey from birth to old age follows an underlying, universal life pattern on which there are endless cultural and individual variations. . . .

Second, there is the idea of *seasons:* a series of periods or stages within the life cycle. . . . A season is a relatively stable segment of the total cycle. Summer has a different character from winter; twilight is different from sunrise. To say that a season is relatively stable, however, does not mean that it is stationary or static. Change goes on within each, and a transition is required for the shift from one season to the next. Every season has its own time; it is important in its own right and needs to be understood in

"To everything there is a season, and a time to every purpose under the heaven."

ECCLESIASTES

its own terms. No season is better or more important than any other. Each has its necessary place and contributes its special character to the whole. It is an organic part of the total cycle, linking past and future and containing both within itself.

There is a biological dimension to this life cycle—birth, childhood, adolescence, adulthood, old age, and death—but it also possesses a psychological and spiritual dimension. Each stage has its own spiritual challenges to be met, its own satisfactions and joys. No one stage is more crucial or valuable than any other. Every moment of our lives is in fact part of the shape of the whole.

Levinsen and his fellow researchers identified the life cycle as evolving through a series of four stages called "eras" lasting roughly twenty-five years each. Each of these eras is "partially overlapping, so that a new one is getting underway as the previous one is being terminated." The sequence goes like this:

1. Childhood and adolescence: age 0–22
2. Early adulthood: age 17–45
3. Middle adulthood: age 40–65
4. Late adulthood: age 60–?

> "Children can be conceptualized as mirrors. If love is given to them, they return it. If none is given, they have none to return. Unconditional love is reflected unconditionally, and conditional love is returned conditionally."
>
> ROSS CAMPBELL, M.D.

The transition between eras, says Levinsen, "requires a basic change in the fabric of one's life, and this takes more than a day, a month, or even a year. The transition consistently takes four or five years—not less than three and rarely more than six. This transition is the work of a developmental period that links the eras and provides some continuity between them."

Childhood

In *How to Help Your Child Have A Spiritual Life*, Annette Hollander, a psychiatrist and mother of two girls, discusses the stages of children's spiritual development from the viewpoint of what she calls the rationalist (Freud and Piaget) and the transpersonal (Steiner and Chilton Pierce) theories.

Those in the rationalist group, she found, "see us as born ignorant, growing in understanding only as the brain

"A child's world is fresh and new and beautiful, full of wonder and excitement. It is our misfortune that for most of us that clear-eyed vision, that true instinct for what is beautiful and awe-inspiring, is dimmed and even lost before we reach adulthood. If I had influence with the good fairy who is supposed to preside over the christening of all children, I should ask that her gift to each child in the world be a sense of wonder so indestructible that it would last throughout life, as an unfailing antidote against boredom and disenchantments of later years, the sterile preoccupation with things that are artificial, the alienation from the sources of our strength."

RACHEL CARSON

"The difference of the soul/spirit dimensions in being with children is the difference from pretty to beautiful, from cute to enchanting, from interesting to awesome, from respect to reverence."

CAROL MANKITI

and body mature. The early stages have no value in themselves, but are necessary way stations to be left behind as we reach the goal of 'maturity.'"

"The second group values the early stages, when children are in touch with the living, interconnected web of the cosmos. For this group, which I have called 'transpersonal,' each stage of childhood develops faculties that we later integrate to reach our full spiritual potential."

"The world of the preschool child is analogous to that of the mystic," Hollander concludes, "alive, and without the concept of space and time as we know it. (Remember, though, that consciousness *before* the concept of space and time develops may not be the same as consciousness that goes *beyond* it.) There is enough overlap so that our children can help *us* enter into 'beginner's mind'—that state before defenses, concepts, and conditioning insulate us from experiencing directly. What we can do for their spiritual life in the first five years is to allow their joyfulness to inspire us, and encourage them to continue to expand their love and wonder even as they enter the age of reason."

As a result of questionnaires she sent out and personal interviews she conducted, Hollander became convinced that children are naturally mystical and will carry on their own spiritual quest with or without the help of their parents. We can as parents, however, actively support them by accepting and acknowledging our children's inner experiences as valid. A high percentage of the adult respondents to Hollander's questionnaire reported that they had had mystical experiences as children, but generally kept quiet about them, sensing that their parents would not understand.

Transpersonal psychologist Frances Vaughan encourages parents to share their own inner experiences with their children as a way of validating the inner realm for them. She reports in her book *Awakening Intuition,* "Many adults in my groups [for developing intuition] have said that they felt they were more intuitive as children, and that they learned to keep their intuitive perceptions to themselves after encountering skepticism or ridicule from adults. . . . Children seldom share their inner world of fantasy and perception with adults, because sympathetic, understanding adults are rare."

"In general," Vaughan says, "intuition flourishes only when it is valued." Children who don't receive a positive response from their parents on this account often learn to turn off those experiences altogether.

Hollander suggests that the reluctance of parents to share these events with their children stems from the taboo in our culture against nonrational experience. "We tend to keep silent about these things, not only because we are afraid others will think us crazy—we ourselves wonder if we are crazy. We have internalized society's judgment."

Meditation is certainly one way to encourage the contemplative side of our children's nature, and according to Theresa Scheining, a family therapist who teaches Christian meditation to children, it can be taught soon after babyhood. In her book *Our Treasured Heritage*, she says she has found children to be natural contemplatives: "What continues to overwhelm me as I prepare children for meditation and contemplation is the undeniable fact that many of them are already familiar with the contemplative experience."

"In the East," says Soto Zen Buddhist abbess Rev. Roshi Jiyu-Kennett in *How to Help Your Child Have a Spiritual Life,* "the average child is taught to meditate as soon as it is possible for it to sit upright; i.e. around one or two years old." She goes on to describe how instruction occurs:

> No doctrine is put into the child's head. The mother and father, and the rest of the family, will sit quietly in front of the family altar; the child, without being restrained, will either sit for a few moments or roll around on the floor with the parents taking no notice. The parents thus express their knowledge of the child's latent understanding and do not treat it like less than themselves. In a very short time the child wants to sit down like the parents, as do, interestingly enough, the dog and cat. . . . Thus, if the parents meditate, the child will meditate too.

Adolescence

"Adolescence," as Annette Hollander writes, "is an age of spiritual hunger and a quest for meaning, as well as a time of tremendous physical and emotional changes."

"In the Jungian view," says Hollander, "we are reborn whenever there is the death of an old attitude and the birth of a new consciousness. The spiritual crisis of the adolescent is programmed by biological necessity: death of the dependent child attitudes, rebirth as a psychological adult."

The spiritual crisis of adolescence tends to be dramatic. According to psychosynthesis, adolescence is a time when there is a sudden surge of both sexual energy and spiritual energy from "the higher self." Mystical experiences and sudden conversions are part of the spiritual life of many adolescents.

Many traditions honor and mark this time with appropriate rituals, such as the bar mitzvah of the Jews or the Vision Quest of the American Indian.

"What can we do to help channel the teenager's spiritual energies?" asks Hollander. "As usual the most important thing is simply to recognize and respect their quest."

The Noon of Life

Carl G. Jung was the first to pay close attention to the stages of the adult life cycle. Jung, writes Levinsen,

"There are . . . parents who know that their children should receive educations and try to give it. But very few among them, even among those who are most serious and sincere, know that the first thing to do, in order to be able to educate the child, is to educate oneself, to become conscious and master of oneself so that one does not set a bad example to one's child. For it is through example that education becomes effective. To say good words, give wise advice to a child has very little effect, if one does not show by one's living example the truth of what one teaches. Sincerity, honesty, straightforwardness, courage, disinterestedness, unselfishness, patience, endurance, perseverance, peace, calm, self-control are all things that are taught infinitely better by example than by beautiful speeches."

THE MOTHER

"distinguished the first half from the second half of life, and placed the dividing period at around 40. . . . Jung observed that a resurgence of 'individuation' may begin at around 40—the 'noon of life' as he called it—and continue through the afternoon and evening of life."

"As Jung conceived the term, and as it is commonly used by psychologists, individuation is a developmental process through which a person becomes more uniquely individual," explains Levinsen. "Acquiring a clearer and fuller identity of his own, he becomes better able to utilize his inner resources and pursue his own aims. He generates new levels of awareness, meaning and understanding."

It is also during this period, according to Jung, that we can begin to pay more attention to the "archetypal unconscious," which speaks to the deepest levels of self and the spiritual journey. In other words, it is during this period, when our physical and biological growth has culminated, and even begun to decline, that our greatest inner and spiritual growth can take place.

Aging: A New and Old View

In most traditional cultures old age is seen as a time worth looking forward to. The elders of the society are treated with respect and admiration. Old age is a time to live more quietly, away from the strivings of life, to develop spiritually and prepare for death. In the modern Western world, however, we see life as going downhill from middle age onward. Old people are considered a bother—we'd rather not see or care for them at all, because we have more important things to do, and perhaps because they remind us of our own inevitable mortality.

But through the efforts of the elderly themselves this view and the isolation it brought are changing. "Old age is not a disease—it is strength and survivorship, triumph over all kinds of vicissitudes and disappointments, trial and illnesses," says Maggie Kuhn, founder of the Gray Panthers, an elderly activism organization. Kuhn originally started the Gray Panthers with a small group of like-minded friends, all of whom had been forcibly retired from national religious and social service organizations. "We de-

"Let's look at the first requirement that is necessary in giving a child that longed for meaning to life. We parents must possess a foundation upon which to base our lives and which can withstand the test of time. Something that will support us through every phase of living: adolescence, young adulthood, middle age, old age, marriage crises, financial crises, children's crises, energy crises, and especially, a rapidly changing society in which spiritual values are swiftly eroding. We parents must have a crucial foundation upon which we base our lives in order to give it to our children. In my opinion, it is the most valuable treasure we can pass on to our offspring."

ROSS CAMPBELL, M.D.

cided to pool our energies to use our new freedom responsibly." Nine years later the Panthers is a large and visible organization working for social change.

There are three excellent reasons to celebrate growing older, according to Kuhn:

> The first thing is you can speak your mind, as I certainly try to do.
>
> The second thing I like about getting old is that I have successfully outlived a great deal of my opposition: many of the people who were my detractors before are not around anymore! And then the third thing that I've especially liked about getting old is that it's really kind of a miracle to be able to tap into the incredible energy of the young, while making use of the knowledge and experience that comes after living a long, full life. Having the power and energy of these two worlds is an enormously vitalizing and inspiring experience.
>
> I think of age as a great universalizing force. It doesn't begin when you collect your social security benefits. Aging begins with the moment of birth and it ends only when life itself has ended. Life is a continuum; only, we—in our stupidity and blindness—have chopped it up into little pieces and kept all those little pieces separate. I feel that the goal of successful aging is to keep on growing and learning and becoming a mature, responsible adult.

Making Friends with Death

"Death is a subject that is evaded, ignored, and denied by our youth-worshipping, progress-oriented society," say Joseph and Laurie Braga in *Death, the Final Stage of Growth*. "It is almost as if we have taken on death as just another disease to be conquered. But the fact is that death is inevitable. We will all die; it is only a matter of time."

For most of us, death takes place in hospitals, behind closed curtains so as not to disturb the living. Many of us had relatives or parents die when we were young. One day they were there, and the next thing we knew, they were gone; we had seen none of the steps in between.

What kind of signal does this treatment of death send a child (or an adult for that matter)? Death is seen as

"Whatever prepares you for death enhances life."

STEPHEN LEVINE

something to be avoided at all costs. So strong is our aversion to death that Dr. Bernie Siegel, a surgeon at Yale New Haven hospital, says that it's not uncommon for even a doctor to go through an entire medical career without ever witnessing a death face to face. The actual moment of death is left for the nurses and orderlies to deal with, he says.

We're coming to realize though that this avoidance of death takes a tremendous toll on our lives. It manifests as a kind of fear that numbs us, causing us to step back from challenges and risks for what seems to be securer ground.

The way through this fear is to begin to see death as a friend. The Bragas tell us that "If you can begin to see death as an invisible, but friendly, companion on your life's journey—gently reminding you not to wait till tomorrow to do what you mean to do—then you can learn to *live* your life rather than simply passing through it."

Being with a friend or relative at their death is a good way of beginning to deal with our own fear of death, says Deborah Duda, author of *A Guide for Dying at Home.* "Like living, dying has its share of sadness and joy. The sadness of letting go of a person we love is tempered if we remember to hold everyone lightly, knowing they are 'just on loan.' When someone we love is dying, we tend to focus on sadness, not on joy. But it's a choice. We can allow joy into this often most painful experience of our lives; the quiet joy of sharing love and caring, of seeing a loved one content, of touching into timelessness."

"It is a rare privilege to be with someone who is dying," she says later in the book. "I suggest you use this time to think about your own death, your own spiritual beliefs."

Conscious Life/Conscious Death

The biggest question about death is what happens to us? Are the near-death experiences reported by people like Dr. Raymond Moody a clear preview of what's in store for us, or are they simply hallucinations? Do we go to a

"If you aim to dispense with method, learn method. If you aim at facility, work hard. If you aim for simplicity, master complexity."

THE WAY OF CHINESE PAINTING

"All goes onward and outward,
Nothing collapses
And to die is different from
What anyone supposes
And luckier,"

WALT WHITMAN

heaven or a hell? Do we experience the realms of the *bardo* as described in the *Tibetan Book of the Dead*. Or, as Hindus believe, are we on a cycle of endless reincarnation?

There is no way, except through faith and intuition, that we can know the answer to these questions—until of course our own time comes. We can however, apply our clearest ideals generated by the hope of a spiritual life right up to the moment of death.

To die consciously is to die in full awareness, awake, open, and fully alive to the last moment. If, as Stephen Levine says in *Who Dies,* we're lucky enough to approach death slowly and know it's coming, we can have the time to finish all of our unfinished business in this life. We can express our love to all those we love, clear up any unspoken conflicts with those to whom we are bound, and we can begin to consciously deal with the deep well of fear that may reassert itself as we approach the moment of our last transition in the world.

Since none of us knows for sure whether or not we'll have that warning, the best advice, of course, is to live each moment as if it's going to be our last. That exercise alone is the only spiritual exercise one would ever need to do.

Lessons From the Light
Contributed by Ken Ring

During the past seven years, I have interviewed hundreds of people who have had near-death experiences—beautiful and life-transformative encounters with what most of them simply call "the Light." Many of these individuals have come to be much more than my "research subjects." By becoming channels for "the Light," they have become my teachers as well. Here, in their own words, is what the universe looks and feels like when perceived within the Light, and some lessons learned from the experience:

It was a total immersion in light, brightness, warmth, peace, security. It's something which becomes you and you become it. I could say, "I was peace, I was love." I was the brightness, it was part of me. It was eternity. It was like I was always there, and I will always be there, and that my existence on earth was just a brief instant.

It was just pure consciousness. This enormously bright light seemed almost to cradle me. I just seemed to exist in it and be part of it and be nurtured by it, and the feeling just became more and more and more ecstatic and glorious and perfect. The *feeling*—if you took the one thousand best things that ever happened to you in your life and multiplied by a million, maybe you could get close to this feeling. I don't know.

I remember I knew that everything, everywhere in the universe was OK, that the plan was perfect. That whatever was happening—the wars, famine, whatever—was OK. . . . The whole time I was in this state, it seemed infinite. . . . I was just an infinite being in perfection. And love and safety and security and knowing that nothing could happen to you and you're home forever. That you're safe forever. And that everybody else was.

I realized that there are things that every person is sent to earth to realize and to learn. For instance, to share more love, to be more loving toward one another. To discover that the most important thing is human relationships and love—not materialistic things. And to realize that every single thing that you do in your life is recorded and that even though you pass it by not thinking at the time, it always comes up later. For instance, you may be . . . at a stop light and you're in a hurry and the lady in front of you, when the light turns green, doesn't take right off, (she) doesn't notice the light, and you get upset and start honking your horn and telling her to hurry up. Those are the little kinds of things that are recorded that you don't realize at the time are really important. One of the things that I discovered that is very important is patience toward other human beings and realizing that you yourself might be in that situation sometime.

You are shown your life—and you do the judging. Had you done what you should do? You think, "Oh, I gave six dollars to someone that didn't have much and that was great of me." That didn't mean a thing. It's the little things—

maybe a hurt child that you helped or just to stop and say hello to a shut-in. Those are the things that are most important.

Ken Ring is a psychologist and near death experience researcher

Rebirth: The Life Circle

The idea of rebirth is prevalent in many traditions, including the pre-Christian West, and is probably the most widespread belief about what happens after death.

In *The Wheel of Death, A Collection of Writings From Zen Buddhist and Other Sources on Death, Rebirth, Dying,* Philip Kapleau writes: "Unlike the linear theology of the West, Buddhism teaches that life and death present the same cyclic continuity observed in all aspects of nature. . . . Men who have seen life and death as just such an unbroken continuum, the swinging of an eternal pendulum, have been able to move as freely into death as they walked through life." And later on in this inspiring and useful anthology, he quotes Zen Master Dogen:

"It is fallacious to think you simply move from birth to death. Birth from the Buddhist point of view is a temporary point between the preceding and the succeeding, hence it can be called birthlessness. The same holds for death and deathlessness. In life there is nothing more than life, in death nothing more than death: we are being born and are dying at every moment."

From this point of view, our life and death together make a circle which, like our truest nature, is fundamentally whole and complete.

"Never the spirit is born
The spirit will cease to be never
Never the time when it was not.
End and beginning are dreams
Birthless and deathless and changeless
Remains the spirit forever.
Death has not touched it at all
Dead though the house of it seems."

Sioux Prayer of Passing

Recommended Reading

Books to Read on Spirituality and Children

Our Treasured Heritage, Teaching Christian Meditation to Children by Theresa O'Callaghan Scheihing with Louis M. Savary (Crossroad, 1981). Written by a family therapist and meditation teacher, this how-to book, exhibits a deep psychological as well as spiritual understanding of children and their desire to experience peace.

Mother Wit, A Feminist Guide to Psychic Development, by Diane Mariechild (The Crossing Press, 1981). Drawn from her experience with Womancraft, a feminist derivative of Silva Mind Control, Mariechild gives a practical introduction to using psychic skills, including experiential exercises for developing healing ability and spiritual awareness.

How to Help Your Child Have a Spiritual Life, by Annette Hollander, M.D. (Bantam, 1980). An all inclusive guide to creating a spiritual life with your child outside of the context of traditional religion.

On Family Togetherness

The Marriage and Family Book, A Spiritual Guide, edited by Ravi Dass and Aparna (Schocken, 1978). This is a collection of writings on marriage, parenting, and family life mostly from the Eastern religious viewpoint.

Lifeways by Bons Voors (Hawthorne Press, 1982; U.S. distributor, St. George Books, P. O. Box 163, Nannet, NY 10977). Inspiring essays on spirituality and family life. This book reflects on finding ways to return to the natural rhythms while living in the modern world.

What We May Be, by Piero Ferrucci (Tarcher, 1982). Written by a student and colleague of Roberto Assagioli, this book is a practical introduction to psychosynthesis. The book includes guided imagery exercises to help develop the various aspects of one's personality and being. These processes could be shared in a family group with older children.

Ways of Being Together, by Michael and Nina Shandler (Schocken, 1980). This is a book of exercises for couples to use to deepen communication, deal with conflicts and enhance trust and mutual acceptance. Most of the exercises could be used in a family setting.

On Birth

The World of the Unborn, Nurturing Your Child Before Birth by Leni Schwartz Ph.D. (March, 1981). A how-to guide for making the most of the months of pregnancy.

The Secret Life of the Unborn Child by Thomas Verney, M.D. (Summit Books, 1981). A report on the scientific evidence on prebirth awareness.

Spiritual Midwifery by Ina May and the Farm Midwives (The Book Publishing Co., 1975). Written by the midwives of The Farm, a large commune in Tennessee, which has an active birthing service, this book tells the tale of several births. The midwives see birth as a spiritual process.

Conception, Birth and Early Childhood, by Norbert Glass, M.D. (Anthroposophic Press, 1972). This book, written over twenty years ago by an English physician who was a student of Rudolf Steiner, looks at conception and birth from a spiritual perspective.

On Death and Dying

Who Dies? by Stephen Levine, (Anchor Books, 1982). Levine, a dying counselor and Buddhist meditator, approaches the experience of death from a Buddhist perspective combined with the richness of his many years working with dying people. It is a deep and excellent book that helps the reader make friends with death.

A Guide to Dying at Home by Deborah Duda, (John Muir Publications, 1982). A down to earth, step by step guide to taking care of a loved one while they die at home. Duda views sharing a death as a precious spiritual experience.

Reincarnation: The Phoenix Fire Mystery, Compiled and Edited by Joseph Head and S. L. Cranston (Julian Press/Crown, 1977). An anthology that brings together diverse thinking on the question of reincarnation, including current and past thinkers in the fields of religion, science, psychology, philosophy, art, and literature.

Resources

Organizations:

Alternative Birthing:

NAPSAC (International Association of Parents and Professionals for Safe Alternatives in Childbirth, P.O. Box 646, Marble Hill, MO 63764, (314)238-2010. A clearinghouse for information on childbirth. Produces a newsletter ($15/year, four issues) and a directory of Alternative Birth Services ($5.95).

Youth:

The Breakthrough Foundation, 1990 Lombard St., San Francisco, CA 94123, (415)563-2100. An organization inspired by est which provides a ten-day course and follow-up community workshops for troubled adolescents.

Aging:

The Gray Panthers, 311 S. Juniper St., Philadelphia, PA 19107, (215)545-6555. Founded by Maggie Kuhn, this activist group has branches in over thirty states. Works to help change ideas about aging in our society. Any contribution of $15 or more includes a subscription to a quarterly newsletter. Topics of concern also include health care, housing, and peace. (No one is excluded from membership due to inability to pay, however.)

Death and Dying:

IANDS (Institute for the Advancement of Near Death Studies), U-20, University of Connecticut, Storrs, CT 06268, (203) 486-4906. Collects information on near-death experiences and produces a newsletter reporting on near-death research. $15/year, quarterly.

The Living/Dying Project, Box 5564, Santa Fe, NM 87502. Under the auspices of the Hanuman Foundation (founded by Ram Dass), this project consciously and compassionately investigates our living and our dying.

National Hospice Organization, 1901 N. Fort Myer Dr., Suite 307, Arlington, VA 22209, (703)243-5900. Publishes a directory of over 2,000 hospices in the United States. $31.50 for members and $45 for non-members (pre-paid orders only).

6

Work

In *Prosperity is God's Idea,* Margaret M. Stevens tells the following story:

> [There was] a man who died and found himself in a beautiful place, surrounded by every conceivable comfort. A white-jacketed man came to him and said, "You may have anything you choose—any food—any pleasure—any kind of entertainment."
>
> The man was delighted, and for days he sampled all the delicacies and experiences of which he had dreamed on earth. But one day he grew bored with all of it, and calling the attendant to him, he said, "I'm tired of all this. I need something to do. What kind of work can you give me?"
>
> The attendant sadly shook his head and replied, "I'm sorry, sir. That's the one thing we can't do for you. There is no work here for you."
>
> To which the man answered, "That's a fine thing. I might as well be in hell."
>
> The attendant said softly, "Where do you think you are?"

This fable strikes a chord, and also suggests an intriguing question: Why is it that so many of us think that *not* to work would be heaven, or something very close to it? Why do we make such clear distinctions between work and play in our lives, often finding it difficult to bring the same quality of joy and attention to our work as we do to our leisure? And what do we miss out on by holding these attitudes?

"Most men would feel insulted if it were proposed to employ them in throwing stones over a wall, and then in throwing them back, merely that they might earn their wages. But many are no more worthily employed now."

HENRY DAVID THOREAU

"Work consists in whatever a body is *obliged* to do, and Play consists of whatever a body is not obliged to do."

MARK TWAIN

"Work is love made visible."

KHALIL GIBRAN

Very possibly the answer has something to do with the way many of us consider work purely in terms of "making a living." Surely this sense of work as survival is an important part of work, but it is hardly the whole story.

In *Identity, Youth and Crisis,* Erik Erikson writes: "Freud was once asked what he thought a normal person should be able to do well. The questioner probably expected a completed 'deep' answer. But Freud simply said, 'Lieben und arbeiten' (to love and to work). It pays to ponder on this simple formula; it grows deeper as you think about it."

"Caring about our work, liking it, even loving it, seems strange when we see work only as a way to make a living," writes Tibetan Buddhist teacher Tarthang Tulku in *Skillful Means.* "But when we see work as the way to deepen and enrich all of our experience, each one of us can find this caring within our hearts, and awaken it in those around us, using every aspect of work to learn and grow."

Work, as can any other activity in our lives, can be a deeply enriching—and meditative—experience. It all depends on the attitude we carry to it. Approaching work with care and awareness can transform even the most mundane task into an exciting opportunity to reflect and grow. This attitude is reflected in most spiritual traditions.

Karma Yoga

In the yogic traditions, for example, work is seen as such an integral part of spiritual development that it is called Karma Yoga. In *Creative Work—Karma Yoga: A Western Interpretation,* the philosopher and philologist Edmund Bordeaux Szekely describes the essence of this teaching:

> In the highest sense, work is meant to be the servant of man, not the master. It is not so important what shape or form our work may take; what is vitally important is our attitude toward that work. With love and enthusiasm directed toward our work, what was once a chore and hardship now becomes a magical tool to develop, enrich and nourish our lives. "Work makes the man" is an old proverb with much more truth in it than appears on the surface. Work can indeed make the man, if the man will use his God-given powers of reason to transform work into the sacred partnership with the Creator it was originally meant to be.

The idea of action without attachment to the results of fruits of your labor is basic to Karma Yoga. Both the Hindu and Christian traditions stress that all work should be dedicated to God and undertaken to serve others. "Labore ut orare," say the Benedictine monks, "To work is to pray."

Ram Das writes of his guru, "Maharajji did not generally encourage severe austerities, nor extensive meditation practice, nor complex rituals. Rather, he guided us to *karma yoga,* a way of coming to God through living life as an act of devoted service . . . But Maharajji made it clear that hard work alone was not the essence of the matter. Rather, it was work carried on with remembrance of God; that is, work done with love in the presence of God's grace."

"The true husbandman," H. D. Thoreau writes in the "Bean Patch" chapter of *Walden,* "will cease from anxiety, as the squirrels manifest no concern whether the woods will bear chestnuts this year or not, and finish his labor with every day, relinquishing all claim to the produce of his fields, and sacrificing in his mind not only his first but last fruits also."

"There is dignity in work only when it is work freely accepted."

ALBERT CAMUS

"Praise Allah, but first tie your camel to a post."

SUFI SAYING

When we work in this way, we offer all we really have to offer: ourselves.

The story about the three masons illustrates how much difference our attitude about our work makes. Margaret M. Stevens writes:

> You know the story of the three brick masons. When the first man was asked what he was building, he answered gruffly, without even raising his eyes from his work, "I'm laying bricks." The second man replied, "I'm building a wall." But the third man said enthusiastically and with obvious pride, "I'm building a cathedral."

The Work Ethic Revised

In our culture, many of our unhealthy attitudes toward work can be traced back to the Protestant work ethic. The work ethic is partially a product of seventeenth century Calvinist theology, a deterministic philosophy which held that only a certain number of people in the world are destined to be saved or chosen by God. Although there was no way to tell for sure whether you were part of the elect, you *could* tell if you were not. Any signs of sloth, lack of prudence and above all lack of worldly success were sure signs that you were not of the chosen.

Though few of us today subscribe to this theological theory, it still forms the unconscious bedrock of our belief about work. In *Person/Planet* Theodore Roszak characterizes this old work ethic as follows:

> 1. Children play, grownups work. Work is what makes you officially grownup. . . .
> 2. Work is something you have to go looking for out there in the world. You apply for it and compete for it. . . .
> 3. Work is what fathers go away in the morning to do all day. It is very serious, because it is what the family lives by, and it is somewhat mysterious, because it happens far away—at someplace called the office or the plant or the shop. Most mothers work at home, but that doesn't count as real work.
> 4. Work is not something you are supposed to like.
> 5. People who don't work are either very poor or very rich. Poor people who don't work are lazy and contemptible.

"Business should be fun. Without fun people are left wearing emotional raincoats most of their working lives. Building fun into business is vital; it brings life into our daily being. Fun is a powerful motive for most of our activities and should be a direct part of our livelihood. We should not relegate it to something we buy after work with money we earn."

MICHAEL PHILLIPS

6. Losing your job is one of the most shameful and terrible things that can happen, because then you have to ask for handouts and people will think you're a freeloader.

By reversing these values in meaning, we can get a fairly good picture of the new work ethic as it is unfolding. Michael Phillips points to this shift of values in the *Briarpatch Book:*

"In the past it was considered reasonable for people to develop a marketable skill and pursue a career that would earn them enough money to do the things they really wanted to do. People worked at their jobs so they could do the things they wanted on weekends, go where they wanted on vacations and, in some cases, earn enough to retire 'early' and *then* do what they wanted. Now our peers are saying, 'that's nonsense; why should I do something I don't like 70% of my life so I can do what I want 30%?'" The old wage-slave mentality of renting ourselves to our jobs for eight hours a day to cover the essentials of life is giving way to the awareness that work is an integral part of our lives. Therefore the quality of our lives and the quality of our work-time are one and the same.

David Gershon, co-leader of "The Empowerment Workshop," drew similar conclusions as a result of his own work, consulting small businesses:

> What I observe happening today is people seeking more than money for their work; they're seeking personal fulfillment as well.
>
> Some of the ways people are seeking this personal fulfillment is through creating businesses that reflect their vision of a world the way they'd like to see it. This growing movement can be capsulized in the term *social entrepreneurship*—people making a statement about their spiritual values through both the content of the business they created and the way it's run.
>
> Other ways people are seeking more fulfillment is by taking more chances, risking by being more vulnerable, honest, and open in their communication with their fellow workers and bosses.
>
> One final observation is that many of the people I come in contact with are seeing their work or business as their teacher—the bottom line, if you will, for applying what they've learned in their spiritual practices—perhaps the most demanding "guru" of all. Work has become the new spiritual classroom.

Right Livelihood

As people begin to seek more fulfilling, rewarding work, some of them are finding that the solution to one problem can lead to the creation of another.

"Now that more people are thinking about doing, working at, and being what *they want*," says Michael Phillips in the *Briarpatch Book*, "the really tough question becomes, 'What do I want?' " Many people find the Buddhist concept of Right Livelihood helpful in answering this question.

The term *Right Livelihood* originates with the Buddha's teaching of the Eightfold Path, and has entered modern culture as a reflection of a general attitude of *caring* about one's work in the same way one cares about one's body.

Theodore Roszak puts it this way:

> The Buddha, in his wisdom, made "right livelihood" (another word, I think, for vocation) one of the steps to en-

lightenment. If we do not pitch our discussion that high, we have failed to give work its true dimension, and we will settle for far too little—perhaps for no more than a living wage. Responsible work is an embodiment of love, and love is the only discipline that will serve in shaping the personality, the only discipline that makes the mind whole and constant for a lifetime of effort. There hovers about a true vocation that paradox of all significant self-knowledge—our capacity to find ourselves by losing ourselves. We lose ourselves in our love of the task before us and, in that moment, we learn an identity that lives both within and beyond us.

What else should the highest yoga be, after all, but the work we turn to each day?

Michael Phillips offers up four qualities that he considers the essentials of right livelihood:

1. Your work should be an area of great passion. Most of the time right livelihood means we get up and look forward to the day with the same excitement that we feel on vacations.
2. Right livelihood is something you can spend your life doing: this means the livelihood should have within it the room for your constant curiosity; it must give you room to keep learning, to grow in compassion; and it should offer you challenges that will try you and yet appeal to you time and again. Most livelihoods actually have this potential, whether it is garbage collecting or systems programming, because the range of subtle and delicate refinements is always present.
3. It should be something that serves the community: you should feel that you are completely serving the community in what you do or you will have a longing as you get older to do something else and may have regrets. . . . But nearly every livelihood has enormous potential to serve people, and you will be serving people best when you are using your unique skills most fully.
4. And last, it should be totally appropriate to you.

How to Find the Right Right Livelihood

"Blessed is he who has found his work," writes Thomas Carlyle. "Let him ask no other blessedness."

"Many men go fishing all of their lives without knowing that it is not fish they are after."

HENRY DAVID THOREAU

All very well, you may say, but how do you achieve this state of blessedness? How do you find work that is right for you and right for the world?

Don't be a Victim of the Victim Mentality

"Playing into the victim mentality is the biggest cause of people failing to find satisfying work," says Richard Bolles, a minister and the closest thing to an enlightened career counselor America has ever seen. In his book *The Three Boxes of Life—and How to Get Out of Them*, Bolles writes:

The Victim Mentality, simply defined, is that outlook or attitude which says: "My life is essentially at the mercy of vast powerful forces (or a vast powerful force) *out there* and beyond my control. Therefore I am at the mercy of—. [Usually at least four are selected]

_____ My history, my upbringing, my genes, or my heritage.

_____ My social class, my education (or lack of it), or my I.Q. (or lack of it).

_____ My parents, my teachers, or an invalid relative.

_____ My mate, my partner, my husband, or my wife.

_____ My boss, my supervisor, my manager, or my co-workers.

—— The economy, the times we live in, the social structure, or our form of government.

—— The politicians, the large corporations, or the rich.

—— Some particular enemy, who is out to get me, and who has great power: an irate creditor, an ex-boyfriend or ex-girlfriend, a combine, or the Devil.

The Victim Mentality ultimately discharges you from any responsibility for your life, since clearly what is happening to you is not your fault. You don't have to lift a finger. . . . Now, to be sure, there is a sense in which we *are* victims, in our culture. We often are at the mercy of forces that we have no control over. A good hurricane or earthquake will remind you forcibly of that fact. So will even a moment's contemplation of what it means to live in The Nuclear Age. . .

Nonetheless, there is a vast difference between being a victim (which we all are, in some areas of our life) and having the Victim Mentality. Being a victim means there are some areas to my life where I am battling powerful forces, *but I will still do battle with them.* Whereas, having the Victim Mentality means giving up: *what's the use? why even try? I have no power at all; the things you suggest may help other people, but they can't offer any hope to me. . . .*

I want to state a simple truth, and that is, I believe every individual has more control over his or her life than he or she thinks is the case. . . . no matter how much of our life we perceive to be unchangeable, because it is in the control of someone or something else, there is always That Part that is under our control, and that we can work on to change. Be it 2%, 5%, 30% or whatever, it is almost always *more* than we think.

Moving in the Right Direction

Danaan Parry, one of the founders of the Holy Earth Foundation and the Earthstewards Network, offers this pragmatic advice on how to move toward right livelihood in one's life. "If your work does not allow you to express your creativity, your joy, your fullness, your own internal code of rightness," he says, "then you have three choices:"

"When the sun rises, I go to work.
When the sun goes down, I take
my rest,
I dig the well from which I drink,
I farm the soil which yields my
food,
I share creation, Kings can do no
more.

ANCIENT CHINESE PROVERB, 2500 B.C.

"A vision without a task is but a
dream,
a task without a vision is drudgery,
a vision and a task
is the hope of the world."

FROM A CHURCH IN SUSSEX, ENGLAND, C.
1730

1. Use your creativity to uncover ways and means to change the system. Introduce concepts of Right Livelihood in your work place. Have patience and persistence; gently assist others to find their point of positive service.

2. Do nothing, but be honest about it. Admit to yourself that you are more interested in not rocking the boat than in changing your life, because Right Livelihood demands change for most of us, away from work-for-security, prestige, and overabundance and toward a positive, right relationship to our labor that is congruent with our roles as planetary stewards.

3. Leave this work and seek other work that has the potential of Right Livelihood. Create a situation wherein you do what you are good at, are who you want to be, and are able to feel what you think is right, all intermingled.

A group of engineers who worked in the nuclear weapons field provide an inspiring example of one innovative way to move toward right livelihood. They had all come to the decision that their work and their spiritual beliefs were out of synch, but, because they all had families to support, they were reluctant to just up and quit their jobs.

So they got together and created a group support system. One at time the engineers left their jobs; they and their families were supported by the others in the group during the months it took them to find a new job in a more benign field.

Zen and the Art of Everyday Work

In *The Turning Point,* Fritjof Capra suggests that our values about what is worthy work are exactly upside down. The work given the lowest value in our culture, he says, is the most "entropic work"—the work "that has to be done over and over again, without leaving a lasting impact"—while high status is given to jobs that create something that lasts: "skyscrapers, supersonic planes, space rockets, nuclear warheads, and all the other products of high technology."

Entropic work, says Capra, is the key to a spiritual life: "Doing work that has to be done over and over again helps us recognize the natural cycles of growth and decay, of birth and death, and thus become aware of the dynamic order of the universe. 'Ordinary' work, as the root meaning of the term indicates, is work that is in harmony with the order we perceive in the natural environment. . . . What we need, therefore, is to revise the concept and practice of work in such a way that it becomes meaningful and fulfilling for the individual worker, useful for society, and part

of the harmonious order of the ecosystem. To reorganize and pratice our work in this way will allow us to recapture its spiritual essence."

Manual labor, called *samu* in Zen, is part of the life of every Zen monk. Every day after breakfast a time is set aside for sweeping, dusting, polishing the floor, scrubbing the toilets, weeding and gardening.

"Since the time when Hyakujo first instituted it, more than a thousand years ago," Roshi Philip Kapleau writes in *The Three Pillars of Zen,* "manual labor has been an essential ingredient of Zen discipline. It is recorded of Hyakujo that one day his monks, feeling he had grown too feeble to work, hid his gardening tools. When they refused to heed his entreaties to return them, he stopped eating, saying, 'No work, no eating.'"

Samu, explains Kapleau, serves two main functions in Zen training. "First, it points up that zazen is not merely a matter of acquiring the ability to concentrate and focus the mind during sitting, but that in the widest sense zazen involves the mobilization of *joriki* (the power generated by zazen) in our every act. Samu, as a mobile type of zazen, also provides the opportunity to quiet, deepen, and bring the mind to one-pointedness through activity, as well as to invigorate the body and thereby energize the mind."

The object of such work, says Kapleau, "as in every other type of zazen, is the cultivation first of mindfulness and eventually mindlessness." (Mindfulness is awareness in which one is aware that one is aware. "Mindlessness" is, on the other hand, "a condition of such complete absorption that there is no vestige of self-awareness.")

"All labor entered into with such a mind is valued for itself apart from what it may lead to," says Kapleau. "This is the 'meritless' or 'purposeless' work of Zen. By undertaking each task in this spirit, eventually we are enabled to grasp the truth that every act is an expression of the Buddha-mind. Once this is directly and unmistakably experienced, no labor can be beneath one's dignity. On the contrary, all work, no matter how menial, is ennobling because it is seen as the expression of the immaculate Buddha-nature. This is true enlightenment, and enlightenment in Zen is never for oneself alone but for the sake of all."

Fourteen Lessons I've Learned Trying to Manage a "Conscious Business"

Contributed by MiraBai Bush

1. See your business as an organism, alive, always changing—a process, not a static institution, requiring continual and spontaneous awareness to be managed effectively. Like the Tao, if you think you know it, you don't.

2. Practice compassion and empathy. The basic truth that we are not separate from one another is as central to relationships in business as it is to relationships in the rest of life. Competition is healthy only when we remember that it is also true that we all are cooperating in a much larger task.

3. Keep close to the ground. Use common sense and simple solutions. Be wary of acting out of a concept of how things should be. The gut (or hara) is the center for business (informed, of course, by love and wisdom).

4. Work on creating a happy workplace. Benefits, like appropriate salary, health insurance, vacations, etc., do not make people happy; they keep people from being unhappy. Happiness in the workplace comes from a challenging and satisfying relationship with one's work.

5. Care about your product. You are adding more "stuff" to the environment. Make sure it's in harmony with your values.

6. Continually rearticulate the values of the business. The daily demands of every work situation tend to eclipse the deeper motivations.

7. Create effective strategies—it helps you remember that business is a game. It also gives flexibility and strength. The martial arts have taught the Japanese a great tradition of honoring strategy. The wider your choice of possible responses to a situation, the greater your chance of success.

8. Always tell the truth. If this seems contrary to the demands of American business, read Gandhi.

9. Don't get in it for the money. Recognize that a healthy, growing business needs to be profitable, but if your central intention is to become rich, it's not worth doing.

10. Keep the rest of your life alive and diverse. Remember your other priorities. Don't get confused about whether to attend a cash-flow seminar or your child's Christmas play. Take lots of vacations. Meditate or do whatever reminds you that you are not only the person behind the desk.

11. Encourage personal growth. It increases productivity.

12. Hire people you trust, people who share your values. It's almost always more important than skills.

13. Know that the end never justifies the means. The process is it. The end is conditioned by the means.

14. Be playful. The world *doesn't* make sense—don't forget!

Ms. Bush is the founder and director of Illuminations.

"Certain professions are more or less completely incompatible with the achievement of man's final end; and there are certain ways of making a living which do so much physical and, above all, so much moral, intellectual and spiritual harm that, even if they could be practised in a non-attached spirit (which is generally impossible), they would still have to be eschewed by anyone dedicated to the task of liberating, not only himself, but others.

ALDOUS HUXLEY

The Path of Business

Although many people view running a business as antithetical to spiritual growth, Bob Schwartz of the Tarrytown Conference Center, for one, sees business as a perfect opportunity to put your ideals into reality. In the past several years, Schwartz has championed the idea that spiritually minded, socially conscious people could best create right livelihood by going into business themselves. According to Schwartz, entrepreneurs stand on the cutting edge of innovation and social change. A small business, being inherently more flexible than a larger institution, offers a good vehicle for bringing new ideas into the culture.

Kenneth Blanchard and Spencer Johnson agree in *The One Minute Manager:* "People who feel good about themselves produce good results," they say. Their book is about people, but it is also about productivity. The ingredients of the one-minute manager are one-minute goal-setting, one-minute praising, and one-minute reprimands. Once you've read how it works—which takes just a little more than a few minutes—this way of managing people, yourself included, may seem obvious. No doubt it is, but the authors have managed to distill a fair amount of wisdom from the obvious.

Here it is in a nutshell:

> You set One Minute Goals with your people to make sure they know what they are being held accountable for and what good performance looks like. You then try to catch them doing something right so you can give them a One Minute Praising. And then, finally, if they have all the skills to do something right and they don't, you give them a One Minute Reprimand.

Behind it all is the thought: "The best minute I spend is the one I invest in people."

One group of people who have clearly proven Schwartz' theory is the Briarpatch Network in the San Francisco area. Originally the brain child of Dick Raymond of the Portola Institute, the publisher of the first *Whole Earth Catalogue,* and Michael Phillips, the Briarpatch Network is a network of small businesses in the San Francisco area, unified around certain common values.

"Briarpatch," says Phillips, "is a word that conveys a set of values: openness, sharing, and serving people through business. The Briarpatch consists of several thousand people throughout America who recognize and have found each other through shared interests. What we have in common are our business values and the joy and excitement we feel about our work."

The Briarpatch Network holds essentially three values in common: "We are in business because we love it; we find our reward in serving people, rather than in amassing large sums of money; and we share our resources with each other as much as we can, especially our knowledge of business." One practice that they all share is that they keep all of their books and financial records open to the public. *CoEvolution Quarterly,* Stewart Brand's spinoff of the *Whole Earth Catalogue,* for example, publishes a financial statement in the back of each issue, along with a column of gossip about the *CoEv* staff and friends.

The Briarpatch Network is active in San Francisco only, but it serves as a model that could be developed

"If you have built castles in the air, your work need not be lost; that is where they should be. Now put the foundations under them."

HENRY DAVID THOREAU

elsewhere. Briarpatch business people have lunch or breakfast together to discuss their common challenges and concerns in their businesses, and they basically make it a policy to help each other: cooperation replacing competition. It is a kind of Right Livelihood Chamber of Commerce.

But Right Livelihood is not restricted solely to the province of small business and cottage industry. Recent studies suggest that even in the largest corporations the best economic results are produced by following the most humanistic approaches in management.

In a best-selling study of successful businesses, *In Search of Excellence,* Thomas J. Peters and Robert H. Waterman, Jr., point out that the key to a successful organization is first of all people. It is the human factor that matters most.

General Shared Values

The Japanese seem to understand this very well. Peters and Waterman report:

> As a senior Japanese executive explained to us: "We are very different from the rest of the world. Our only natural resource is the hard work of our people."
>
> Treating people—not money, machines, or minds—as the natural resource may be the key to it all. Kenichi Ohame, head of McKinsey's Tokyo office, says that in Japan organization and people (in the organization) are synonymous. Moreover, the people orientation encourages love of product and requires modest risk taking and innovation by the average worker.

Kenichi Ohame described it to Peters and Waterman this way: "Japanese management keeps telling the workers that those at the frontier know the business best. . . . A well-run company relies heavily on individual or group initiatives for innovation and creative energy. The individual employee is utilized to the fullest extent of his creative and productive capacity. . . . The full organization—the proposal boxes, quality circles, and the like—look 'organic' and 'entrepreneurial' as opposed to 'mechanical' and 'bureaucratic.'"

"Every kind of work can be a pleasure. Even simple household tasks can be an opportunity to exercise and expand our caring, our effectiveness, our responsiveness. As we respond with caring and vision to all work, we develop our capacity to respond fully to all of life. Every action generates positive energy which can be shared with others. These qualities of caring and responsiveness are the greatest gift we can offer."

TARTHANG TULKU

Zen and the Art of Ordinary Work

Whether we work in a large corporation or driving a cab, we tend to forget the value of hands-on work as a part of daily life. These three stories can serve as a reminder.

Other People Are Not Me

The first is from the Japanese Zen master Dogen, who went to China to study Zen in the twelfth century. His celebrated *Instructions to the Zen Cook* tells how, in China,

he learned the importance of the cook in Zen training and life. The following story is taken from a masterful new translation with commentary of Dogen's instructions. Writes Dogen:

"When I was at Mount Tiantong, a monk called Lu from Qingyuan Fu was serving as tenzo. One day after the noon meal I was walking to another building within the complex when I noticed Lu drying mushrooms in the sun in front of the *butsuden*. He carried a bamboo stick but had no hat on his head. The sun's rays beat down so harshly that the tiles along the walk burned one's feet. Lu worked hard and was covered with sweat. I could not help but feel the work was too much of a strain for him. His back was a bow drawn taut, his long eyebrows were crane white.

"I approached and asked his age. He replied that he was sixty-eight years old. Then I went on to ask him why he never used any assistants.

"He answered, 'Other people are not me.'

"'You are right,' I said; 'I can see that your work is the activity of the *buddhadharma,* but why are you working so hard in this scorching sun?'

"He replied, 'If I do not do it now, when else can I do it?'

"There was nothing else for me to say. As I walked on along that passageway, I began to sense inwardly the true significance of the role of tenzo."

Years later, when he had returned to Japan, Dogen instructed his monks in the proper way to cook—or to do any kind of work, for that matter.

"Keep your eyes open," he wrote. "Do not allow even one grain of rice to be lost. Wash the rice thoroughly, put it in the pot, light the fire, and cook it. There is an old saying that goes, 'See the pot as your own head; see the water as your lifeblood.'"

"It is vital that we clarify and harmonize our lives with our work," said Dogen, "and not lose sight of either the theoretical or the practical."

"Handle even a single leaf of a green in such a way that it manifests the body of the Buddha. This in turn allows the Buddha to manifest through the leaf."

Making Shoes

"You know," André Gregory writes, "somebody once told me that in France in medieval times, if you wanted to go on some kind of spiritual journey, if you were really lucky you would meet somebody who might have been a teacher (you were never quite sure), and that person would say to you, 'What is it that you wish to do?' And you would say, 'Well, I want to be a shoemaker.' He'd say, 'There's a wonderful shoemaker in Lyons who may be somebody quite spiritual. I'll send you to him and you can apprentice with him. The only rule is that you must never, ever discuss anything spiritual with him.' And so you would go off and work for this person for four or five years as an apprentice, and then you would really get to know how to make shoes, and he would say, 'You know, you really know how to make very good shoes now. There is an opening in a partnership in Dijon with a very special man who makes shoes. I can get you that partnership, but you must never,

ever discuss anything spiritual with him. You must concentrate on making very beautiful shoes.' And so off
you'd go to Dijon and work for years, and shortly before
his death the old man would say, 'Well, soon this business will be yours. You've become a really fine shoemaker. Now, one of these days, someone who is younger
than you may come wanting to learn something sprir-
itual from you. Only tell him about making shoes.'"

Finally: What Else Is There?

Joko-sensei, a teacher at the Zen Center of San Diego,
tells that one morning she was working putting the finish-
ing touches on a remodeled kitchen at the Zen Center of
Los Angeles, when the teacher, Maezumi-roshi, walked in
to see how things were going.

"Everything's going fine," she said. "There are only
a few details to finish up."

At this the roshi scratched his head. "Only a few
details?" he asked, looking puzzled. "But details are all
there are."

Recommended Reading

Creative Work, Edmond Szekely (Academy Books, 1973). Szekely
presents the idea of Karma Yoga, union of all things through
work. An excellent primer on treating work as a spiritual practice.

The Briarpatch Book, the Briarpatch Community (New Glide/
Reed, 1975). True tales from a network of small businesses dedicated to open, supportive cooperation and public service.

Honest Business, Michael Phillips and Salli Rasberry (Random
House, 1981). This book is about bringing love, hard work,
honesty, and social responsibility together to develop useful and
fulfilling small businesses.

Skillful Means, Tarthang Tulku (Dharma Publishing, 1978). Ap-
plying spiritual insight to work, and using meaningful work to
contribute to life and society.

Resources

Organizations:

Association of Humanistic Business, c/o Swankin and Turner, 1424 16th St., N.W., Washington, D.C. 20036. An association of business people who share humanistic values. Organizes educational events and publishes a members list.

The Business Initiative, c/o Betsy Combier, 315 E. 65th St., New York, NY 10021, (212)794-8902. A membership organization for people interested in bringing about social change within the business world. Sponsors regular meetings in New York City and publishes a monthly newsletter.

The Meta Network, Metasystems Design Group, Inc., 1401 Wilson Blvd, Suite 601, Arlington, VA 22209. A network of people interested in transformation and business which communicates via a computer conferencing system.

TWG (The Washington Group), c/o John Adams, Resources for Human Systems Development, 2914 27th St. N., Arlington, VA 22207, (703)524-8126. A loose-knit network of people interested in Organizational Transformation—looking at practical approaches for transformation as it applies to large organizations. Produces a bimonthly newsletter ($12/year) and a members list.

What Color Is Your Parachute?, P.O. Box 379, Walnut Creek, CA 94597. This is perhaps the only spiritually oriented career development project in North America. Directed by Richard N. Bolles, the author of *What Color Is Your Parachute?* Bolles offers one two-week training program in Life/Work Planning, held the first two weeks of August.

Magazines and newsletters:

In Business, (Box 323, Emmaus, PA 18049, $18/year, six is-
sues). A sensitive guide to running a small business with heart
and integrity.

7

Money

"The rich man," suggests the Talmud, "is the man who is satisfied with what he has."

It sounds simple enough, but few of us are able to heed the advice of the Talmudic sages. Money bestows power in our society, and this power, we think, will bring us freedom, happiness, security, and the fulfillment of all our desires.

This belief is both a tempting and a grand illusion. "In fact," as Mike Phillips, author of *The Seven Laws of Money*, writes, "the wisdom of millions of our ancestors has been very consistent on the point of money, the goal of amassing money is traditionally called 'greed' and regardless of your motives for getting the money (freedom, charity or anything else), the results will not be what you hope for. Instead the wise teachers of tradition tell us to go ahead and do the things we want and become good at them. In that lies our freedom."

Many people on the spiritual path, recognizing the suffering that the endless pursuit of money can cause, remember the biblical warning that "money is the root of all evil." But what St. Paul actually said is, "The *love* of money is the root of all evil." It is our attachment to money—and our mistaken belief that money is the key to a fulfilling life—that is the problem, not money itself.

"On the whole we should regard money as mother's milk: it nourishes us and it nourishes others. That should be our attitude to money. It's not just a blank coupon that we have in our wallet. Each dollar contains a lot of past; many people worked for that particular one dollar, one cent. They worked so hard, with their sweat and tears. So it's like mother's milk. But at the same time, mother's milk can be given away and we can produce more mother's milk. So I wouldn't hang on to it too tightly."

CHOGYAM TRUNGPA RINPOCHE

Money As Energy

But what is money? Nothing in itself; it exists only because it stands for something else. To some economists it symbolizes labor, goods, or property. To others it represents gold or silver stored in bank vaults. A final definition seems elusive. As Georg Simmel writes in *The Philosophy of Money,* "The question as to what value really is, like the question as to what being is, is unanswerable."

There does, however, seem to be general agreement from a spiritual point of view that money may most usefully be viewed as a symbol of energy. Money stands for energy that passes between us. It is not a thing but a transaction, a transfer, an exchange.

When we see money in this way, we begin to change our usual attitude towards it. You can't, for example, own energy or treat it as a thing or possession. You can care for it properly, but you can't hoard it or hold on to it. Energy is not energy unless it is used, and you cannot use it unless you let go of it.

Once we realize this, we can begin to unravel the "problem" of money in our own lives. Freed from attachment and greed, money could become a symbol of our interconnectedness, a medium for the exchange of human energy and values—manna rather than Mammon.

In many ways, our relationship to money is an accurate mirror of our spiritual development. When we call someone a miser or spendthrift, we make an observation about that person's relationship to both money and the world in general. Money invites us to work with our own desires in a specific way. The illusion of money is very powerful, but as we acknowledge it, we find that money turns into an ally and teacher on the spiritual path.

Swami Kriyananda, founder of Ananda Coop Village in Nevada City, California, makes a similar point in a little pamphlet called *How to Use Money for Your Own Highest Good:*

> I used to be strongly opposed to the business consciousness of America. In college, so great was my aversion to business that at meals I even avoided sitting at the same table with business majors. To me (philosopher and poet, as I fancied myself) they represented Crass Materialism.
>
> Well, much to my surprise, when I came onto the spiritual path, I encountered true saints who were also highly successful businessmen. Moreover, a major impetus toward my own spiritual search had already been the discovery that an interest in philosophy and the arts didn't necessarily make a person *less* materialistic. Conversion to the spiritual path forced a radical shift in my beliefs! What I realized, belatedly, was that it isn't a question of whether or not one makes money, but of *how* one makes it, and how one uses it.

Kriyananda reminds us again, "Money is merely a symbol of energy. One can use energy wisely or foolishly; generously or selfishly; freely, or with greedy attachment. Money is capable of doing a great good. To use it rightly is to perform a useful, even a spiritual service; it is not materialism."

Mike Phillips, a Bank of America banker, instrumental in developing Master Charge, had an experience that brought him to the same conclusion. At the age of thirty-

"Always leave enough time in your life to do something that makes you happy, satisfied, or even joyous. That has more of an effect on economic well-being than any other single factor."

PAUL HAWKEN

"The cost of a thing is the amount of what I call life which is required to be exchanged for it, immediately or in the long run."

HENRY DAVID THOREAU

one, having never taken a vacation in his life, he took a cruise on the advice of one of his clients.

"Once I was on board and realized that there was nothing to do," Phillips remembers, "I just about had a nervous breakdown. I even tried to get a helicopter to come pick me up. Finally, I was faced with the choice between going insane and just sitting in a deck chair and looking out at the ocean for several days straight."

It was the beginning of a great change. Phillips realized that "because I wanted freedom, and thought that money could get me freedom, I had ended up working in a job where I had very *little* freedom to do the things I really cared about. I thought that people with more money would be more loved and respected—and yet when I looked at the qualities that made me care for them, money had absolutely nothing to do with it. I wanted security for my family and friends, yet I was hardly even able to *see* my family and friends because my life had become so excessively work-centered.

"In thinking about old age, I looked at my parents and saw that their most important asset in dealing with being older was their ability to be competent, helpful, flexible, curious, generous, and involved with others. Money had very little to do with it."

Mike is an advisor to Briarpatch, and a former president of Point, the foundation set up by the Whole Earth Catalogue. He spends at least one month a year in Kyoto, Japan, sits zazen, and has recently cut down his possessions to 250. Seven years after its publication, *The Seven Laws of Money* continues to sell exactly the same number of copies it has since its publication: 125 a week.

> "Superfluous wealth can buy superfluities only. Money is not required to buy one necessity of the soul."
>
> HENRY DAVID THOREAU

> "I have no money, no resources, no hopes. I am the happiest man alive."
>
> HENRY MILLER

The Seven Laws of Money

The first step in seeing through an illusion is to understand how it works. There are thousands of books about how to turn money into more money (the best way to get rich, as someone once said, is to tell other people how to get rich), but Mike Phillips' *Seven Laws of Money* is the only book we know of that deals with the illusion of money and the way that illusion works in our lives. *The Seven Laws* have been reprinted a number of times, but we feel that they are solid gold, and well worth contemplating again.

1. Do it! Money will come when you are doing the right thing. The first law is the hardest for most people to accept and is the source of the most distress. The clearest translation of this in terms of personal advice is "go ahead and do what you want to do." Worry about your ability to do it and your competence to do it, but certainly do not worry about the money.

2. Money has its own rules: records, budgets, saving, borrowing. The rules of money are probably Ben Franklin-type rules, such as never squander it, don't be a spendthrift, be very careful, you have to account for what you're doing, you must keep track of it, and you can never ignore what happens to money.

3. Money is a dream—a fantasy as alluring as the Pied Piper. Money is very much a state of mind. It's much like the states of consciousness that you see on an acid trip. . . . It is fantasy in itself, purely a dream. People who go after it as though it were real and tangible, say a person who is trying to earn a hundred-thousand dollars, orient their lives and end up in such a way as to have been significantly changed simply to have reached that goal. They become part of that object and since the object is a dream (a mirage) they become quite different from what they set out to be.

4. Money is a nightmare—in jail, robbery, fears of poverty. I am not expressing a moral judgment. I am making very clear something that many people aren't conscious of: among the people we punish, the people we have to take out of society, 80% or more are people who are unable to deal with money. . . .

    Money is also a nightmare when looked at from the opposite perspective—from the point of view of people who have inherited a lot of money.

    The Western dream is to have a lot of money, and then you can lead a life of leisure and happiness. Nothing in my experience could be further from the truth.

5. You can never give money away. Looked at over a period of time, money flows in certain channels, like electricity

through wires. The wires define the relationship, and the flow is the significant thing to look at. The fifth law of money suggests that by looking at the gift in a larger or longer-term perspective, we will see that it is part of a two-way flow.

6. You can never really receive money as a gift. Money is either borrowed or lent or possibly invested. It is never given or received without those concepts implicit in it. . . . Giving money requires some repayment; if it's not repaid the nightmare elements enter into it. A gift of money is really a contract; it's really a repayable loan, and it requires performance and an accounting of performance that is satisfactory to the giver.

7. There are worlds without money. They are the worlds of art, poetry, music, dance, sex, etc., the essentials of human life. The seventh law is like a star that is your guide. You know that you cannot live on the star; it is not physically a part of your life, but rather an aid to orientation. You are not going to reach this star, but in some sense neither are you going to reach your destination without it to guide you.

Creative Financing

If Michael Phillips is right, then there are many creative ways to go about funding the great things we might want to do. Spiritual literature as well as the many quasi-spiritual, think-and-grow-rich, prosperity consciousness type texts have a good deal of advice to offer on this account. If, in fact, money is energy, then it follows that our attitudes can play a significant role in creating financial well-being. Following are some guidelines:

Practice Abundance Consciousness

The term "prosperity consciousness" refers to a basic attitude toward life—one in which we see our lives as rich and abundant rather than scarce in resources. Some proponents of abundance thinking take this quite literally.

"The fact is that there is more than enough to go around for every being on earth, if we are willing to open our minds to that possibility," writes Shakti Gawain in her book *Creative Visualization*. "The universe is a place of great abundance and we are all naturally prosperous, both in material and spiritual wealth."

"Money talks because money is a metaphor, a transfer, and a bridge."

MARSHALL MCLUHAN

"The use of money is all the advantage there is in having money."

BENJAMIN FRANKLIN

"Often people attempt to live their lives backwards: they try to *have* more things, or more money, in order to *do* more of what they want, so they will *be* happier.

"The way it actually works is the reverse. You must first *be* who you really are, then, *do* what you need to do, in order to *have* what you want."

MARGARET YOUNG

"Manifestation is not magic. It is a process of working with natural principles and laws in order to translate energy from one level of reality to another."

DAVID SPANGLER

"You already possess an infinite amount of wealth," Jack and Lois Johnstad concur in *The Power of Prosperous Thinking*. "You don't realize this fact because most of your wealth is in forms you don't recognize as wealth. You possess time, energy, skills, ideas. You have not yet acquired the specialized knowledge to convert your already possessed wealth into other, more negotiable, forms of wealth."

No doubt this is true as far as it goes, but as some critics point out, the enthusiasts of prosperity consciousness too often forget that the transformation of inner wealth into outer wealth is not always easily done—or even desirable.

True abundance, as David Spangler, an early leader of the Findhorn community reminds us, is more than material. "To have a consciousness of abundance on a soul level," Spangler writes in *The Laws of Manifestation*, "does not mean having a sense of access to many things, seemingly stored in some treasure house, but rather being at one with the Essence behind and within all things. True abundance is a consciousness of wholeness, oneness and quality, not of separateness, multiplicity and quantity."

Be Grateful

One way to encourage a personal attitude of abundance is to be grateful for all that we *do* have rather than focusing on what we lack. Brother David Steindl-Rast, in fact, sees the practice of gratefulness as the essence of his spiritual practice. He says in a *New Age* interview: "That would be my practice: to try and live gratefully." The practice of gratefulness, he says, trains you to see all of life as an opportunity. "If you train yourself to be grateful for everything, every moment, then when you come to something you don't like, you realize it's still given and you have to deal with it. You will be alert to the gift within every gift, which is opportunity."

Practicing gratefulness can take the form of very specific practices such as this one suggested by Caroline Kirby, our classified advertising manager at *New Age Journal:* "I actually write the word 'Blessings!' on each check that I write. This helps me to remember to thank all involved with making the goods and services that I am purchasing available to me. I always feel refreshed from it. It's easy to bless and be thankful for what comes in, but it requires an effort at first to bless and be thankful for that which goes out."

Surrender Your Project to a Power Greater than Yourself

A cornerstone of Alcoholics Anonymous, turning your life over to a power greater than yourself, can also help in keeping projects of good works afloat financially. Prosperity consciousness books are full of anecdotes that attest to the power of this act, but the best way to test it out is to try it. One way to begin is to use the phrase from the Lord's Prayer, "Thy will be done." See your project as being watched over and cared for by a higher power. Imagine that every need has been or will be taken care of. This does not mean you should sit by passively. This attitude helps you to let go of trying too hard and allows you to notice opportunities when they arise.

"All substance is energy in motion. It lives and flows. Money is symbolically a golden flowing stream of concretised vital energy. This golden stream is enslaved by man's selfishness, greed, fear of insecurity, love of power, etc. Money which has been the slave of man's selfishness, must become the instrument of man's goodwill. Money is magnetically bound to selfish purposes by the power of selfish desire. It can be equally attracted and bound to unselfish purposes by unselfish desire."

THE MAGICAL WORK OF THE SOUL

"Money is God in action."

RAYMOND CHARLES BARKER

"You are prosperous to the degree that you are experiencing peace, health, and plenty in your world. While prosperous thinking means many things to people, basically it gives you the power to make your dreams come true, whether those dreams are concerned with better health, increased financial success, a happier personal life, more education and travel, or a deeper spiritual life."

CATHERINE PONDER

"Save and invest as though you would live forever. Share and spend as though you would die tomorrow."

JACK AND LOIS JOHNSTAD

One spiritual healer offers another approach to the same thing. She suggests seeing your plan or project as a seed in an apple. That seed already contains all of the information necessary to grow into a tree and create more apples. In that sense it already has everything it needs. Seeing your project in this light, affirming that it has a purpose of its own, a purpose that is greater perhaps than you're even aware of, can help develop the faith and courage necessary to go on during times of uncertainty.

Positive Thinking

Proponents of the power of the mind in financial matters tell us that our thinking is the key to creative financing. "Our belief at the beginning of a doubtful undertaking," says the great American psychologist William James in *The Varieties of Religious Experience*, "is the one thing that ensures the successful outcome of the venture."

"When you expect the best," says minister Norman Vincent Peale in the classic *The Power of Positive Thinking*, "you release a magnetic force in your mind which by law of attraction tends to bring the best to you."

"As a man thinketh, so he is," runs one of the most oft-quoted mottoes of the positive thinkers. And lest you think the idea of positive thinking is simplistic and obvious, consider the words of the Babylonian in another prosperity consciousness classic, *The Richest Man in Babylon:* "Deride not what I say because of its simplicity. Truth is always simple."

Visualization and Affirmation

Visualization and affirmation, as used in prosperity consciousness, are both essentially advanced forms of positive thinking.

Affirmations consist of repeating positive statements so that they take root in the mind. According to Leonard Orr, one of the most active teachers of prosperity consciousness (as well as the founder of a controversial tool called "rebirthing"), affirmations may be spoken aloud, read into a tape recorder and played back or written down.

Writing down affirmations seems to have certain advantages. When we write affirmations, the mind, hand, and eye are all involved. Many people resist the unsophisticated "simple-minded" notion of writing down affirmations in this manner, but it is perhaps just because of this simplicity that this method often works so powerfully for many people.

One of the most effective ways of using written affirmations is to write an affirmation such as "I am prosperous in everything I do," or "All of my needs are taken care of," on the right side of a page. As you repeatedly write the affirmation, stop to write the negative responses that arise in your mind on the left side of the page. Once this is done you can see what your habitual negative response to positive thoughts about money is. Next, convert your negative responses into positive statements, making new affirmations for yourself. Rephrasing your negative beliefs into affirmations, says Orr, can transform your habitual thinking at the subconscious level.

Visualization also transforms negative conditioning at the level of imagination, reprogramming the unconscious. In her book *Creative Visualization,* Shakti Gawain gives these four basic steps for effective visualization as an aid to prosperity consciousness:

1. Set your goal—decide on something you would like to work toward, realize, or create.

2. Create a clear idea or picture—create an idea or mental picture of the object or situation exactly as you want it. You should think of it in the present tense, as already existing the way you want it to be.

3. Focus on it often—bring your idea or mental picture to mind often, both in quiet meditation periods and also casually throughout the day when you happen to think of it.

4. Give it positive energy—as you focus on your goal, think about it in a positive, encouraging way. Make strong positive statements to yourself: that it exists, that it has come or is now coming to you. See yourself receiving or achieving it. These positive statements are called "affirmations."

"There is a certain Buddhistic calm that comes from having . . . money in the bank."

AYN RAND

One caution: Affirmations and visualizations are powerful tools that call for careful use. Pouring attention and energy into one area of your life will have an effect, but will it be the effect that is truly the best for you and other people? For this reason, practitioners of prosperity consciousness, affirmations, and creative visualization are warned to not be too specific in their attempts.

Shakti Gawain recommends always adding the following phrase to the affirmation process: "This, or something better, now manifests for me in totally satisfying and harmonious ways to the highest good of all concerned."

Prosperity Conscience

Living well does not necessarily depend on having more money or more things. Expenses and expenditures, as many people have noticed, have an astonishing way of rising to keep up with income.

If, like most of us, you don't have enough money, there are two things you can do. The first one, which occurs to everyone, is to increase your income. The second is simply to simplify your life. This trend toward simplicity is a significant and growing one, as Stanford Research Institute social scientist Duane Elgin points out in his book *Voluntary Simplicity*. (Elgin took the title of his book, and the name for this movement, from an essay published by a Harvard-educated American disciple of Gandhi, Richard Gregg.)

Gregg wrote: "Voluntary simplicity involves both inner and outer condition. It means singleness of purpose, sincerity, and honesty within, as well as avoidance of exterior clutter, or many possessions irrelevant to the chief purpose of life. It means an ordering and guiding of our energy and our desires, a partial restraint in some directions in order to secure greater abundance of life in other directions. It involves a deliberate organization of life for a purpose."

Elgin expands on that definition in *Voluntary Simplicity:*

> What does it mean to live more simply? To consciously bring greater simplicity into our lives does not mean that we must live in a primitive or rudimentary manner. Voluntary simplicity is an aesthetic simplicity because it is consciously chosen. Few people will choose deliberately to make their lives ugly when they, instead, can choose to bring a functional beauty and integrity into their lives. Yet how we simplify is a very personal affair. We all know where our lives are unnecessarily complicated. We are all painfully aware of the distractions, clutter, and pretense that weigh upon our lives and make our passage through the world more cumbersome and awkward. To live with simplicity is to unburden our lives—to live a more direct, unpretentious, and unencumbered relationship with all aspects of our lives: consuming, working, learning, relating, and so on. Simplicity of living means meeting life face to face. It means confronting life clearly, without unnecessary distractions, without trying to soften the awesomeness of our existence or masking the deeper manifestations of life with pretentions, distractions and unnecessary accumulations. It means being direct and honest in relationships of all kinds. It means taking life as it is—straight and unadulterated.

Thoreau and Gandhi Agree

"The essence of civilization consists not in the multiplication of wants but in their deliberate and voluntary renunciation," said Gandhi.

"Money, young man, is good for the nerves."

J. P. MORGAN

After meeting the King of England, a reporter commented to Gandhi on how scantily dressed he had been in the presence of the King. Gandhi replied, "It's okay. The King had on enough for both of us."

Henry David Thoreau said, "An honest man has hardly need to count more than his ten fingers, or in extreme cases he may add his ten toes, and lump the rest. Simplicity, simplicity, simplicty! I say, let your affairs be as two or three, and not a hundred or a thousand; instead of a million, count half-a-dozen, and keep your accounts on your thumbnail."

And Finally—Giving Money Away

A spiritual accountant might say that getting and managing money properly is half of it—giving it away wisely is the other half. Tithing, the practice of giving away ten percent of one's income to a church or spiritual organization, is one of the oldest forms of giving. Practiced by the ancient Jews and recommended by Jesus, the custom is making a comeback among contemporary spiritual seekers. Though it inevitably seems as if we can't afford it, it is also inevitable that we can't afford not to: How can we truly receive unless we give.

Jim Guiness had this to say about tithing in a very early issue of *New Age:*

> During the past year my wife and I have had the good fortune to discover that giving away one-tenth of our money enriches us spiritually and even financially. A year ago I was unemployed. We had a new baby and were beginning to dip into our small savings in order to meet living expenses. Our financial problems were compounded by fuel shortages and the price of food. Prospects for the winter looked bleak, to say the least.
>
> It was about this time that we heard of the practice of tithing. Giving away one-tenth of our money seemed like a very extraordinary way of relieving our financial problems, since we had far too little money to begin with. We thought of a multitude of convincing reasons why we shouldn't or couldn't tithe, but we took the plunge.
>
> We began to give our ten percent on a weekly basis, and we've had no financial worries since. I now have any

"The lack of money is the root of all evil."

GEORGE BERNARD SHAW

number of opportunities for employment, and all our needs are easily and promptly met.

It seems impossible to give anything to God, but it does seem important to give to something larger than oneself.

Conscious Giving

Robin Hood Was Right is a book published by the Vanguard Public Foundation, a group of thirty people who have been giving away more than $250,000 a year for social change and community projects in San Francisco. In Boston, another active organization, the Haymarket Foundation, helps people give their money away intelligently and sensitively.

In 1981 a group was founded with the expressed goal of providing funding for projects furthering the spiritual transformation of the world community. The group ("who by unique circumstance have personal wealth and who have experienced an awakening to great feelings of love") call themselves the "Donuts" (motto: "Keep Your Eye on the Whole"), have maintained a low profile, do not accept written proposals, and only deal through the amorphous network of spirituality-oriented groups and individuals. In this way they manage to avoid the trappings and bureaucratic bogs of big-money "Foundations."

The most important thing about giving, the Donuts have found, is giving with a clear heart. Don't give and hang on, but rather give and let go. Don't try to use your gifts to control. The spirit with which you give is the best insurance that the gift will do some good.

In the Donut Newsletter, one conscious philanthropist writes, "Everything is alive, everything is interrelated; all life is sacred. . . . Sharing fully of what I have in every sense completes the spiritual loop. It's my way of saying thanks to God."

Resources

The Power of Positive Thinking, Norman Vincent Peale (Fawcett, 1978). Minister Peale's basic primer is still one of the best.

The Success System That Never Fails, W. Clement Stone (Prentice-Hall, 1962). Another classic of ageless wisdom from a self-made millionaire.

Think and Grow Rich, Napoleon Hill (Fawcett Crest, 1960). First published in 1937, Hill promises to reveal the "magic formula" that made Andrew Carnegie his millions. He doesn't quite do that—you have to read between the lines to find it—but he does give a good rundown of prosperity-consciousness thinking.

The Dynamic Laws of Prosperity, Catherine Ponder (Prentice-Hall, 1962). The basic book by the Unity Church minister who is one of the most respected and popular prosperity-consciousness authors.

Newsletters:

Good Money (28 Main St., Montpelier, VT 05602, $36/year). A bi-monthly newsletter with information on socially conscious investing. Subscriptions are offered on a trial basis (cancel if not satisfied) and come with two companion newsletters, *Catalyst* and *Netbacking.*

Insight (Published by the Franklin Research and Development Co., 222 Lewis Wharf, Boston, MA 02110, $36/year). A quarterly newsletter with monthly updates on socially conscious investing. An introductory copy is available free.

The Resource Group, U.S. Curator, P.O. Box 38, Monterey, MA 01245. A foundation that's concerned with second order change (that affect the way we think about particular problems) and that have global implications.

The Threshold Foundation, c/o Tides Foundation, 873 A Sutter St., San Francisco, CA 94109. Funds projects focused on transformational approaches to peace, the environment, personal growth, social justice, and arts and media.

8

Play

In *Golf in the Kingdom,* Mike Murphy writes:

> It cannot be argued that golf was the first human game played on another planetary body. Those two shots Alan Shepard hit . . . have brought a certain stature and gleam of the eye to golfers the world over. . . . Golf on the moon!
>
> Had NASA put him up to it for public relations reasons? Maybe they wanted some humor in the enterprise or the backing of certain rich and powerful golfing senators. . . . Or could it simply be that all his golfer's passion to hit the ball a mile now had a chance to express itself, indeed the chance of a lifetime, the chance of history! Indeed, the cry came down from space, ". . . it's sailing for miles and miles and miles," Alan Shepard was giving the mad cry of golfers the world over who want to put a ball in orbit and reassume their god-like power.

Apparently, the impulse to play can burst forth anywhere, even on the moon. Play is something that unites adults and kids, opposite sexes, different races, in fact it binds humans and animals together. It is at this interspecies level that playfulness deepens gracefully into an act of communication. When a dolphin and a human play together, they also "talk."

From the divine play of the universe—which the Hindus call *lila*—to the innocent self-absorbing play of the child and puppy, play is something wonderfully free and aimless, the spark that makes life worth living. As Plato once said, "Life must be lived as play, playing certain games,

"Since everything is but an apparition, perfect in being what it is, having nothing to do with good or bad, acceptance or rejection, one may well burst out in laughter."

LONG CHEN PA

making sacrifices, singing and dancing, and then a man will be able to propitiate the gods."

A sense of humor is one of the most important qualities of the truly spiritual person. A sense of humor is the result of a true sense of proportion; it is the opposite of self-importance. Real sages, for example, have a certain childlike character, and more often than not their eyes are full of laughter.

On the occasion of his 66th birthday, Joshu Sasaki-Roshi, the contemporary Zen master of the Cimmaron Zen Center in Los Angeles, wrote:

> As a butterly lost in flowers
> As a child fondling mother's breast
> As a bird settled on the tree
> For 66 years of this world
> I have played with God

Sasaki-Roshi was once asked why he had come to America. "I have come to teach people to laugh," he said. True to his word, he has advised his students to start the day by standing straight up and laughing out loud, from deep in the belly. This practice, he says, is equal to many hours of zazen.

Rajneesh has given his students similar advice: "Laughter is tremendously healthy," he says. "Playfulness is as sacred as any prayer, or maybe more sacred than any prayer, because playfulness, laughter, singing, dancing will relax you. And the truth is only possible in a relaxed state of being."

And Long Chen Pa, a Tibetan yogi, once said, "Since everything is but an apparition, perfect in being what it is, having nothing to do with good or bad, acceptance or rejection, one may well burst out in laughter."

The Game of Sports

For many Westerners, play most often takes the form of sports and athletics. This type of play, according to George Leonard and Michael Murphy, offers an often overlooked opportunity for spiritual development.

"We may discover that sports and physical education, reformed and refurbished, may provide us the best possible

path to personal enlightenment and social transformation in this age," says George Leonard in *The Ultimate Athlete*. Michael Murphy, the founder of Esalen Institute, agrees. He found that the practice of sports has so much in common with the practice of a spiritual discipline that he once wrote an essay, "Sports as Yoga." More recently Murphy and Rhea White, a librarian and parapsychologist, coauthored *The Psychic Side of Sports*, documenting what the authors call "The Spiritual Underground of Sports." They collected tales of mystical sensations, altered perceptions, and extraordinary feats that parallel ancient legends about yogis, saints and magicians. In fact, the world documented in *The Psychic Side of Sports* is a sports edition of the old classic, *The Varieties of Religious Experience*. In a chapter on Sports and Mysticism, Murphy explores the similarities between these two seemingly disparate realms:

> Games often create an order that resembles the cadenced life of ashrams and monasteries, and sporting expeditions are in certain respects like religious pilgrimages. The acts

"At the height of laughter the universe is flung into a kaleidoscope of new possibilities. High comedy, and the laughter that ensues, is an evolutionary event. Together they evoke a biological response that drives the organism to higher levels of organization and integration. Laughter is the loaded latency given us by nature as part of our native equipment to break up the stalemates of our lives and urge us on to deeper and more complex forms of knowing."

JEAN HOUSTON

they comprise are invested with special meaning and are pointed toward perfection. Athletes feel the effect of a playing field in their bones. Fenway Park or an Olympic stadium or a famous golf course like St. Andrews can bring a quickening of the spirit, a concentration of energies, a connection with heroes past and future that give performances in these places a heightened quality. . . .

Like yoga, sport invites and reinforces an ever-deepening attention to the task at hand. The thousands of miles a distance runner covers, all the shots a golfer makes in practice, the hours each day a gymnast spends perfecting each maneuver lead to moments that resemble religious ecstasy.

Murphy and White have identified at least eleven categories of "transcendent feelings commonly described by artists, mystics, and lovers—and also by athletes." These eleven categories include: Acute Well-Being, Peace, Detachment, Freedom, Ecstasy, Power, Control, Being in the Present, Instinctive Action and Surrender, Mystery and Awe, Feelings of Immortality, and Unity. They also report on many instances of Altered Perceptions, such as extrasensory perception, out-of-the-body experiences, and pre-cognition. Examples of these range from auto racing and boxing to mountain climbing and aikido.

Synchronicity: Playing with Time and Space

Many games with a spiritual or mystical significance seem to work according to the principle of *synchronicity*. Synchronicity is psychiatrist C. G. Jung's term for the relationship between two seemingly unrelated events. "Synchronicity," says Jung, "takes the coincidence of events in space and time as meaning something more than mere chance." This "something more," says Jung, is "a peculiar interdependence of objective events among themselves as well as with the subjective (psychic) states of the observer or observers." Synchronicity, we might say, is a kind of coincidence of cosmic proportions.

Astrology, for example, is based on the correspondence between the positions of the planets and a person's inherent propensities, opportunities, and challenges. The Tarot cards, which are believed to derive from an ancient Egyptian system, reflect a person's state of mind through the prism of visual archetypes, and the celebrated *I Ching*, or Book of Changes, yields Taoist and Confucian wisdom derived from a chance toss of coins or, more traditionally, yarrow stalks.

Each toss or shuffle of these games calls forth our own lives, and makes us visible to ourselves. Games such as the Tarot or *I Ching* are not meant to tell the future—though they may indicate a general direction or course—but to reveal the present. "If a handful of matches is thrown to the floor," writes Carl Jung, "they form the pattern characteristic of that moment."

One word of advice from Carl Jung on the use of the *I Ching:* Do not ask more than once. It is true, as Jung says in his introduction to the Wilhelm/Baynes edition of the *I Ching* (published by the Bollingen Foundation), that "any number of answers to my question were possible, and I certainly cannot assert that another answer would not have been equally significant." However, as Jung continues, "the answer received was the first and only one; we know nothing of other possible answers. It pleased and satisfied me. To ask the same question a second time would have been tactless, and so I did not do it: 'the master speaks but once.'"

Playing the Inner Game

Whether you are a seasoned athlete or a casual player, the key to turning sports into yoga is to play what Tim Gallwey calls "the inner game." By playing the inner game, all of our play becomes a lesson in learning and awareness itself.

"Every game we play is composed of two parts, an outer game and an inner game," says Gallwey in *The Inner Game of Tennis*. "We've been taught to play the outer game—trying to beat our opponent or to reach a new goal." But it is the inner game—the game that, according to Gallwey, takes place in the mind of the player—that allows for the most fascinating learning. The inner game, says Gallwey, "is played against such obstacles as lapses in concentration, nervousness, self-doubt, and self-condemnation."

While working as a tennis pro, Gallwey observed that there are two selves within each of us that are engaged in play. One is the director and the other the doer. The director is the one that says, "do it this way, shoot a good ball this time, over to the left." The doer accomplishes the directive as best it can. Gallwey believes that it's the relationship between the two selves within the player that is "the prime factor in determining one's ability to translate his knowledge of technique into effective action."

There are several keys to getting the two selves together in sports. First of all, Gallwey found that we learn best by observation and by learning to trust ourselves. He found that if he visually demonstrated a swing to a student several times, for example, with very little verbal instruction, the student would often copy the swing perfectly. And learning to "trust thyself" results in a relaxed attitude that will produce better playing.

Learning to see "nonjudgmentally," that is, to see *what* is happening rather than how well or how badly you think it is happening is another important inner game skill. This practice corrects the problem of "trying too hard." Gallwey points out that there is no absolutely good or bad event in a tennis game. If the server serves out of bounds, for example, the server considers that bad, but the opponent considers the same ball good, while the referee just considers it "out of bounds." Our labeling things as "good" and "bad" gets in the way of clear observation and learning says Gallwey. It is by seeing things as they are that we can learn to change them.

The final key to the inner game is concentration. This is the master skill, says Gallwey: "Concentration is not staring hard at something. It is not *trying* to concentrate. It is not thinking hard about something. Concentration is fascination of mind . . . it is effortless and relaxed, not tense and purposeful."

He offers several simple techniques for tricking yourself into entering a state of relaxed concentration. A typical
exercise is the following: while playing tennis, listen to the
sound of the ball as it first makes contact with your racket,
and then the court, and then your opponent's racket. Each
time the ball bounces, say to yourself "bounce" and each
time it hits a racket say "hit." Almost as soon as you start
saying "bounce, hit, bounce, hit," you can see your tennis
game improve as your mind, which is normally preoccupied with chatter and anxiety quickly settles into a state
of relaxed attention.

New Games

For many of us a competitive instinct encouraged by
our culture not only can get in the way of achieving pro-
ficiency, but can turn the experience of playing into an
isolating and stressful one. One of the best ways to learn
a different way of playing is to play games where personal
victory is not the object. In 1973, a different and unusual
approach to play was inaugurated by the *Whole Earth
Catalogue*'s Stewart Brand and friends. "Why not apply

the notion of cooperation and creativity directly to game-playing?" they wondered. New Games are a never-ending series of improvised games with three basic rules, as expressed in the New Games Association's motto: "Play hard, play fair, nobody hurt."

The organization that grew out of the first New Games Tournament provides training for physical education teachers, community recreation administrators, or interested families, and it has published two books full of games and ideas on how to create your own games as you go along. Whereas some games are totally new, others are a new twist on an old game. Take infinity volleyball, for example. Here's the rules: "The object of this game of cooperation is to keep the ball on the volley indefinitely. In general, the normal rules of volleyball apply, except that no specified number of players is required. As in regular volleyball, one team may hit the ball no more than three times before sending it over the net. Players of both teams chant aloud the number of times the ball has been volleyed. Both teams share the final score. For average players, any score over fifty is very good; a one hundred or more is phenomenal."

It may sound sappy and even boring, but it's surprising how much fun playing this way can be and how much in the case of a game like volleyball your game actually improves while doing it.

The games can be played in small groups or large. One tournament in Boston, for example, partially funded by the city recreation department, attracted well over 2000 people of all ages and races. There was not one scratch or unhappy incident reported all afternoon. The final game of the day, in which everyone made one long line and walked across the park slowly picking up every tiny bit of trash, left the park sparkling clean.

The Value of Competition

This is not to suggest that competition is in and of itself bad, any more than money is. As with money, your attitude toward the subject and the nature of your goals determine whether competition is a productive or destruc-

"Disciplined running is a kind of meditation in itself, without the addition of any specific mental exercise. But by paying attention to the mental side of it you can deepen and enlarge the experience. Here are some meditation exercises.

"Sit in a place near your running course, eyes shut (or open just enough to focus softly on the ground in front of you), and simply count your breaths. Don't force your breathing, just let it happen, and when you have counted ten exhalations start again and count to ten once more. Do this for fifteen or twenty minutes. If your mind wanders and you miss a breath, start again. Don't be discouraged if your mind wanders; simply stay with the exercise and see what develops.

"Now start walking, holding the same kind of focused awareness. Focus on the feeling at the soles of your feet, or upon the ground directly in front of you. After a minute or two begin to run at a shuffle or fresh swing, keeping your attention on your feet or the ground. If thoughts intrude, return to the first place of focus.

"You can experiment with other ways to place your awareness, for example on the feel of your gait or tempo, or on a point of tension in your body, or upon the stream of consciousness itself. The main thing is to take the spirit of meditation directly into your running."

MIKE SPINO

"To win one hundred victories in one hundred battles is not the acme of skill. To subdue the enemy without fighting is the acme of skill."

SUN TZU

tive force. Tim Gallwey discovered this for himself after rejecting competition as harmful and unnecessary while developing his inner game technique.

"When I was in the process of writing *The Inner Game of Tennis,*" Tim Gallwey said in a magazine interview, "I began to see that there really was some sort of value in competition."

I really respected the people who made comebacks, who were down five-love or forty-love and then somehow got it together in the middle of the game and went on to overcome all that. I could see the determination to win, which was only motivated because of the competitive situation, and the power of that determination, and it really impressed me. So, just going on that, I wondered: Is there some motivation to win at tennis besides the ego's motivation to win? I began asking myself that question, and then after a conversation I had with my father, I really had to change my mind.

I was arguing that the benefit of sports didn't derive from the competitive aspects of it. I used surfing as an example. That's when Dad brought up the point that the surfer was competing against the wave. I almost argued

against that, saying that, no, he was really just trying to be one and in harmony with the wave and get high on it, when I realized that he *did* wait for the largest wave to come by. That meant he appreciated the obstacles, appreciated the difficulties. And that was the primary value of competition—the opportunity to overcome obstacles, something that elicited a person's highest response.

So I began seeing that the goal is not to eliminate competition, but to eliminate the ego—the thing that makes it difficult for you to perform well in the face of a challenge.

This is the sense in which Zen archers (and in fact all martial arts masters) understand competition. In that small masterpiece *Zen and the Art of Archery*, German philosophy professor, Eugene Herrigal, writes:

> Should one ask, from this standpoint, how the Japanese Masters understand this contest of the archer with himself, and how they describe it, their answer would sound enigmatic in the extreme. For them the contest consists in the archer aiming at himself—and yet not himself, and thus becoming simultaneously the aimer and the aim, the hitter and the hit. Or, to use some expressions which are nearest the heart of the Masters, it is necessary for the archer to become, in spite of himself, an unmoved center. Then comes the supreme and ultimate miracle: art becomes "artless," shooting becomes not-shooting, a shooting without bow and arrow; the teacher becomes a pupil again, the Master a beginner, the end a beginning, and the beginning perfection.

The Master of Go

Sports and athletics are not the only games that can teach us the lessons of life in microcosm. Board games and card games can do the same. Indeed, every game can be seen as an analogy for life itself; each one provides a rich body of folk-wisdom about the rules of life, as demonstrated through the rules of the game. Poker players, bingo players, cribbage players, bridge players, chess players, Go players, Mah Jongg players—each see the world through the peculiar prism of their favorite game.

One game little known to Westerners that stands out in particular as a tool for learning about oneself is the ancient Chinese game of Go. Skip Ascheim, a writer, teacher, and president of the Massachusetts Go Association, had this to say about it:

Go is a game of pure strategy, basically a competition for territory. Two players alternately place black and white pieces (called 'stones') on the intersections of a 19 × 19-line grid. Eventually the stones of each color form continuous boundaries that surround and control empty areas. When the board has been completely divided up, the player with the larger total area is the winner. Combining these simple elements according to a few easy rules has produced the most complex and profound board game ever invented by humans. It is thought to have arisen 4000 years ago in China or the Himalayan region of central Asia.

It is possible to be content with Go as a fascinating intellectual recreation, yet most players who get reasonably good at it notice that it affects their way of thinking, and that situations on the board appear to mirror or model situations in life and personality characteristics. Two aspects of the game intersect to create this dimension: its inner structure and its social organization.

The system of Go is rooted in the idea of (yin/yang) balance, the principle of harmonizing opposing forces. Neither excessive aggression nor extreme timidity is rewarded, and intuition is as important as analysis. The need for a balanced approach is, in effect, a 'law' of the game: it cannot be overcome by clever play.

Go also encourages a balanced emotional posture: patience (alert, not lazy) and a dispassionate attitude toward winning and losing. Amateur players are linked worldwide by a common ranking system, the purpose of which is to facilitate the handicapping of games between unequal players. The range of skill is so great (some 40 ranks separate raw beginners from the best professionals) that, without handicapping, the stronger player would win virtually every game, and both would quickly become bored. However, by reference to the players' relative standing in the ranks, every game can be handicapped so that each player has an equal chance to win.

The ranking system itself is self-perpetuating and self-policing: your correct rank is the level at which you can win roughly half your games. When you start to win disproportionately you know you've improved, so you promote yourself. Thus your progress is graphically measured, and you are forced to come to terms with any residual need to win every time, or a need to slaughter your opponent. The effect of all this is that you begin to compete less with your opponent and more with your own current level of skill.

This redirection of the competitive impulse opens up more cooperative, ultimately more satisfying, levels of play while preserving the excitement and unpredictability of a game. Go then functions more as a dance, or negotiation, between alternative versions of reality (guesses about the nature of the system). The winning side has more nearly harmonized the active and passive elements of play.

The Game of Life

Whether or not we play a formal game, from a cosmic point of view, we might say that we are all players in the game of life. The playing field is the earth, the game lasts as long as our life (or longer, if we think in terms of more than one life), and the aim is enlightenment, awareness, love or realization, or whatever we conceive as our highest and ultimate goal. This metagame is referred to in many esoteric traditions. It is the largest game we can imagine, the most serious, the most real (so real we tend to forget, in the heat and excitement of the play, that we are playing), and also, if we play with the right spirit, the most enjoyable and satisfying game of all.

Best Books on Tarot and Symbols

Contributed by Angeles Arrien

Jung and Tarot, Sallie Nichols, (Samuel Weiser, N.Y., 1982)
Dictionary of Tarot, William Butler
Choice Centered Tarot, Gail Fairfield (Iowa City Women's Press, Iowa City, 1981)
The Tarot, Paul Foster Case (MaCoy Publishing Co., 1947)

Astrology Classics for Beginners

Contributed by Hank Stine

Astrology for the Millions, Grant Lewi (Lewellyn, 1978). Simplicity and depth. Contains charts and tables that allow the beginner to cast a fairly accurate chart without using math or any other books.
Principles and Practice of Astrology, Noel Tyl (Lewellyn, 1979). A definitive twelve-volume series that makes drawing mathematically accurate charts and advanced interpretation like child's play. Tells everything you could conceivably want to know.
Astrology, Ronald Davidson (Arco, 1967). A handy one-volume paperpack for those wishing an inexpensive introduction.

Merely Playing

The late Alan Watts, the philosopher who did as much as anybody to communicate and popularize hitherto "inscrutable" Oriental ideas such as Zen and Tao in the West, wrote in *The Book On The Taboo Against Knowing Who You Are:*

The idea of "play" has two distinct meanings which are often confused. On the one hand, to do something *only* or *merely* in play, is to be trivial and insincere, and here we should use the word "toying" instead of "playing."

On the other hand, there is a form of playing which is not trivial at all, as when Segovia plays the guitar or Sir Laurence Olivier plays the part of Hamlet, or, obviously, when someone plays the organ in church. In this sense of the word Saint Gregory Nazianzen could say of the Logos, the creative wisdom of God:

For the Logos on high plays,
stirring the whole cosmos back and forth, as he wills,
into shapes of every kind.

And, at the other end of the earth, the Japanese Zen master Hakuin:

In singing and dancing is the voice of the Law. . . .

You have seen that the universe is at root a magical illusion and a fabulous game, and that there is no separate 'you' to get something out of it, as if life were a bank to be robbed. The only real "you" is the one that comes and goes, manifests and withdraws itself eternally in and as every conscious being. For "you" is the universe looking at itself from billions of points of view, points that come and go so that the vision is forever new . . . Yet just as there is no time but the present, and no one except the all-and-everything, there is never anything to be gained—though the zest of the game is to pretend that there is.

Resources

Organizations:

American Go Association, P.O. Box 397, Old Chelsea Station, New York, NY 10113. Membership in the Go Association ($25/year) gives you a subscription to a quarterly journal and a zip coded list of members and Go clubs.

Inner Game Corporation, Attn: Joann Kailikea, 127 Berrington Place, Los Angeles, CA 90049. Provides workshops and clinics in tennis and golf using sports as a metaphor for learning about business, relationships and life.

The New Games Foundation, P.O. Box 7901, San Francisco, CA 94120, (415) 526-7774. Provides educational materials, books, and trainings on playing and leading New Games.

9

Tuning the Body

There is an Indian or Tibetan story about an old, blind turtle who lives in the depths of the ocean. Once every thousand years, the turtle swims to the top of the sea, and sticks its head up through the waves, surfacing for air.

Now imagine that there is a wooden ring floating somewhere on the surface of the ocean, and think of how rare it would be for the blind turtle, coming up for air once every thousand years, to put its head through the wooden ring. It is just that rare, say the Tibetans, for a being to gain human birth.

Obviously, an occasion as rare as this is to be highly prized. To the Tibetans, to be born with a "precious human body" (as they call it) is to be born with the perfect vehicle for obtaining realization or enlightenment. Other spiritual traditions make the same or similar points in their own way. The human body is considered a temple, the reflection or embodiment of the cosmos, the form of divinity.

Unfortunately, this ancient view of the body has, for the most part, not been in the mainstream of spiritual life in the West. As Sri Aurobindo, the modern Indian sage and philosopher, says, "In the past the body has been regarded by spiritual seekers rather as an obstacle, as something to be overcome and discarded than as an instrument of spiritual perfection and a field of spiritual change. It has been condemned as a grossness of Matter, as an insuperable impediment and the limitations of the body as something unchangeable, making transformation impossible."

"To keep the body in good health is a duty . . . otherwise we shall not be able to keep our mind strong and clear."

BUDDHA

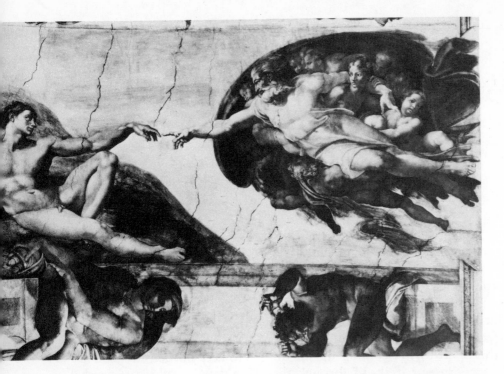

Christianity, especially as institutionalized by St. Paul, added a definite moral twist to these ideas. The body was seen as the cause of sin and corruption. The only answer was asceticism, to deny, subjugate, and master the body.

In the last decade, however, the body has once again become more recognized as a vehicle for spiritual growth. And for good reason.

The body holds the potential of being one of our greatest teachers. Both the Eastern and the Western traditions have taught that the microcosm of the human body is a mirror and reflection of the macrocosm, the entire created universe. "I am a little world," wrote the Renaissance poet John Donne. Manly P. Hall, in *The Secret Teachings of All Ages,* his encyclopedic compendium of Western esotericism, writes that "The oldest, the most profound, the most universal of all symbols is the human body. . . . The Mysteries of every nation taught that the laws, elements, and powers of the universe were epitomized in the human constitution; that everything which existed outside of man had its analogue within man."

According to the ancient Indian yogic tradition, the spine is analagous to Mt. Meru, the mythical center of the world. There are seven chakras (from the Sanskrit for "wheel") that are focal points of energy along this central axis. In some systems of meditation, concentration on certain chakras is used to awaken or develop a particular kind of energy. For example, concentration on the heart chakra awakens compassion.

On a symbolic level, the chakras provide a rich and evocative system, a reminder that when we see our body as only so much flesh and bone, we miss an essential dimension of ourselves.

The Alexander Method

F. M. Alexander was an actor and elocutionist. In the 1880s he suddenly and unaccountably lost his voice. After finding that none of the doctors or specialists he consulted could help him, Alexander began looking for a cure himself. He spent hours every day in front of a mirror, until he noticed that every time he tried to speak, he unconsciously pulled his head down and back. By paying close attention to the way his posture affected his behavior, Alexander restored his voice.

The Alexander method that grew out of this experience was one of the first techniques to explore the connection between body and mind. The Alexander teacher works, in part, by gently correcting the way you carry yourself, with particular attention to the relationship between head and neck, until you get the feel of a more natural posture. The Alexander exercises focus on how you go about the simplest of everyday activities—how you stand, walk from one room to another, how you sit down in a chair.

Many of our problems, according to Alexander, are the result of our being "inveterate end-gainers." That is, we care only about the end of an action, and totally ignore how we get there. Alexander's method, then, apart from its considerable therapeutic value, teaches about the importance of attention to the moment. This aspect drew the early enthusiastic support of Aldous Huxley, who wrote of the method: "We are so anxious to achieve some particular end that we never pay attention to the psycho-physical means whereby that end is to be gained. So far as we are concerned, any old means is good enough. But the nature of the universe is such that ends can never justify the means. On the contrary, the means always determine the end."

Learning from the Body

The best way to begin to learn from our bodies is to enter into the practice of one of the many mind/body disciplines that are proliferating today.

As Jean Houston tells us: "We have a veritable potpourri of possibilities—tai chi, aikido, kundalini yoga, methods of ancient Tibetan energy harvesting, acupuncture as orthodoxy, shamanic exercise, Sufi dancing, polarity balancing, rebirthing, biofeedback, the varieties of Reichian experience. It is as if every discipline of healing, health, and becoming whole that ever was has suddenly been called back into practice all over the earth in order that we might have the richest possible inventory of psychophysical opportunities with which to reinvent ourselves. The planetary memory banks of body-mind transformation are available in ways that they could never be before."

Many of these techniques for transforming and perfecting the body were raised to a fine art in the East long ago. Probably the most widely known of all systems is yoga—with the martial arts running close behind.

Hatha Yoga

Yoga, which derives from the same root as "yolk," essentially means union or communion. Hatha Yoga is one form of yoga (Patanjali gives us sixteen) that makes use of physical postures, gestures, and breath. Hatha Yoga *asanas* (postures) stretch, massage, and relax the body. Each asana, says Ram Dass, "embodies a specific attitude and relationship to the universe. It's as if you're changing the receiving channel of your body by changing position. . . . Hatha Yoga postures open the energies of the body; each position becomes a meditative posture that allows you to tune in to a different space."

Hatha Yoga is actually a precise method for fine-tuning body and mind, and it is best approached as a spiritual discipline rather than calisthenics. Jon Kabot-Zinn, director of the stress reduction program at the University of Massachusetts Medical Center and a Yoga teacher, suggests approaching Yoga with the long term in mind, noticing the changes as they slowly occur over a lifetime.

Yoga means extending your limits, getting to know your body inside and out. "Don't push it," advises Kabot-Zinn, "just notice how your body feels in each asana, notice what happens if you slowly stretch just a little further. Notice the limits give way a little bit." And one day, says Kabot-Zinn, "you will come to a certain moment when you can suddenly do something that you could never do before."

Martial Arts

Many people come to the martial arts for exercise and sport, or as a means of self-defense, but in the deepest sense these disciplines are actually a kind of moving meditation.

The martial arts are thought to have originally been developed in ancient China, where wandering Buddhist and Taoist monks needed to defend themselves against bandits. The skills and techniques the monks developed were refined and developed by the samurai warriors of Japan, who reinterpreted the practice of martial arts in the light of Zen Buddhist philosophy. The samurai combined discipline, commitment, and skill into a whole life-style known as "the way of the warrior," living on the sword's edge of life and death.

The foundation of all the martial arts is a series of basic exercises known as a *kata* or form. These movements, practiced again and again, train the body to react spontaneously and immediately. The true contest, as many mar-

"Here in this body are the sacred rivers: here are the sun and moon, as well as all the pilgrimage places. I have not encountered another temple as blissful as my own body."

SARAHA

tial artists teach, is really with oneself rather than with any opponent. Pursued to the end, the physical technique becomes a path to the highest spiritual realization, in which body and mind are one.

Tai Chi and Aikido are two of the most valuable and spiritual of the martial arts. Both place a great deal of emphasis on the development of the vital energy—called *chi* in Chinese and *ki* in Japanese—as a source of strength and power.

Tai Chi Kuan is possibly the oldest of the martial arts. It is based on Taoism and many of its movements are inspired by the way animals move and fight. The practice of these movements is considered a very effective way of exercise and meditation. Millions of Chinese workers practice the Tai Chi form in groups every morning before work.

Tai Chi is based on allowing the *chi,* or vital force, to sink to the tan tien—the hara, or spot just below the navel—and then move throughout the body. The idea, writes the late Professor Cheng Man-ch'ing, is to "concentrate your chi and bring about the pliability like that of an infant's." The key is complete relaxation: "Throw every bone and muscle of the entire body wide open without hindrance or obstruction anywhere."

Aikido

Aikido is the most recently developed of the martial arts and some would say the most spiritual. Its founder, Ueshiba Morihei, was considered to be one of the world's greatest living martial artists. Though he was a very small man, those twice his size were unable to attack him without quickly finding themselves on the ground.

When he was a young man, he mastered nearly all the martial arts. He felt, though, that there was something beyond what he had learned, and went off to the mountains to sit with a Zen master. There he attained a deep realization, discovering that "True budo [the way of the warrior] is love. It involves giving life to all that exists and not killing or opposing one another."

Aikido, which the master developed as a synthesis of all the martial arts as seen from a perspective of love, means the way of harmony. It is a dynamic kind of meditation, one that always involves another person. It is thus about relationship and the peaceful resolution of conflict. "The secret of Aikido," writes Ueshiba Morihei, "is to harmonize ourselves with the movement of the universe and to bring ourselves into accord with the universe itself." "The genius of aikido," writes George Leonard, a black belt, "is to transform the most violent attack, by embracing it, into a dance."

One of the first moves itself embodies the principles of Aikido. This is a half-turn in which the defender, grasped at the wrist, turns in the same direction as the attacker—so that the defender is looking at the world through the attacker's eyes. By first blending with the attacker's energy and then leading that energy down to the mat, the defender can easily make the throw.

An Aikido Exercise

The development of *ki* is essential to Aikido. To see how the energy of ki is superior to muscle strength, hold out your arm and tighten the muscles as hard as you can. Ask a friend to bend your arm using all of his strength. Chances are he will be able to do so easily. Now, extend your arm in a relaxed way, and visualize your ki pouring through it and extending through the fingertips. Chances are your friend won't be able to budge it (especially if you center yourself first).

Massage and Bodywork

Bodywork and massage, essentials for tuning the body, are often viewed as mechanical healing techniques that are done *to* us. But in actuality, most approaches to bodywork are learning tech-

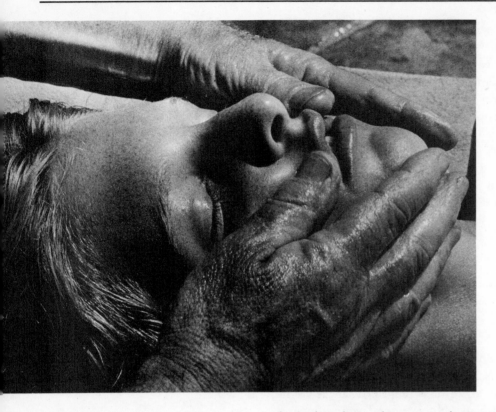

niques that give us the opportunity to attain greater awareness and mental freedom using the body as the point of access. For some, working with a particular form of bodywork on a long-term basis can even become a spiritual path in itself in the same way that martial arts is for others. Two of the most well-known forms of bodywork, Feldenkrais work and Rolfing, exemplify two very different approaches.

Moshe Feldenkrais, an Israeli physicist who holds a black belt in judo, began investigating the connections between mind and body after he had a debilitating knee injury. Using the wisdom he had learned through physics and judo, he literally taught himself to walk again. Feldenkrais discovered, quite simply, that our minds and bodies have far more flexibility and potential than we ever put to use. We are limited, he says, by the way we learn to move as small children. Once we learn a move that works, we repeat it the same way our entire lives with very little variation. These limitations, while reflected in our bodies, influence all other aspects of our being: how we think, feel, and live.

Although Feldenkrais work deals directly with the body and in many cases "undoes" conditions that have been deemed unhealable, Feldenkrais views his work as an approach to learning rather than healing. The Feldenkrais exercises are gentle and subtle. Feldenkrais has designed thousands of these movements—exercises, says Ken Dychtwald, that "are so unusual in their form and practice that they force people to explore and integrate aspects of themselves that have probably been out of awareness for years."

Feldenkrais himself says his exercises are designed "to clear, to purify, take away the dust, the rot, the rust that was introduced in improper education." We "patterned" and "wired" our learning once, he says, and we can do it again. By working directly and consciously with your nervous system—how you send it messages, how those messages move muscles—you can re-educate yourself and create new pathways for "the genius within."

Feldenkrais work has two basic forms. Table work is done by a practitioner who works on you, moving your body for you. Floor work is exercise that you do yourself without the physical aid of a practitioner.

Rolfing, or structural integration, which looks like a form of deep massage, also works to free up the relationship between body and mind, teaching us a new way of being in the world. According to Ida Rolf, a one-time biochemist and yoga student, our bodies tend to be pulled out of proper alignment by the psychological and physical pain we suppress and store in them as well as by the inexorable pull of gravity. Rolfing seeks to liberate us from this condition by realigning the body through deep massage and manipulation of the muscles and the fascia, the tissues holding the muscles to the bones.

To have your body rolfed usually takes ten sessions. Along the way it is common for "rolfees" to re-experience the memories and emotions that are locked within their bodies. Because of the intensity of the pain—"resistance," according to Rolfing theory—that many people experience, this form of body work is not for everyone. It is, in general, for those people who are ready to work on what Ken

"When the lowest vertebrae are plumb erect,
The spirit reaches to the top of the head.
With the top of the head as if suspended from above;
The whole body feels itself light and nimble."

THE CLASSICS OF TAI-CHI-CH'UAN

Dychtwald calls "the edges," that place where our pain defines "the boundaries that exist between what we have created for ourselves as possible and what we have created as impossible."

Massage, which would appear to be the most mechanical type of body work can also be approached in a way that both tunes the body through relaxation and at the same time enhances self-awareness. Massage releases blocked energy in the body, allowing the chi, or life force, to flow more freely. When our bodies open, energy of the universe can move through us.

Deep massage is the most useful for working directly on our habitual body blocks and tensions. As Wilhelm Reich and others have discovered, unexpressed or suppressed emotions such as fear, anger, or grief can freeze our bodies. Since body and mind each reinforce and influence the other, this "body armor" (to use Reich's term) tends to further inhibit and block feelings.

Purification

While doing a physical practice is an obvious key to tuning the body, a less obvious, but equally important approach is "not doing"—practicing the various forms of purification and simplification that have been used by most spiritual traditions. Purification becomes all the more important in our modern world, where we are faced with so much clutter and complexity that we can find ourselves spending all of our time simply responding to external stimuli.

Traditional techniques of purification range from the practice of austerities to eating a balanced diet. Some forms of purification today might include eating simply, rising a half-hour early for meditation or yoga, or abstaining from watching TV for two hours each night.

Eating

Most would accept that what we eat affects how we feel. But beyond this point, it is difficult to say anything about food on which everyone would agree. There are few subjects that inspire more fanaticism than diet. Perhaps this is because, as B. K. S. Iyengar writes in *Light on Yoga,* "Men are the only creatures that eat when not hungry and generally live to eat rather than eat to live." There are people who swear by a diet of almost pure protein, carbohydrates, vegetables, rice, fruit, wheat grass or seaweed, or honey. There are even people who make the questionable

"All Bibles or sacred codes have been the causes of the following errors:

"1. That Man has two real existing principles Viz: a Body and a Soul.

"2. That Energy, call'd Evil, is alone from the Body, and that Reason, call'd Good, is alone from the Soul.

"3. That God will torment Man in Eternity for following his Energies.

"But the following Contraries to these are True:

"1. Man has no Body distinct from his Soul for that call'd Body is a portion of Soul discern'd by the five Senses, the chief inlets of Soul in this age.

"2. Energy is the only life and is from the Body and Reason is the bound or outward circumference of Energy.

"3. Energy is Eternal Delight."

WILLIAM BLAKE

claim of being able to live on air and sunlight alone. (They are called "Breatharians.")

In general, most people who become interested in the spiritual path tend towards a diet that is lighter, more natural, and less reliant on heavy red meat than the traditional American diet. "The yogi believes in harmony," says Iyengar, "so he eats for the sake of sustenance only. He does not eat too much or too little. He looks upon his body as the rest house of his spirit and guards himself against overindulgence."

Many people would say that *how* you eat is as important or more important than *what* you eat.

Nearly every spiritual tradition advises an attitude of gratitude and thankfulness—either to God or to the plant or animal that provided the meal. Zen Buddhism includes an awareness of all the labor that goes into bringing us our food—from the plowing of the soil to the person who sells it to you. When we are mindful of all that goes into putting our breakfast on the table every morning, it is natural to acknowledge it with a moment of silence or grace.

Fasting

In addition to its physical benefits, many people find that moderate fasting (for a few days) has the power to purify their mind and spirit. Some say that fasting gives them a light and "high" feeling that is conducive to meditation. (Take care not to get too attached to this aspect; there have been isolated cases of people seriously harming their health by getting too fixated on the "high.")

Fasting is also very useful in showing you what functions, other than nutrition, food has for you. Most people who fast, even for a short time, are astonished by how much of their lives are built around eating, either by themselves (as an outlet for anxiety or boredom) or with others, as a social occasion. Fasting can bring the way you use food into sharp relief. Ultimately, fasting can help you achieve a truly balanced life—one in which food plays its proper part. It is not easy to do, however, and is best done with some kind of guidance either from a dietician or a holistic physician.

Dr. Carol Englander, the *New Age* Health columnist, offers six pointers for beneficial fasting:

1. Ease in and out of a fast. If you're a meat eater stop eating meat for two or three days, and then eat only raw fruits and vegetables for another day or so.

2. During the fast, drink two or three quarts of fluids a day to flush out waste products that accumulate as your body breaks down old tissue.

3. Many experts feel that juice fasting helps to detoxify the body more quickly and gently than water alone.

4. There are no special precautions you need to take while fasting for short periods. Go about your life normally, but don't overdo exercise. Brisk walking is fine; forget your eight-mile run.

5. Ease out of a fast gradually by eating small amounts of fresh and cooked vegetables and fruits, yogurt, then grains and heavier foods. If you eat slowly and chew food well, your digestive system will readjust easily.

6. It's reasonable to fast on your own for up to a week. For longer, it's best to be supervised by a physician or nutritionist or other health practitioner.

Breathing

Breath is the essence of life and of spirituality. In fact, the word *spiritual* itself is derived from *spiritus,* which means breath in Latin. Breathing is the link between our bodies and the world outside us. It is not surprising then that awareness of breathing is the basis of meditation in many traditions, particularly the Buddhist.

In the East, breathing is considered to be our connection with the universal life energy of the cosmos. With smog and pollution in the air all around us, tainting even the most remote regions of the country, it is impossible to purify the air we breathe in any immediate sense. However, we can get the maximum benefit out of breathing by learning to do it in the right way.

How to Breathe

Ken Dychtwald suggests asking yourself questions such as, "Are you a shallow breather? A deep breather? Do you breathe into your chest or into your belly when you inhale?

Is it more pleasurable for you to inhale or to exhale?" It might help to observe your breathing pattern in a mirror, or to watch your breathing while lying down, a position that makes it easier to notice the rise and fall of your diaphragm.

The idea is not to change your breathing, but to become aware of it, to bring this usually unconscious process into consciousness. When you watch, you generally find that your mind becomes calmer, and that your breathing, consequently, slows down.

Breathing Out

Breathing out is connected with letting go. When you become aware of your breathing, you may notice that you tend to hold your breath. In Zen sitting (*zazen*), meditators are taught to breathe out completely by giving a little extra push with their diaphragms on the out-breath. When you try this you will find that the in-breath is automatic. There is nothing to be afraid of. We can afford to let go.

When we breath this way, says Taisen Deshimaru, a Zen master and author of *The Zen Way to the Martial Arts,* "the life energy of the universe that is contained in the air is transformed into human energy."

"It was as he was breathing out," Deshimaru tells us, "that the Buddha achieved enlightenment under the Bodhi tree."

Bathing

Water is the great purifier of life. In addition to its cleansing qualities, water has a deep relaxing and restorative function. In India, orthodox Hindus begin every day by bathing in a river. In Japan, the bath—heated near to scalding—is an integral part of every day, and in the Scandinavian countries the sauna is a common communal ritual. Heat is often used in bathing in order to open the pores of the skin and flush out wastes and toxins. Usually, a hot bath or sweat in a sauna is followed by a cold shower to close up the pores and restore vigor.

Immersion in water can include a state of natural meditation—or at the very least, relaxation. Water returns us to the source of life. Floating in a hot tub, we are held gently and freed from gravity. Let your mind follow your body into relaxation. The Japanese say that the bath is a gift from the gods. At Tassajara Zen Mountain Monastery a bath in the hot springs—originally used for healing by the local Indians—is a required part of the daily schedule, as much a part of practice as anything else. Silence is maintained to encourage a restful attitude, and a stick of incense burns before a small shrine. Some Zen students even claim that a half-hour in the bath equals half a day of meditation!

"Sometimes [when surfing] you reach a point of being so coordinated, so completely balanced, that you feel you can do anything—anything at all. At times like this I find I can run up to the front of the board and stand on the nose when pushing out through a broken wave; I can goof around, put myself in an impossible position and then pull out of it, simply because I feel happy. An extra bit of confidence like that can carry you through, and you can do things that are just about impossible."

MIDGET FARRELLY

Leonard Orr, who invented the technique of rebirthing while lying in a hot bath, says, "Since we spend nine months immersed in warm water in the womb, total immersion in a comfortable bathtub or hot tub is the bridge between the invisible and the visible worlds. Thinking or daydreaming totally immersed in water bridges these two worlds."

Orr also points out that the United States has more bathtubs and available hot water than any other country in the world. Some cities now have spas, similar to those in Japan or Scandinavia, where you can find a sauna, hot tub, and cold shower.

My Daily Tools for Re-connecting

Contributed by Paul Winter.

I'm intrigued with daily rituals. I have some I call "The Seven S's:"

    Sun

        Song

          Sax

            Stretch

              Sprint

                Stough

                  Smile

"Sun" is the outdoors, in any weather. Both Thoreau and Scott Nearing swore by a regimen of four hours a day outside. It works. When I can get these hours, my life comes into balance.

"Song" is any king of singing, chanting, humming. Music is an alternative floppy-disc to put into your computer, to replace the chatter-thoughts which run our lives most of the time. But listening is not enough. You have to *be* the music, so you have to make the sounds yourself.

"Sax" is my horn. If I play for even five minutes in the morning, it is transforming. Something happens when you awaken the respiratory system and get vibrations going through your being. I come away from this with melodies in my head which will revolve in my memory-wheel for hours.

"Stretch" is hatha yoga. I do the postures while listening to a cassette from Swami Satchidananda's ashram ("Yoga: Beginner's II). The guide on the tape is a woman with a wonderful soothing voice, that calms my runaway brain into slowing down and *being* there. I have learned from her that the most important part of hatha is not just the postures themselves, but the relaxing in between.

"Sprint" is running, jogging. I have just learned the difference in the experience of going five miles versus three. I am looking ahead to the kind of exhilarations reported by my ten-mile friends.

"Stough" is a series of breathing exercises taught by an extraordinary teacher, Carl Stough, a breathing therapist in New York with whom I study.

"Smile," when I don't have time to do any of the above, I can still smile, even in the taxi on the way to the airport. I have heard that smiling releases certain endorphins into the system that actually effect a chemical change in your being.

For me, the path toward re-connecting is a physical one. It's a simple process of reversing that downward spiral so often created by our hungry and domineering minds, the scenario for which may go like this: We gobble input, the mind-computer starts whirring and takes over the ship, feelings and instincts disengage, we stop breathing, the body gets tense, circulation slows and what's left is the rigid robot, thinking its way through life, punched into survival mode.

To break out of this, and reverse the spiral, I see the process as this: You do something physical that gets the breathing going, then the nervous system relaxes, circulation increases, the mind eases its grip (as it always does when the heart revives), and you get your life back. And "spirit" is there by definition. We *are* spirit, when we are alive.

Paul Winter is a sax player who specializes in earth music and ecology.

Final Note: On the Transformation of the Body

The vision of the perfected and transformed body is a part of a very ancient tradition. Catholics look towards a Resurrection of the Glorified Body; certain yogis are said to be able to manifest their bodies in different forms at will. The Word is made Flesh; the Rainbow Body dissolves into light.

Sri Aurobindo, whose Ashram in Pondicherry, India, Michael Murphy studied at for a year before starting Esalen Institute, hints at the possibility of bodily transformation throughout his writings. Intrigued by Aurobindo's writings, Murphy began The Transformation Project, an ongoing research effort to collect all sorts of evidence of supernormal physical functioning. So far, Murphy and his colleagues have collected over 8000 articles from scientific journals relating to bodily transformation and consciousness: research on sports, hypnosis, shamanism, healing, drug research, and more.

In an interview in *Yoga Journal,* Murphy sums up his vision. "Historically," he says, "there's always been this blind spot, I would argue, about the truly dynamic role of the body and the future of the illumined form—the future of, let's call it the 'Evolutionary body on Earth.'

"I don't like to say too much about what it might be. But yes, we can say it will be an illumined body, a body with new powers, a body that manifests the glories of the spirit more fully than our body does now. Eventually, I see us stimulating a direct attempt to achieve this transformed body—way down the road. Maybe that's hundreds of years down the road. But I think the culture can wake up."

Recommended Reading

Spiritual Cookbooks

While there is no one diet that is required or necessarily recommended for living a spiritual life, certain ones have become popular among spiritual devotees in America. A number of good cookbooks have come out of new spiritual communities or restaurants that spiritual communities have started. Here are five of our favorites:

Tassajara Cooking, Edward Brown (Shambhala, 1973). A Zen and vegetarian cookbook filled with recipes from the Tassajara Zen Mountain Center, plus good advice about cooking and life. In many ways, the classic in the field.

The Findhorn Family Cookbook, by Kay Lynne Sherman (Findhorn, 1981). Findhorn is as famous for its good food as it is for its gardens. This cookbook shares not only the recipes, but the philosophy that made Findhorn possible.

Laurel's Kitchen, Laurel Robertson and friends (Bantam, 1978). Laurel Robertson discovered natural foods and vegetarianism in her quest for spirituality. Unable to find the kind of comprehensive cookbook/nutrient resource guide she was looking for, she decided to write one with the help of several friends. The result is an excellent introduction to cooking consciously with natural foods.

The Moosewood Cookbook and *The Enchanted Broccoli Forest,* Mollie Katzen (Tenspeed Press, 1982). Probably the best-selling vegetarian cookbooks in America; also our favorites.

Diet for a Small Planet, Francis Moore Lappe (Ballantine, 1982). Political economy, nutrition, cooking. The classic statement on how a meat-centered diet squanders the earth's protein, with recipes for high-protein, meatless meals. Good ideology equals good eating.

On the Body:

Bodymind, Ken Dychtwald (Jove Publications, 1978). A good overview of the theories of bodymind.

On Body Work:

Awareness Through Movement: Health Exercises for Personal Growth, Moshe Feldenkrais (Harper and Row, 1972). A good introduction to Feldenkrais's work with exercises. Moshe Feldenkrais's most readable book.

The Massage Book, George Downing (Random House/Bookworks). A good basic introduction to massage with beautiful illustrations by Anne Kent Rush.

The Resurrection of the Body: the Writings of F. Matthias Alexander, edited by Edward Maisel (Universe Books, 1969). A good introduction to the philosophy of Alexander's work.

Rolfing, Ida Rolf (Dennis-Landman, 1977). A good introduction to the theory and practice of Rolfing written by its founder.

Be a Frog, a Bird or a Tree, Rachel Carr (Doubleday, 1973). An excellent book on yoga for children.

Light on Yoga, B. K. S. Iyengar (Shocken, 1966). The most consistently recommended book on yoga.

Tai Ch'i Ch'uan, Cheng Man-ch'ing (North Atlantic Books, 1981). A very clear step-by-step illustrated guide to the tai ch'i form.

On Martial Arts and Yoga:

Aikido, the Way of Harmony, John Stevens (Shambhala Publications, 1983). A good basic introduction to the practice of aikido.

Resources

Yoga

Compiled by Linda Klein, Managing Editor, *Yoga Journal*
Here are six of the major yoga centers in the United States and Canada. Most of them can put you in touch with teachers and centers in your area.

Ananda
14618 Tyler Foote Road
Nevada City, CA 95959
Founder: Swami Kriyananda

Satchidananda Ashram-Yogaville
Rt. 1, Box 172
Buckingham, VA 23921
Founder: Rev. Sri Swami Satchidananda

Himalayan Institute
RD 1, Box 400
Honesdale, PA 18431
Founder: Swami Rama

Sivananda Yoga Vedanta Center
243 West 24th St.
New York, NY 10011
Founder: Swami Vishnu Devananda

Publications

The best way to find out about and keep up with yoga in America is to subscribe to the *Yoga Journal,* a bimonthly national magazine published by the California Yoga Teachers Association (2054 University Avenue #604, Berkeley, California 94704). They also publish a yearly *National Directory of Yoga Teachers, Centers, and Training Programs* in the July/August issue.

A good way to start and keep up in comfort and privacy of your living room. Tune in to "Lilias, Yoga, and You" (PBS) or Richard Hittleman (also PBS). Check your TV listings for times and channels to see these local yoga and stretching shows.

Magazines and newsletters:

American Health, Fitness of Body and Mind, (P.O. Box 10034, Des Moines, IA 50347, $14.95/year, monthly.) Health news and information, oftentimes with a holistic perspective.

East West Journal, (P.O. Box 970, Farmingdale, NY 11737, $18/year, monthly.) A magazine which reflects the macrobiotic approach to life. Articles on natural food and natural living.

Vegetarian Times, (P.O. Box 570, Oak Park, IL 60303, $24.95/ year, monthly.) Articles about vegetarians and the vegetarian life-style. Recipes and nutritional information.

Healing

10

In *Getting Well Again,* Carl and Stephanie Simonton tell the story of two men who responded in very different ways to the same life-threatening illness: "[One man] stopped working practically the day he received his diagnosis. He had gone home to sit in front of the television set all day. . . . He could not even bring himself to go fishing, which was something he liked to do. He died in a short period of time."

The other man took quite a different attitude: "[He] had had the disease for over a year but had not missed work other than a few hours each time he had a treatment. Early in the development of his disease he had gotten in touch with a lot of things that were causing life to lose meaning for him. He started to spend more time with his family, taking them on business trips with him. I remember his saying one day, 'You know, I had forgotten that I didn't look at the trees. I hadn't been looking at the trees and the grass and the flowers for a long time and now I do that.' It was interesting to watch him. Every week he improved, getting stronger, healthier."

In our culture illness is often viewed as a calamity that strikes from outside of us. If it's serious—"terminal"—life is over. If it's not serious, it's an inconvenience that we must endure with the help of palliative medications. But from another perspective, illness can be seen as a teacher, alerting us to disharmonies in our lives and demanding that we pay attention to finding a new sense of balance. In some cases, the crisis of illness serves as a gateway to

"The greatest force in the human body is the natural drive of the body to heal itself—but that force is not independent of the belief system, which can translate expectations into physiological change. Nothing is more wonderous about the fifteen billion neurons in the human brain than their ability to convert thoughts, hopes, ideas, and attitudes into chemical substances. Everything begins, therefore, with belief. What we believe is the most powerful option of all."

NORMAN COUSINS

spirituality. Faced with our own mortality, we are propelled to take stock of our lives and look for a new sense of meaning and happiness. Sometimes, as in the case of the second man in the story, this awakening seems to enhance the healing process leading to a physical healing.

According to holistic physician Charles Steinberg, our symptoms contain very clear metaphors for what's missing or out of balance in our lives. When we discover the symbolic meaning of the symptoms, the next step in our healing process often becomes apparent. Steinberg gives as an example the case of a very high-strung woman who came to his office because of spasms of tension in her neck. "She was talking a mile a minute," he reports, "and when I encouraged her to slow down, she looked at me and said, 'I always go at *breakneck* speed.'"

In another instance, a man came in to Dr. Steinberg suffering from tendonitis in his foot. "For months and months, he kept trying to work with his running to make the tendonitis better, with no success. It just so happened that during this entire period his wife was having an affair. When he finally 'put his foot down' about the affair, the tendonitis in his foot disappeared. It was that literal." Not surprisingly, the kind of advice we get by paying attention to our symptoms is more like what you'd expect to hear from a spiritual counselor or a therapist. If followed, not only might it enhance the healing of the physical symptom, but the overall quality of our lives as well.

"We are not troubled by things, but by the opinions which we have of things."

EPICTETUS

Since life is a dynamic and ever-changing process, all of us occasionally lose our balance, so illness is in fact an inevitable part of our lives. When we begin to see it as a part of our spiritual path, our experience of it takes on a whole new dimension. As holistic physician Paul Brenner says, "Illness is a friend . . . [for] suffering has the propensity to heighten one's awareness. Illness has the potential to place one in a higher state of consciousness. It may provide the opportunity to exercise options and establish priorities. It's an internal psychiatrist. Use it—you paid for it!"

Religion and Medicine

Throughout human history, spirituality and healing (or religion and medicine) have been inextricably intertwined. It is not a coincidence that many of our greatest spiritual teachers have been well known for their healing abilities. The root meaning of health is *wholeness,* which comes from the same Anglo-Saxon root for whole, hale, and holy. In many religions, wholeness and health were equated with salvation, which according to theologian Paul Tillich also has the same etimology. "The word salvation," he says, "is derived from the Latin word *salvus,* which means heal and whole." In *The Meaning of Health,* Tillich tells us that "Salvation is basically and essentially healing, the re-establishment of a whole that was broken, disrupted, disintegrated."

Throughout history, in traditional cultures worldwide, the powerful and esteemed positions of medicine man, shaman, and priest were often held by the same person. Magic, medicine, and religions were practiced as one discipline, and in fact illnesses of the soul were considered the root cause of bodily illness. In some cultures this approach persists today. As Dr. Andrew Weil, an expert in alternative medicine, reports in *Health and Healing:* "The shaman of tribal peoples in northern Asia and the Americas is the doctor of bodies, souls, and situations. He has learned to be a personal mediator between the everyday world and the 'other world,' leaving his body to commune with spirits and learn the specific causes of illness. . . ." In the West, the Christian church has a long, though somewhat submerged, tradition of healing, but in general, Western cul-

"The soul becomes dyed with the color of its thoughts."

MARCUS AURELIUS

"The Buddhist concept of healing marvelously anticipates the growing realization in the West that most illnesses, however physical their symptoms, are in fact psychosomatic disorders, or arise therefrom."

JOHN BLOFELD

tures over the centuries have tended to treat the body in isolation from the spirit. According to Plato, this was a problem, even in his time: "For this is the great error of our day, in treatment of the human body, that physicians separate the body from the soul," he said. The growing reliance on technological medicine in the twentieth century has resulted in doctors narrowing their view even more to pay attention only to the physical body and the material aspects of illness.

But as John Naisbitt suggests in his book *Megatrends,* high technology usually results in what he calls a "high touch" alternative. In the past few decades a revival of Christian healing has begun to permeate Christian churches of every denomination, both Protestant and Catholic. Hand in hand with this revival, we have seen the development of the holistic health movement, which is providing us with a new, more spiritual understanding of health and healing.

From the holistic perspective, health is seen as the balanced integration of body, mind, and spirit. Rather than merely being the absence of disease, health is viewed as a positive state of creative self-expression, usually accompanied by feelings of joy, vitality, happiness, and love.

Transpersonal Psychology and the Healing Mind

Transpersonal psychology is referred to as the *fourth force* in psychology. First there was Freudian psychoanalysis, with its emphasis on psychopathology and unconscious instincts. The second force was behaviorism, with the human being treated as a mechanism to be manipulated and controlled through external reinforcement. The third force in modern psychology is humanistic psychology, where the major focus is on psychological health and expanding human potential. As Abraham Maslow, one of the founders of humanistic psychology, put it: "To oversimplify the matter somewhat, it is as if Freud supplied us the sick half of psychology and we must now fill it out with the healthy part."

Psychologist Gordon Allport wrote that "by their own theories of human nature, psychologists have the power of elevating or degrading that same nature. Debasing assumptions debase human beings; generous assumptions exalt them." Transpersonal psychology goes beyond humanistic psychology in the generosity of its assumptions about human nature. It is concerned with expanding the field of psychological inquiry to include healing the spirit as well as the mind.

Transpersonal psychotherapies are really a marriage of Eastern and Western approaches to healing and spiritual evolution. All of them are concerned with the realms of human consciousness that go beyond the ego—transcendent or transpersonal experience. The notion that expanded states of consciousness can facilitate healing is certainly not a new one, but the rigorous study and comparison of various psychotherapeutic and spiritual disciplines is providing fertile ground for spiritual development in the context of psychotherapy. Many types of mystical and spiritual experience that were considered pathological or abnormal in traditional psychology are understood in the transpersonal approach to be a part of the evolution of the human spirit.

There are many different schools of thought and techniques included in this burgeoning field. Carl Jung's depth psychology, with its emphasis on dream work, archetypal symbols, and analysis, is an example of a Western approach. Roberto Assagioli's psycho-synthesis is a similar Western model, using imagery, meditation, drawing, and writing to develop intuition and will. Stanislav Grof and others have developed therapies which utilize psychedelic drugs and other techniques to alter states of consciousness to explore the unconscious and the transpersonal realms. Still others use esoteric systems like tarot, astrology, and the *I Ching* as adjuncts to their work. There are many more examples, but the important thing to realize is that transpersonal therapists are available to guide anyone interested in exploring the spiritual aspects of healing the mind. These therapists tend to be open-minded about mystical experiences and religious ecstasy because they have had these experiences themselves.

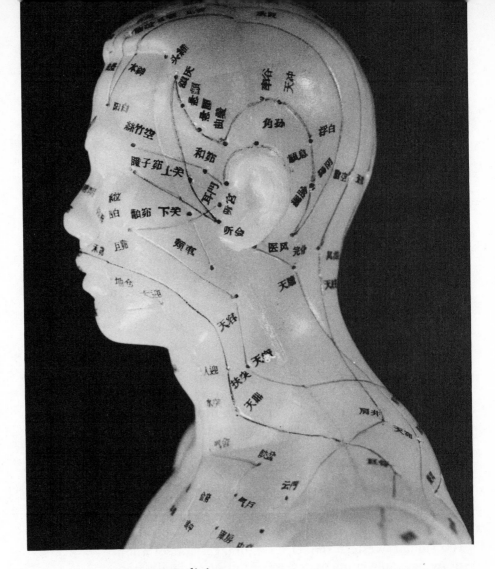

Energy Medicine

All of the healing systems that can be called "holistic" share a common belief in the universe as a unified field of energy that produces all form and substance. As it says in the classic text on Chinese medicine, *The Yellow Emperor*, "Pure energy is the root of the human body." This vital force, which supports and sustains all life, has been given many names. The Chinese call it "chi'i," the Hindus call it "prana," the Hebrews call it "ruach," and the American Indians name it "the Great Spirit." Physicists also postulate that the universe is made up of unified fields of energy, a complex web of relationships between the various parts of a unified whole. Some people call this power-that-connects, love, or divine energy.

According to these theories, we are healthy when this energy is flowing through us in a balanced and unrestricted fashion. When the energy is blocked in some way, be it through poor life-style habits, stress, or negative emotions, then in time these constrictions manifest as physical or mental disease. The energy is blocked by "swimming against the Tao," says Chinese herbalist Stephen Fulder in *The Tao of Medicine*. In the Taoist philosophy underlying Chinese medicine, Fulder says, man is seen as "a temporary assemblage of parts in a continually changing and interacting universe: a wave on the ocean, with a tendency to feel himself superior to the rest of the water. But the essence of health," he says, "is to fall in with the patterns of life. To be in harmony with the Tao."

Most of the alternative approaches to healing in the West are also based on the notion of spiritual or universal energy. Homeopathy, a system of medicine developed by German physician Samuel Hahnemann in the early nineteenth century, is a good example. In spite of its esoteric philosophy, it became a popular medical practice in much of the Western world until the early twentieth century. Homeopathy is based on the Law of Similars—"like cures like"—a minute amount of substance that produces a certain set of symptoms in a healthy person is seen to have the power to cure a sick person with the same symptoms. The homeopathic dosage is so infinitesimal that homeopaths believe the "energy" of the substance, rather than its material, induces healing. In *Health and Healing* Andrew Weil points out the extreme dichotomy between homeopathy and allopathic (scientific) medicine:

> Here is the essence of an unreconcilable philosophical difference between allopathy and homeopathy. Regular doctors give drugs because they value properties attributed to the substance of those drugs. It is the *material* aspect of a drug that counts. Homeopaths use remedies containing no drug materials, yet they believe in the existence and therapeutic power of some other aspect of the drug—of its idea, if you will, or its ghost or spirit. Truly, homeopathy is a spiritual medicine, consistent with its founder's views on the relative importance of spiritual versus material reality.

There are many other healing disciplines—from Zone Therapy to Rudolf Steiner's Anthroposophical Medicine—

Dr. Irving Oyle's Guide to Good Health
1. Eat when you are hungry.
2. Sleep when you are tired.
3. When nature calls, answer.
4. When it's cold, go inside.
5. Don't think of anything else while making love.

"Your health is bound to be affected if, day after day, you say the opposite of what you feel, if you grovel before what you dislike and rejoice at what brings you nothing but misfortune. Our nervous system isn't just a fiction; it's a part of our physical body, and our soul exists in space, and is inside us, like the teeth in our mouth. It can't be forever violated with impunity."

BORIS PASTERNAK

that reflect a spiritual view of life at their core. All of these systems share the fundamental assumption that the highest spiritual aspect of our being becomes manifest in our health.

Spiritual Healing: The Ultimate Form of Energy Medicine

Spiritual healing is the oldest form of healing. The earliest primitives had their witch doctors and shamans who could commune with the spirits to heal physical, emotional, and social ills.

The role of the spiritual healer is to serve as a "channel" for universal energy to unblock the natural flow of the life force in the patient, and to help the person to reconnect with his or her spiritual essence and re-establish balance. Spiritual healing is generally practiced in two forms—contact and non-contact healing. Contact healing, often called the "laying-on-of-hands," is a very old method in which healers place their hands on the head or shoulders of the patient or on the part of the body that is diseased or in pain. They might then pray for healing and mentally picture the healing energy passing through their hands to the one in need. A modern version of contact healing called Therapeutic Touch has been developed and researched by Delores Krieger, R.N., Ph.D., and is now being successfully practiced by thousands of nurses all over the United States.

Non-contact healing, often called absent healing, does not involve any physical contact between the two parties. Many consider this the highest form of healing because it can take place at a distance of thousands of miles, and frequently the one seeking help is unknown to the healer. The healer may receive the name of the person in need in the mail or by phone and simply pray to God for the sick person. Or the healer may project unconditional love or a ray of white light to the one in need. Olga Worrall, the best-known spiritual healer in the United States, offers absent-healing services for thousands of people each year, reportedly with remarkable effectiveness. Dr. Worrall has been the subject of numerous scientific studies, and her ability to influence living organisms and laboratory instruments at great distances is well documented.

"As a man thinketh, so will he be."

BIBLE

"Lord grant me the ability to change what I can change, the ability to accept what I can't, and the wisdom to know the difference."

FROM THE ALCOHOLICS ANONYMOUS PRAYER

In England there are over 5000 healers accredited by the National Federation of Spiritual Healers, and they work side-by-side with doctors in over 1500 hospitals. Here in the United States, the New Thought Churches (Christian Science, Unity, Science of Mind, Religious Science), evangelical and charismatic faith healing, and many other forms such as Psychic Surgery, Reiki Healing, Therapeutic Touch, and Polarity Therapy represent different approaches to spiritual healing.

Seven Tips for Healing Yourself

Contributed by Bernard Siegel, M.D.

1. *Accept your illness:* Being resigned to an illness is destructive, allows the illness to run your life, but accepting allows energy to be freed for other things in your life. Acceptance is like saying, "I'll leave it to God." You know that the illness is there, but you also know that the future will be something you can handle, so it's no longer a burden.

2. *See the illness as a source of growth:* The symbolism I often use here is the salamander. If the salamander loses its tail, it doesn't get emotionally involved, it simply regenerates a new one. I think our primitive nervous system tells us that if you have a loss you grow something to replace what was lost. If you begin to grow psychologically in response to your losses, then you don't need to have a physical illness or growth anymore.

3. *View your illness as a positive redirection in your life:* This means that you don't judge anything that happens to you. If you get fired from a job, for example, you assume that you are being redirected toward something that you're supposed to be doing. Your whole life changes when you say that something is just a redirection. You are then at peace. Everything's okay and you go on your way, knowing that the new direction is the one that is intuitively right for you. After awhile you begin to feel it. And, of course, fewer and fewer misdirections begin to occur in your life because of the person you become.

4. *Understand that death or recurrence is not a failure if steps one, two, or three are accomplished, but a further*

choice or step: If staying alive is your sole goal, you have to be a failure, because you have to die someday. When you begin to accept the inevitability of death and see that you only have a limited time (including the only time you *really* have, which is right now) you begin to realize that you might as well enjoy where you are at the moment to the best of your ability.

5. *Learn self-love and peace of mind and the body responds:* Your body gets what I call "live" messages when you say, "I love myself." And that's not the ego talking, it's just self-esteem. It's as if someone else is loving you, saying you are a worthwhile person, believing in you, and telling you that you're here to give something to the world. When you do that, your immune system says, "This person likes living, let's fight for his or her life."

6. *Don't make physical change your sole goal:* When someone comes to our groups saying, "I've come to get over my sickness," I tell them that's the wrong reason. Come to obtain peace of mind, acceptance and forgiveness. Learn to love. In the process, the disease isn't totally overlooked, but we look at it as one of the problems they are having and perhaps one of the fears. Learn about hope, love, acceptance, forgiveness, and peace of mind, and the disease may go away in the process.

7. *Achieve immortality through love:* The only way you can live forever is to love somebody—then you really leave a gift behind. When you live that way, as I have seen with people with physical illness, you literally have a choice of when you die. You can say, "Thank you, I've used my body to its limit. I have loved as much as I possibly can, and I'm leaving at two o'clock today." And you go. Then maybe you spend half an hour dying and the rest of your life living. When these things are not done, you spend a lot of your life dying and only a little bit of time living.

Dr. Siegel is a surgeon at Yale/New Haven Hospital.

Stress and the Mind

Western medicine has been most clearly influenced by the holistic perspective through the concept of stress. The National Institute of Health now considers that most of the major diseases afflicting the Western world, such as heart disease, stroke, high blood pressure, colitis, ulcers, and headaches, have a stress component. This indicates a growing recognition that our mental and emotional states play some role in the onset of disease. Carl and Stephanie Simonton, who have done seminal work with stress and cancer, believe that stress also plays a role in the onset of cancer. In *Getting Well Again,* they report: "We believe that cancer is often an indication of problems elsewhere in an individual's life, problems aggravated or compounded by a series of stresses six to eighteen months prior to the onset of cancer. The cancer patient has typically responded to these problems and stresses with a deep sense of hopelessness or 'giving up.' This emotional response, we believe, in turn triggers a set of psychological responses that suppress the body's natural defenses and make it susceptible to producing abnormal cells."

The key word here is "response," because according to Hans Selye, the father of stress research, stress in and of itself is neither good nor bad. It is a fact of life. Stress technically means the response of an organism to change. It's the quality of our response to the change that makes it either a positive force (eu-stress, according to Selye) or a negative force (distress) in our lives.

The major influence on the level of "dis-tress" in our lives, according to Dr. Richard Moss, is our self-identity—who we think we are. "A rigid identification with the personal 'me' causes us to overreact to the events in our lives," he says, and can contribute to stress-related illness. Our best path to health, according to Moss, is to enlarge our sense of who we are: "Individuals of expanded consciousness are no longer exclusively concerned with 'me.' They perceive issues differently and thus behave differently."

This quest for an enlarged sense of identity, which is fundamental to many spiritual teachings, is also the purpose of healing, according to the teachings of Christian Science. According to *A Century of Christian Science Healing,* "The purpose of spiritual healing is never simply to produce physical ease. It is rather to put off the limited, physical concept of man which binds thought to matter, and thus bring to light Paul's 'new' man. This is the man

"There are a number of techniques that can bring about healing at various levels and integration of all levels. These healing processes can be divided into three major groups: first are those involving the physical body and its energies—these are usually techniques that are done to a patient by a physician or other therapist. Second are those processes that involve our minds, and emotions and our resulting life-styles and habits—these are things that we consciously do to ourselves. And third are those processes that involve our spiritual selves and our basic attitudes and our values toward life—these are things that we do unconsciously or unwittingly to ourselves.

"A fourth process is our way of life, as a holistic approach to living and being, in which the highest spiritual aspect of our being becomes manifest in our personality and ultimately in our physical body, bringing about integration of all the dimensions of the individual and the state of wholeness."

—HOLISTIC HEALTH REVIEW

Health and Healing
In the World's Religions
Christianity: "The prayer of faith shall heal the sick, and the Lord shall raise him up."
Confucianism: "High mysterious Heaven hath fullest power to heal and bind."

Loving Kindness Meditation
(Theravada Buddhism)

If anyone has hurt me or harmed
me knowingly or unknowingly in
thought, word, or deed, I freely
forgive them.

And I too ask forgiveness if
I have hurt anyone or harmed
anyone knowingly or unknowingly
in thought, word, or deed.

May I be happy
May I be peaceful
May I be free

May my friends be happy
May my friends be peaceful
May my friends be free

May my enemies be happy
May my enemies be peaceful
May my enemies be free

May all beings be happy
May all beings be peaceful
May all beings be free.

whom Christian Scientists understand to be the 'real' man, created by God in His own image, spiritual and whole."

Another basic factor determining the level of distress in our lives is attitudes. Attitudes are the stances we take in life, the perceptual filters through which we give meaning and understanding to all of our experiences. If we believe that we are loving, caring individuals who belong in this world, our reaction to the vicissitudes of life might be quite different than if we feel we are unloved and isolated. Our attitudes are a direct reflection of our basic state of consciousness.

Negative, inflexible, rigid attitudes such as pessimism, depression, or cynicism decrease our ability to cope with the stress of life, and ultimately lead to suffering and disease. Flexibility is the essential quality inherent in all spiritual attitudes, including forgiveness, compassion, empathy, renunciation, humility, faith, and hope. To be flexible is to bend like a branch in the wind. It is the ability to accept reality as it is. Ultimately, flexibility in body, mind, and spirit promotes both health and healing. A healthy mind means a healthy body. It's almost that simple.

Since change is constant, stress is a given in life. The real question then is how one *responds* to stress. As Albert Schweitzer once said, "The greatest discovery of any generation is that human beings can alter their lives by altering their attitudes of mind." This is particularly true for the healing process.

Eight Healing Attitudes

There are a number of attitudes that ancient and modern authorities agree do a great deal toward promoting mental and *physical* health. The most important of these are love and laughter.

Love and Laughter

Jesus said, "Love thy neighbor as thyself." This may well be the single most concise and powerful bit of medical advice any of us could follow. Catherine Ponder, in her book *The Dynamic Laws of Healing,* says: "Love has been described as the 'physician of the universe,' because it has the power to heal all ills, when invoked. We have often thought of love as an emotion," she says. "We have often thought of love as a spiritual quality. It's both; love is also a mind power native to man, existent in every one of us."

Whether it's through chicken soup made with loving hands or a warm hug or kiss, all of us have experienced the soothing and healing effect of love. Immunological research clearly shows that negative feelings close down the immune system, while positive feelings turn it on to its optimum. For example, researchers found the men whose wives recently died of breast cancer had a large decrease in lymphocyte activity for the six months following the death of their spouses—their grief and depression making them more susceptible to illness. On the other hand, students at Harvard who watched a film about Mother Teresa that was filled with positive images of her loving charity were found to have improved immune efficiency directly following the film, increasing their ability to ward off disease.

Eileen Garrett, a well-known healer, puts it this way in *Frontiers of Healing:*

> The techniques and therapies of healing are numberless— chemistry, the readjustment of physical malformations, surgery, spiritual healing, the laying on of hands, prayer, meditation, hypnosis, psychoanalysis, electricity, diet, magnetism . . . Yet most of our cures are of the simplest kinds. It is not without natural warrant that the mother kisses her child's scratched hand or bruised knees. He comes to her in tears, and goes away laughing. Yet the mother is just a human being—sometimes a very ignorant one. But having love, she is always ready for service, and when the need arises she gives what she has—herself. Usually she contributes some kind of direct attention and a soothing bit of admonition and advice; but love is always included in her ministrations, and there is no one who can adequately fill her place. This, I suppose, indicates the foundation on which all healing is based. One must love enough to be pure, in the sense of being quite selfless, and ready for service. The magic which is effective in the laying on of hands, or in any other type of helpfulness, must reach down to the subtle will to live that lies at the very heart of the individual existence; and it, being undeceivable, must gather the positive reassurance that it is fully related to the vitality of life itself. There is only one kind of healing—the reassurance of the vital center within the physical form—the will to live.

"Your health is bound to be affected if, day after day, you say the opposite of what you feel, if you grovel before what you dislike and rejoice at what brings you nothing but misfortune. Our nervous system isn't just a fiction; it's a part of our physical body, and our soul exists in space, and is inside us, like the teeth in our mouth. It can't be forever violated with impunity. I found it painful to listen to you, Innokentii, when you told us how you were reeducated and became mature in jail. It was like listening to a horse describing how it broke itself in."

BORIS PASTERNAK

"So when the shoe fits
The foot is forgotten,
When the belt fits
The belly is forgotten,
When the heart is right
'For' and 'against' are forgotten."

THOMAS MERTON

Ever since former *Saturday Review* editor Norman Cousins described in *The Anatomy of An Illness As Perceived by the Patient* how he cured himself of an allegedly terminal illness, using large doses of Vitamin C and Marx Brothers movies, much attention and research has focused on the role of positive emotions for enhancing the healing process. Many hospitals have set aside "laughter rooms" where patients can listen to comedy and enjoy the healing release of humor. Allan Funt has even set up a Laughter Therapy Institute through which he makes old "Candid Camera" shows available to institutions for use in laughter therapy.

Cousins sums it up "ILLNESS IS NOT A LAUGHING MATTER. Perhaps it ought to be. Laughter is a form of internal jogging. It moves your internal organs around. It enhances respiration. It is an igniter of great expectation."

Laughter is one of the best medicines. And you can't get too much of it!

Here are seven other healing attitudes that promote spiritual and emotional as well as physical well-being:

Humorous Healing

Raymond Moody, M.D.

I have a very good friend who is a very warm and wise person, and an internationally known clown. He has made a rule for himself that as often as he can, after a performance, he'll go by the local children's hospital and just walk through the wards, entertaining people. Otherwise, he says, he feels like its a waste of makeup. As long as you have the makeup on, you go and help the people that need it.

One day I was talking with him about my observations about medical uses of humor and how humorous interventions can sometimes help people back to health. He looked at me like: "Oh yeah? So what else is new?"— not in a hostile way, but he seemed rather amazed that I was amazed by all this. He said, "Sure, I do that all the time," and he described a case involving a little girl of about twelve who was in a kind of catatonic state:

she'd been unresponsive and hadn't been talking for a long time. So he walked in on this little girl to entertain her, and she immediately perked up and started to say his name over and over, whereupon the nurse who had been feeding the child just threw down the spoon and went running off to get the doctors, because this was a miracle. My friend was able to work with this child in such a way that she started talking again, and this effect lasted.

Subsequently, I have been to conventions of clowns, and I've been amazed by how many professional clowns will tell you about this kind of thing, where they've been able to go into hospitals and bring back people who are just terribly despondent—so despondent that they hadn't talked in a long time. And yet the clown could go in and bring them back to reality as it were—at least into the consensual reality.

Another clown friend of mine told me about how he went in to see a ninety-year-old man who was literally dying of depression: he was so depressed he wouldn't talk or eat, and he was starving himself to death. The doctors had said, "There's nothing we can do." They had tried everything to intervene with the depression. But nothing had worked. This clown friend of mine went in and within about thirty minutes this fellow was laughing and talking and eating again, and he actually went on to live several more years. This intervention brought him back."

Dr. Moody is the author of *Life After Life*.

Willingness

Question: How many transpersonal therapists does it take to change a lightbulb? Answer: Only one, but the lightbulb has got to be willing to change! This joke speaks to the importance of the will in self-healing: if you are in conflict about becoming well on a physical or spiritual level, then chances are that self-healing techniques won't work for you.

Healing is a basic human function;
not a medical touch or a
supernatural power.

Nonjudgment

Nonjudgmental acceptance means just that—not
evaluating things or people as bad or good, positive or
negative, but simply accepting this moment exactly the way
it is. This attitude, referred to as "equanimity" by the
Buddhists, is a habit that can be learned and has direct
application for dealing with everything from pain to add-
ictive behaviors.

Jon Kabat-Zinn, the director of the Stress Reduction
and Relaxation Program at the University of Massachusetts
Medical Center, uses the concept of acceptance in working
with chronic-pain patients. "What frequently happens to
people in chronic pain," he says, "is that they get so focused
on their pain as being 'bad' that their entire lives begin to
revolve around it." When they relax during meditation and
begin to observe the pain as mere sensation, without making any judgment about it, their relationship to the pain
begins to change. In some cases, the pain decreases. In
others, the pain is still there but it interferes less in their
daily life and with their ability to function." Kabat-Zinn
suggests the practice of Insight (Vipassana) meditation for
learning the art of nonjudgmental acceptance.

Forgiveness

"Forgiveness is the key to happiness," says *A Course
in Miracles,* and certainly the Bible advocates it strongly
as a healing remedy. To forgive is to let go of negativity.
It is the ego surrendering all judgment of self and others
in order to allow the healing power of inner serenity to
manifest. Many of us find it very difficult to let go of our
anger at life's injustices, whether real or imagined—but,
in fact, we only hurt ourselves by holding on to negative
feelings.

The good news about forgiveness is that it is a skill
that can be learned. The Buddhists use a loving-kindness
meditation to learn to replace negative states, such as anger
and hatred, with love. Spiritual healer Ruth Carter Sta-
pleton advocated practicing forgiveness using a guided imagery technique, meeting those you need to forgive in your
imagination, with the light of Jesus or divine energy pro-
tecting and healing you.

Renunciation

When you let go of possessions and pride, you let go of a principle source of stress in your life. As Arthur Deikman, M.D., says in *The Observing Self:* "Renunciation means giving up one's attachment to the things of the world, an attachment based on the wish to possess them. A Zen master remarked, 'Renunciation is not giving up the things of this world, it is accepting that they go away.' The result of such acceptance is fulfillment, not deprivation."

Faith

"Thy faith has made thee whole," said Jesus. Faith is a deep intuitive knowledge that a higher spiritual power is at work in our lives. In simply surrendering to it ("Thy will be done") a great burden seems to be lifted from our shoulders, and the self-healing capacity of the body is enhanced. A Unity Church aphorism for developing faith is to "let go and let God."

Hope

"In the face of uncertainty, there's nothing wrong with hope," says Dr. Bernie Siegel, a surgeon who works with cancer patients who are trying to heal themselves. Hope is an attitude of positive expectancy; it enhances the will to live, as well as the immune system, making even the most unbearable situations bearable. A hopeful attitude is also contagious—it inspires others and therefore amplifies positive expectations. One method Dr. Siegel uses for inspiring hope in his patients is finding case histories of other people with similar conditions who have recovered, in some cases against all odds.

Compassion

Both Jerry Jampolsky, a psychiatrist who works with children who are facing catastrophic diseases, and Bernie Siegel stress the role of compassion as a healing force. Jampolsky runs peer support groups in which children of various ages (all facing serious illnesses or disabilities) can counsel with and care for each other. The results are self-evident, says Jampolsky: "As we focus on helping others and do away with focusing on our own problems and

"Your mind will be like its habitual thoughts: for the soul becomes dyed with the color of its thoughts."

MARCUS AURELIUS

"Giving and receiving are one in truth."

A COURSE IN MIRACLES

bodies, fears seem to dissolve, and peace of mind takes their place. Visitors to our group constantly tell us how impressed they are with the feelings of mutual respect, joy, lightheartedness, and love that we all experience. Words fail to adequately describe the experience and its value to those who participate in it. Perhaps it can be most simply stated by saying that we all learned that giving and receiving are one in Truth."

Healing Ourselves, Healing the World

Healing often begins with our bodies, but it does not end there. If we view ourselves as the universe in microcosm, then our lives become a laboratory for testing the power of healing attitudes. When we find that meditation and prayer, for example, bring peace and health to our bodies, then by expanding our awareness we can begin to trust that these same healing attitudes and practices can bring healing to families, societies, and the planet as a whole. In this sense, healing becomes a way of being in the world—one in which we are living to bring greater flow and harmony to all.

Lame Deer, a Sioux Medicine man, reflects: "I believe that being a medicine man, more than anything else is a state of mind, a way of looking at and understanding this earth, a sense of what it is all about. . . . I've been up to the hilltop, got my vision and my power; the rest is just trimmings."

Recommended Reading

Alternative Healing

The Alternative Health Guide, Brian Inglis and Ruth West (Alfred Knopf, 1983). A comprehensive and fully illustrated guide to the principles and practices of seventy alternative therapies.

Health for the Whole Person, edited by Arthur Hastings, James Fadiman, and James Gordon (Westview Press, 1980). The most complete guide to holistic medicine available. Contains a critical annotated bibliography.

Transpersonal Psychology

What We May Be, Pierro Ferrucci (J. P. Tarcher, 1982). A concise introduction to psychosynthesis with many practical exercises.

Beyond Health and Normality, edited by Roger Walsh and Deane Shapiro (Van Nostrand Reinhold, 1983). Transpersonal explorations of states of exceptional psychological well-being.

Psychotherapy East and West, Alan Watts (Vintage, 1961). The classic book on Eastern philosophy and Western psychology. Beautifully written.

On Love and Laughter

Love Is Letting Go of Fear, Gerald Jampolsky, M.D. (Celestial Arts, 1979). A book about love and healing based on material from *A Course in Miracles.*

On Spiritual Healing

Realms of Healing, Stanley Krippner and Alberto Villoldo (Celestial Arts, 1977). An overview of healing and healers from many cultures. Includes laboratory research and scientific theories about healing.

Frontiers of Healing, ed N. Regush (Avon, 1977). A collection of articles by and about healers. An excellent introduction to spiritual healing.

On Holistic Health

Healing From Within, Dennis Jaffee (Knopf, 1980). A discussion of stress-related illness, with many useful exercises.

Wellness Workbook: A Guide to Attaining High Level Wellness, Regina Ryan and John Travis, M.D. (Tenspeed Press, 1979). An excellent guide to whole-body fitness.

Resources

Healing Tapes

The Stress Reducer System, Robin Casarjian and Naomi Raiselle. A self-healing system consisting of six audiocassettes and a 142-page manual. Tapes include processes for relaxation, awareness meditation, love and forgiveness, inner guidance and self-fulfillment. (Soundiscoveries, $75.00, Box 194, Back Bay Station, Boston, MA 02117.)

The Healing Journey, by Emmett E. Miller, M.D. A guided imagery tape with music for relaxation and self-healing. Dr. Miller has also produced several specific healing tapes for smoking, weight loss, insomnia, stress, and chronic pain. Send for a free catalogue to: SOURCE Cassette Learning Systems, Inc., P.O. Box W, Stanford, CA 94305.

Relaxation Training by Thomas Budzinski. A three-cassette training program that will help you to relax from head to toe. (Guilford Publications, Inc., 72 Spring St., New York, NY 10012, (800)221-3966 or in NY, (212)431-9800. $40 for 3 cassettes.)

Sources of Spiritual Healing:

The New Life Clinic: Founded by the well-known spiritual healer, Olga Worrall, this is an ecumenical healing service that prays for the sick. You can call them and have your name or the name of a friend put on their prayer list. Address: 5800 Block, Falls Rd. and Smith Ave., Baltimore, MD 21209, (301)323-4080.

Silent Unity: A twenty-four hour prayer service and telephone line run by Unity School of Christianity. If you write or call in your name, it is put in the prayer room for thirty days. This prayer service has been going on for nearly 100 years and receives as many as 600,000 calls and two and a half million letters a year. Address: Unity Village, MO 64065, (816)251-2100 or (800)669-7729. (Does not include Alaska or foreign countries.)

Organizations that aid personal growth, attitudinal healing, and help for the seriously ill:

The Center for Attitudinal Healing, 19 Main St., Tiburon, CA 94920, (415)435-5022. Founded by Dr. Jerry Jampolsky, this center provides psycho-spiritual support groups for children and adults with catastrophic illnesses and their families.

A Place for Miracles, the Option Institute and Fellowship, R.D. #1, Box 174-A, Sheffield, MA 01257, (413)229-2100. Founded by Barry and Suzi Kaufman, this center offers year-round programs on a group and individual basis for people wanting to be more comfortable and effective in a variety of life situations, as well as persons confronting difficult or tragic circumstances. A separate program trains families of "special" children to create a loving alternative for autism, cerebral palsy, etc.

Simonton Cancer Center, P.O. Box 1055, Azle, TX 76020, (817)444-4073. Founded by Dr. Carl and Stephanie Simonton who did the pioneering work on the role of stress in cancer. Provides workshops for clergy, therapists, and cancer patients. Healing tapes and books are available (order number (800)338-2360).

Professional Organizations and Newsletters:

American Holistic Medical Association, 6932 Little River Turnpike, Annandale, VA 22003, (703)642-5880.

The Association for Humanistic Psychology (AHP), 325 Ninth St., San Francisco, CA 94103, (415)626-2375.

Association for Transpersonal Psychology (ATP), P.O. Box 3049, Stanford, CA 94309, (415)327-2066.

National Center for Homeopathy, 1500 Massachusetts Ave., N.W., Washington, D.C. 20005, (202)223-6182.

Other Information:

Homeopathic Educational Services, 2124 Kittredge St., Berkeley, CA 94704, (415)653-9270. Provides books, tapes, homeopathic medicines, plus lists of practitioners, national organizations and homeopathic pharmacies.

Technology

According to physicist and philosopher Hans Kung, the standard answer to "Do you believe in Spirit?" used to be, "Oh, of course not, I'm a scientist!"; but it might very soon become, "Of course I believe in Spirit. I'm a scientist."

Because science and technology have such a tremendous impact on our lives, it is heartening to realize that the new scientific worldview that has emerged in the twentieth century agrees with what mystics and spiritual masters have been telling us for thousands of years. We are One. Not in just some trivial sense, but at the essential core of our beings. Everything is alive. Matter is not the solid stuff it appears to be; it is a stable form of energy. We are dynamic patterns of cosmic energy, connected to the whole of life in some wonderfully mysterious way.

At a time in human history when science and technology have given us the capability of destroying ourselves and the entire planet, it is fortunate that scientific and mystical views are rapidly converging. As Amaury de Riencourt points out in *The Eye of Shiva,* this convergence is probably not an accident, and may be the key to the transformation in human consciousness that will allow us to survive. He says:

> It might well be that mankind is now on the threshold of a psychological and physiological revolution of a magnitude that will overshadow all the social and political revolutions of our century—made possible by the seemingly incongruous, yet perfectly logical marriage between science and Eastern mysticism's insights.

"Yes, there is That which is the end of understanding
Yes, there is That which you will only understand
At the mind's flowering time
When she shall leaf and bud and burst
Into her fullest inflorescence of fine flowers,
But should you try to trammel up the mind,
And bind her, confine her, and *strive* to turn her inwards
You will not understand

For there is a power of the mind's prime
Which, rising like the sun in all its majesty,
Shines forth with rays of thought at one with feeling.
Hold still the vision of thy Soul in purity
Freed from all else
Let but thy little mind be empty of all things else
All things save one—thine aim
To reach the end of understanding
For that subsists beyond the mind."

THE CHALDEAN ORACLE

"There will be no conflict between religion and science in the future . . . A higher human culture will be established in the ultimately unknowable Paradox of the Divine Unity, the ultimate Identity of God and Man and World."

DA FREE JOHN

The modern scientists, then, are on a spiritual quest, whether they know it or not! In the process of analyzing physical matter into smaller and smaller parts, scientists have come face to face with the spiritual dimension of reality. Outer knowledge and inner knowledge turn out to be the same thing and, in *Space, Time, and Medicine,* Larry Dossey says that no scientist worthy of the title can deny this:

Man's search for unity with nature has gone beyond poetry and mysticism—or perhaps has fused to some degree with them—to form a vision that is unique for our time. This interweaving of science and mysticism is a new event in human history, and it places fresh demands on the scientist. These interconnections are so profound that it can safely be said that the scientist who does not perceive them not only does not understand mysticism, he does not understand his own science.

Until recently, the dominant scientific assumption, developed in the seventeenth century by Newton, Descartes, and Galileo, has been that there is a "real," objective universe made up of inanimate matter, and that one could come to know reality by analyzing and reducing that matter to its smallest component. This approach has, in fact, proved very successful when it comes to understanding and manipulating most physical objects. Its successes range from producing automobiles to landing men on the moon.

The belief that science should be an objective analysis of reality leads to a cold-hearted, rational approach to knowledge, a fundamental split between the two separate realms of mind and matter. Feelings were relegated to the back burner of this scientific world view, and religious and spiritual beliefs were seen merely as primitive superstition that had been debunked by Newtonian, mechanistic inquiry. The new "religion" of scientism became accepted as correct, and was not seriously questioned until very recently.

Fritjof Capra, author of *The Tao of Physics,* stated: "Whenever psychologists, sociologists, or economists wanted to be scientific, they naturally turned toward the basic concepts of Newtonian physics, and many of them still hold to these concepts, even though physicists have now gone far beyond them."

Choosing the Future

"With the splitting of the atom, everything has changed save our mode of thinking. Thus we hurl ourselves toward unparalleled catastrophe."

ALBERT EINSTEIN

With the advent of modern science we have reached a point in our technological evolution that is totally unprecedented on earth. We have developed technologies capable of destroying all life on Mother Earth. Our ability to manipulate and control the human mind is steadily increasing, and the prospect of the genetic engineering of all life forms is on the horizon. We have become *conscious* of the process of evolution, and are beginning to realize that we are the first species that must *choose* the direction of its own evolution.

Consciously choosing which technologies to develop and utilize and which not to has raised (and will continue to raise) many difficult ethical, moral and religious questions. Until now these questions have hardly been addressed, but left in the hands of a scientific/technological elite. The nuclear age began in the secrecy of scientific laboratories (supposedly to meet the needs of the Allies in World War II) and it is proving to be very difficult to get

"We are seeking another basic outlook: the world as organization. This would profoundly change the categories of our thinking and influence our practical attitudes. We must envision the biosphere as a whole with mutually reinforcing or mutually destructive interdependencies."

LUDWIG VON BERTALANFFY

the nuclear "genie" back into the bottle. We seem to be rushing headlong into the Age of Biotechnology with its genetic engineering, cloning, and development of new life forms. In June, 1980, the U.S. Supreme Court ruled that novel, new forms of life engineered in the laboratory are patentable. So far the level of public discussion and concern has been focused on whether or not it is safe to have a genetic engineering lab in your neighborhood, but who is going to determine whether or not we should deploy these biotechnologies at all? We can no longer simply follow the technological imperative that "if we can manipulate and control it, then we should." A different kind of knowledge other than scientism is required at this point in human evolution.

Why? Because science is not a form of knowledge which can answer questions about values, purpose, or meaning. Many scientists are fully aware that modern science is not relevant to the search for the new underlying metaphysical and moral truths by which we live. As physicist Erwin Schrodinger says, such truths must be arrived at through intuition. Or, as science philosopher Henry Morgenau says in *The Nature of Physical Reality:*

> In my view . . . natural science contains no NORMATIVE principles dealing with ultimate goals. . . . To know physical reality is to know where to look when something is wanted or needed to be seen; it is to be able to cure when a cure is desired, to kill when killing is intended. But natural science will never tell whether it is good or bad to look, to cure or to kill. It simply lacks the premise of an 'ought.'

The Rediscovery of Oneness

In the twentieth century, modern physics has brought spirit back into science. Einstein's theory of relativity and quantum mechanics led to the development of a new paradigm, one which emphasizes the fundamental interconnectedness of all things. Fritjof Capra describes this new paradigm in the following way:

> The material world, according to contemporary physics, is not a mechanical system made of separate objects, but rather appears as a complex web of relationships. Subatomic par-

ticles are not made of any material substance; they have a certain mass, but this mass is a form of energy. Energy is always associated with processes, with activity; it is a measure of activity. Subatomic particles, then, are bundles of energy, or patterns of activity. The notion of separate objects is an idealization which is often very useful but has no fundamental validity. All objects are merely patterns in an inseparable cosmic process, and these patterns are intrinsically dynamic, continually changing into one another, in a continuous dance of energy.

When Werner Heisenberg's principle of uncertainty proved that the observer's consciousness influenced what was being observed, human consciousness was once again restored to a fundamental position in the universe. As the British physicist, Sir James Jeans, put it, "The universe begins to look more like a great thought than a great machine." Quantum physics tells us that the universe is not a fixed, given, objective reality.

There are multiple realities rooted in consciousness, a transcendental ground which underlies all the explicit realities. Or, as physicist J. A. Wheeler puts it: "The universe is preselected by consciousness." In other words, our minds construct and maintain the realities which we experience, and all of these realities emerge from a unified field of consciousness, a timeless and spaceless ground of being which seems identical to the "Godhead" described by all the great mystics and sages throughout history.

English physicist David Bohm, who was a colleague of Einstein, maintains that the information of the entire universe is contained in each of its parts. Ken Wilbur summarizes Bohm's theory in *The Holographic Paradigm*:

> In Bohm's terminology, under the *explicate realm* of separate things and events is an *implicate realm* of undivided wholeness, and this implicate whole is simultaneously available to each explicate part. In other words, the physical universe itself seems to be a gigantic hologram, with each part being in the whole and the whole being in each part.

David Bohm puts it this way in his book *Wholeness and the Implicate Order*:

> Parts are seen to be in immediate connection, in which their dynamical relationships depend, in an irreducible way, on

"What's your view of things, Coyote?"

"Well, it mostly depends on how I'm looking at them, I guess. The angle of perception is important, too, of course. And the whether or not of open or closed eyes and mind.

"All in all, I'd say I tend to view things thru my crystal. Much more clarity there, and it tends to filter-out misconceptions, too."

"You know what, Coyote? You talk too damned much!"

"Yes, I agree. And you, Asshole, ask too many questions."

PETER BLUE CLOUD

the state of the whole system (and, indeed, on that of broader systems in which they are contained, extending ultimately and in principle to the entire universe). Thus, one is led to a new notion of *unbroken wholeness* which denies the classical idea of analyzability of the world into separately independently existing parts.

Further support for the holographic paradigm comes from Stanford neurosurgeon Karl Pribram, whose studies in brain memory and function led him to suggest that the brain functions like a hologram. Pribram concludes that the brain is a hologram perceiving and participating in a holographic universe. From this perspective, the experience of mystical oneness can be understood to be a genuine, direct experience of the implicate order that Bohm postulates (or perhaps, the transcendent realm is the source of both the implicate and the explicate realms).

Toward a Science with a Heart

One very important point to keep in mind is that whenever scientists or mystics attempt to talk about the absolute, the "One," paradoxical statements are the result. In *The Holographic Paradigm* Ken Wilber describes the problem:

> Reason generates paradoxical statements when it tries to grasp the absolute. . . . It is true that reality is one, but equally true that it is many; it is transcendent, but also immanent; it is prior to this world, but it is not other to this world—and so on. Sri Ramana Maharshi had a perfect summary of the paradox of the ultimate: "The world is illusory; Brahman alone is real; Brahman is the world." There is no way to directly understand spirit except by radical spiritual transformation, or the direct opening of the eye of contemplation. You can read, think and write about the Tao all day, and none of that is the Tao. No mental theory is even close to Brahman.

In other words, you cannot become a mystic simply by learning a new mental world view. The new paradigm is perhaps a better model with which to order our lives, but by merely learning the new paradigm, you will not transcend. Transcendence requires spiritual practice (for most of us!). The transformation in attitudes, values, and beliefs that seems to be required is from materialism to spiritualism. If you substitute the word "science" for "magic" in the following quote by Evelyn Underhill, in her book *Mysticism*, the difference in value orientation will be apparent:

> The difference between magic and higher mysticism finally boils down to this, that "magic wants to get, mysticism wants to give," which is all due to the lack of feeling love in the magic world. Whereas in magic the will unites with a primitive and rudimentary intellect in search of knowledge and power over countless forces, deities or demons, in mysticism the will unites also with loving emotion in order to transcend the sensuous universe.

This empathetic approach to science and knowledge could be called "science with a heart." This means that science would take its place in a value system that focuses on living in harmony and balance with all life-stewardship for the earth. Fortunately, this spiritually oriented value system is totally compatible with the new science and the systems view of life.

Living Systems and the Habits of the Universe

The resurgence of spirit in science becomes even more apparent when we focus on the new concepts in biology and the life sciences.

Our modern understanding of the role of creative intelligence in the evolutionary process has moved science far beyond Darwin's mechanistic notions of random mutation and natural selection as the major sources of evolutionary change. The key concept in the systems view is the fact that living organisms are self-organizing systems, that is, structure and function are not imposed by the environment but are established by the system itself. But how does a less complex system evolve into a more complex one? Ilya Prigogine won the Nobel prize for his answer to this question, with his theory of dissipative structures. Marilyn Ferguson summarized Prigogine's work in an article in her *Brain-Mind Bulletin:*

"Scientists are, as yet, only barely acquainted with the implicate order which has, however, apparently been explored experientially by mystics, psychics and others delving into paranormal phenomena . . . At the moment this order appears so indistinguishable from the mental operations by which we operate on that universe that we must conclude either that our science is a huge mirage, a construct of the emergence of our convoluted brains, or that indeed, as proclaimed by all great religious convictions, a unity characterizes this emergent and the basic order of the universe."

CARL PRIBRAM

How did life develop in a universe of ever-increasing disorder? How do order and complexity emerge from entropy?

This riddle has been plaguing science for centuries, of course, and it has created a wide gap between biology and physics—between the study of living systems and the study of the apparently lifeless universe in which they arise.

Now Ilya Prigogine, a physical chemist, offers a startling explanation, complete with mathematical proofs: Order emerges *because* of entropy, not *despite* it!

Prigogine's theory applies to open systems, in which a structure exchanges energy with the surrounding environment. It can be a laboratory chemical solution, an amino acid, a human being.

These are what he calls "dissipative structures." Their form or pattern is self-organizing, maintained by a continuous dynamic flow.

The more complex such a structure, the more energy it must dissipate to maintain all that complexity. This flux of energy makes the system highly unstable subject to internal fluctuations—and sudden change.

If these fluctuations, or perturbations, reach a critical size, they are amplified by the system's many connections and can drive the whole system into a new state—even more ordered, coherent and connected.

The new state occurs as a sudden shift, much as a kaleidoscope shifts into a new pattern. It is a nonlinear event; that is, multiple factors act on each other at once.

With each new state, there is greater potential for change. With new levels of complexity, there are new rules. As Prigogine put it, there is a change in the nature of the 'laws' of nature.

The capacity for self-transcendence which all self-organizing systems exhibit can be viewed as a scientific metaphor for the process of spiritual transformation, the "quantum leap" in consciousness that results in a higher level of integrative awareness. "Ephemeralization," as Buckminster Fuller calls it—the nonlinear evolution from matter toward mind toward spirit.

The Age of the Scientist-Mystic

As a result of this modified view or paradigm of reality, we are beginning to see the emergence of what might be called the "scientist-mystic." Fritjof Capra is only one of many modern scientists who have publicly discussed how they have combined the new scientific knowledge with the direct experience of higher states of consciousness. Scientists are opening the "third eye," the Eye of Shiva, and glimpsing into hidden levels of existence impervious to normal sight. This convergence of rational and intuitive knowledge can help humankind to more clearly see the nature of reality.

Examples of this new hybrid scientist/mystic are abundant. Dr. Fritjof Capra not only does research in theoretical high energy physics at the Lawrence Berkeley Laboratory, he does Tai Chi and meditates. *The Tao of Physics* is not only a product of left-brain, analytical thinking. Mind researchers such as Stanislow Grof, M.D., John Lilly, M.D., and Jean Houston, Ph.D., have documented many of their "travels" into other realms of consciousness, and their ability as scientists to order and analyze their own subjective experiences as well as those of their patients have resulted in unique and brilliant contributions to our understanding of the human mind.

Our personal favorite example of a scientist/mystic was Itzhak (Ben) Bentov, a brilliant inventor and consciousness researcher. Bentov had very little formal education, yet he earned his living as a biomedical inventor and all-around creative problem solver. During his early years he would soak in a hot bath and wait for intuitive flashes to solve the problems he was working on. Later he became an avid meditator and his rapidly expanding consciousness took him to the ends of the universe. Yet he always considered himself a "nuts and bolts" man, a plumber whose job was to figure out the basic structure of the universe. He developed one of the first holographic models of the universe, which he describes in *Stalking the Wild Pendulum: On The Mechanics of Consciousness* and he went on to describe his version of the creation in his posthumous sequel *A COSMIC BOOK: On the Mechanics of Creation.*

Bentov had an uncanny ability to order his subjective experiences in profoundly insightful ways. He combined his abilities as a scientist and inventor with his spiritual insights in a truly inspiring way. His human qualities as a

"The changes that appear to occur in the empty world we call real only because of our ignorance. Do not search for the truth; only cease to cherish opinions . . . Make the smallest distinction and Heaven and Earth are set infinitely apart."

SENGSTAN
THIRD ZEN PATRIARCH

"What science has to give is epistemology first, foremost. All the rest is only parables, ONLY PARABLES. But the business of discovery, creating, analyzing, synthesizing, understanding and communicating these parables is not a branch of amateur musing or political journalism. It is as rigorous as Buddhist theology or epistemology, call it what you will. It is art, it is science, it is life."

GREGORY BATESON

loving, caring (and extremely humorous) and compassionate person were present in all aspects of his life. His spirituality and gentleness even shows up in his light and humorous writing style. He was truly a scientist with a heart.

According to Fritzof Capra in his new book *The Turning Point: Science, Society and the Rising Culture,* the shift from material growth to inner growth is at the core of all of the major movements that make up what he calls the "rising culture." This creative minority includes the movements in ecology, feminism, holistic health, appropriate technology, human potential, and the spiritual movement.

According to Jeremy Rifkin, author of *Algeny,* "You can look at every department in every university in the country and see two different worldviews emerging—an ecological approach to the age of biology versus a biotechnical approach to the age of biology—a nurturing, stewardship approach based on participating with the why of things versus a controlling technological approach based on developing the how of things in order to orchestrate our own future."

The development of a spiritual context for our scientific endeavors is going to require much more participation in the decision-making process by all of us. We cannot "leave it to the experts" because the spiritual wisdom in which major cultural choices must be made is unlikely to be held exclusively by our scientific specialists. To allow the power of science to concentrate into the hands of a privileged few who will be in a position to determine the future of life for all of us.

This means that each of us must take responsibility for learning the basic language of science in order to be able to discuss the critical issues and to be prepared to participate in the major social choices that will affect all future life on the planet. In a sense, science will, of necessity, become a part of all of our spiritual paths!

The Message in the Rubik's Cube

If learning basic science sounds like an overwhelming or difficult task, consider this hopeful sign: In 1981 the largest-selling toy in the world was the Rubik's Cube. It was the first global game, and it burst onto the scene as if it were the answer to our deepest collective need. Maybe it was.

To solve the puzzle of the Rubik's Cube, one must accept a very important rule: an answer to a problem on one face of life may cause untold havoc elsewhere. Any solution has to be a *total* solution, acknowledging every facet of life. In a word, wholeness.

> "By plucking her petals, you do not gather the beauty of the flower."
>
> RABINDRANATH TAGORE

The fact that most Rubik's Cube champions are under the age of 17 may give us a shock, but could also give us hope. Maybe they got the message.

In a sense, we are all kids today, because our world is in fact going through exponential (increasing *rate*) growth in every area including communications, scientific theory, spiritual diversity and living styles. Learning how to operate a computer is no harder or easier than solving the Rubik's Cube, it's kid's stuff: that is, it takes a beginner's mind, which is one characteristic required for the spiritual path.

"We say you cannot divert the river from the river bed. We say that everything is moving, and we are a part of this motion. That the soil is moving. That the water is moving. We say that the earth draws water to her from the clouds. We say the rainfall parts on each side of the mountain, like the parting of our hair, and that the shape of the mountain tells where the water has passed. We say this water washes the soil from the hillsides, that the rivers carry sediment, that rain when it splashes carries small particles, that the soil itself flows with water in streams underground. We say that water is taken up into roots of plants, into stems, that it washes down hills into rivers, that these rivers flow to the sea, that from the sea, in the sunlight, this water rises to the sky, that this water is carried in clouds, and comes back as rain, comes back as fog, back as dew, as wetness in the air. "We say everything comes back."

SUSAN GRIFFIN

Children today will grow up knowing how to operate a computer just as their parents knew how to operate a television set. The possibilities of computer technology vary from the benign to the frightening, from concepts of a global network of interdependent communities to concepts of computer-programmed genes inserted into living organisms including humans.

The key principle in computer programming is known as Turing's Theorem; it says: "You can make a computer do anything that (1) you can do, and (2) you know what steps you go through to do it." Thus computers go to the moon, take pictures of the earth from space, and balance our checkbooks; they also design nuclear bombs, and guide nuclear missiles.

One of the biggest questions facing humankind today is whether or not we can use our intelligence.

As science-fiction writer Frank Herbert, author of the *Dune* saga, says, "One of the best things to come out of the home computer revolution could be the general and widespread understanding of how severely limited logic really is—that plus a new appreciation of our own capabilities."

If new technology creates new perils, it also creates new hope. The Industrial Revolution, for all its drawbacks, was a spiritually liberating force. Computer scientist Francis Jeffrey offers consolation, "Technology and consciousness interact in ways that produce new consciousness, new technologies, and new possibilities for the future."

How Much Is Too Much?

Now we come to a final, but equally important question regarding technology and consciousness that everyone on the spiritual path seems to ask themselves at some time or another: Is it possible to live in and utilize the products of modern industrial society without hopelessly compromising one's own spiritual development?

Ivan Illich once commented that the bicycle was perhaps the paragon of technological achievement: it efficiently augments human energy while requiring only a small amount of natural resource materials and no nonrenewable fuels. Using a nuclear power plant to boil water to generate electricity, on the other hand, is in Amory Lovins' words, "like using a chain saw to cut butter."

Any person trying to live conscientiously and gently on this planet will be confronted by questions about the appropriate use of technology and energy: How much is enough? Where do the materials I use come from, and where does the fuel to run my machines come from? What is the real cost, the total cost, including human oppression and ecological degradation?

None of us would willingly see someone contract leukemia so that we could have electricity for our toaster, yet with the advent of nuclear power, this trade-off has become a reality. No one would perhaps be willing to accept a military dictatorship in Chile, Zaire, or Indonesia so that we in North American could enjoy copper, molybdenum and oil, but these are the sort of contradictions we live with every day. What then is the appropriate use of technology, one tht is neither oppressive of other people nor destructive of the environment?

One of the first criteria might be to ask ourselves what is the most *efficient* way to meet our needs, not just the fastest way or the easiest way. Perhaps we could do most of our near-home errands on a bicycle rather than in a car. Most households, it is estimated, could reduce electricity consumption by 25 to 30 percent simply by being more mindful of waste. Less consumption of electricity means less rivers dammed, fewer nuclear power plants built.

As we become more conscious of the repercussions from our uses of technology, we begin to face the contradictions head on, and we learn to be more comfortable with what we do use. It seems a great irony that North Americans fill their houses with electrical gadgets that save labor, then create a multibillion-dollar "fitness" industry to get back into shape. It seems as if a great energy source— human energy—is being jogged, bounced, and stretched away at thousands of fitness centers. Nowhere else in the world do people have so much energy to burn.

Why not try a "fitness" program that *uses* the energy you are burning off? Try hooking up a weight-reduction bicycle to a mill, and grind your own flour while you are

> "And this, our life, exempt from public haunt, finds tongues in trees, books in the running brooks, sermons in stones, and good in everything."
>
> WILLIAM SHAKESPEARE

> "Epistemology is always and inevitably *personal*. The point of the probe is always in the heart of the explorer: What is *my* answer to the question of the nature of knowing? I surrender to the belief that my knowing is a small part of a wider integrated knowing that knits the entire biosphere of creation."
>
> GREGORY BATESON

exercising. Get rid of your gas-guzzling lawn mower, and get a push mower that gives you some exercise while you cut your grass. In short, incorporate your fitness program into your life. Our bodies evolved doing the work of survival. Naturally, if we let machines do all of our work, then our bodies are going to cry out for the exercise for which they are suited.

Once you begin to establish such a routine in your life, you will find where technology fits into your life naturally and appropriately. You can begin to feel at peace with your home computer or your food chopper. One does not have to purge his or her household of technological appliances in order to live a spiritual life. There is a middle path that balances human energy and technology. As we find this balance, technology becomes a friend, rather than a hidden demon.

We may conclude that our hand calculator is appropriate, but that our electric razor is not; we may feel instinctively that a wood stove is an appropriate augmentation to our heating system. We might find that trading in our power boat for three kayaks leads to less consumption and more family fun. The choices, ultimately, are personal with a view toward the social and ecological.

Before one chooses a particular technological solution, one might try running through this simple checklist:

1. Is the task to be performed *needed*?
2. Does the technological solution oppress someone else?
3. Does the technological solution degrade the environment?
4. Do the technology, materials or fuels steal nonrenewable resources from the future? Will our great-grandchildren still have access to this solution?
5. Does the technological solution create negative by-products or effects?
6. Can the task be performed by available human energy?
7. Does the solution create new problems?

Every task, every problem has a vast array of possible solutions. As conscientious individuals, responsible for the effects of our living patterns, responsible to the future, and capable of making choices, we must not take the simplest, easiest, or quickest solution to be the best solution. Neither are we morally bound to forsake technology or treat it as inherently evil. Moderation and common sense will likely lead us to an appropriate balance.

> "There should be no 'science program' distinct from other programs. As I see it, 'science' is a fiction of the same formal nature as the ego. Just as the 'ego' does not exist because it has no boundaries, so precisely 'science' does not exist because it has no boundaries."
>
> GREGORY BATESON

Recommended Reading

The New Physics and New Cosmologies

Stalking The Wild Pendulum, Itzhak Bentov (Dutton, 1977). An easy-to-read yet profound introduction to Bentov's holographic model of the universe.

The Medium, The Mystic, and the Physicist, Lawrence LeShan (Ballantine, 1974). A scholarly theory of the paranormal with quotes from physicists and mystics.

Space, Time, and Medicine, Larry Dossey (Shambhala, 1982). A well-written book about the new physics and holistic medicine.

Biology and Systems Theory

Uncommon Sense, Mark Davidson (Tarcher, 1983). Biography of Ludwig von Bertalanffy. Good introduction to general systems theory.

A New Science of Life, Rupert Sheldrake (Tarcher, 1982). Radical new theory of life called "formative causation."

Mind and Nature: A Necessary Unity, Gregory Bateson (Bantam, 1979). Systems view of the mind as the dynamics of self-organization. A very important book.

Gaia, John E. Lovelock (Oxford University Press, 1979). Lovelock's "Gaia Hypothesis," in which he views Planet Earth as a living organism.

Science, Society and Values

The Turning Point, Fritjof Capra (Bantam, 1983). Comprehensive vision of the reality and culture emerging from the new paradigm in science. Must reading.

Beyond the Post-Modern Mind, Huston Smith (Crossroad, 1982). Brilliant discussion of the limitations and consequences of the Western mind-set, plus a vision of the way out.

Modern Science Books for Kids

The Kids' Whole Future Catalog, Paula Taylor (Random House, 1982). Pictures, mail order, things to make, things to do, and a vast catalog of future possibilities; excellent access information on every subject from health care to space travel.

The Way the New Technology Works, Ken Marsh (Fireside, Simon & Schuster, 1982). Computers, cable-TV, holograms, lasers, and easy explanations about how it all works.

The Sub-nuclear Zoo, Sylvia Engdahl and Rick Roberson (Atheneum, Vreeland Ave., Totowa, NJ 07512). The subatomic world of modern physics explained in simple language.

Resources

Staying up to Date

Brain/Mind Bulletin, edited by Marilyn Ferguson; published every three weeks. A current events newsletter in the field of neurological research written for the lay reader.

Science for the People (P.O. Box 7229, Baltimore, MD 21218).

ReVision (P.O. Box 316, Cambridge, MA 02138); The best journal of holistic scientific thinking, bringing together new ideas in the fields of consciousness research, neurology, physics, and other areas with a dedication to holism and a general systems approach.

12

The Earth

According to an old Jewish folktale, one day a child, Honi, saw an old man digging a hole in the earth. Honi asked the man, "Must you do heavy work at your age? Have you no sons to help you?" The man kept digging. "This work I must do myself." Honi asked, "How old are you?" "I am seventy years and seven," answered the man. "And what are you planting?" "I am planting a bread fruit tree," was the answer, "and the fruit of this tree can be made into bread." "And when will your tree bear fruit?" asked Honi. "In seventeen years and seven." "But you surely will not live that long," said Honi. "Yes," said the old man, "I will not live that long, but I must plant this tree. When I came into this world there were trees here for me. It is my duty to make sure that when I leave there will be trees here also."

At its base, ecological awareness is spiritual; it is a return to the simple, profound respect for and responsibility to the earth that our ancestors knew and practiced. Ecological philosophy, like spiritual philosophy, teaches that we are all one, all united. No matter how deeply we look into the fabric of material being—the biological level, chemical level, subatomic level—we see that life forms are interdependent, co-conditioning and co-evolving. Every human effort, civilization, thought, and spiritual insight, requires and is supported by the whole of organic life.

"Patanjali, Buddha, Moses and Jesus did not go to workshops or seminars or even churches," says Dolores LaChapelle, author of *Earth Wisdom*. "They went directly to nature: sat under a Bodhi tree or on top of a mountain or in a cave. We've been living off the residual remains of their inspiration for thousands of years, but this has about run out. It is time to return to the source of this inspiration—the earth itself."

The first step toward rediscovering this spiritual fountainhead is simple: go out and observe the natural world. We need simply to look very closely. In this way the earth teaches us its eternal message, quietly, in a way unlike the textbook learning *about* nature.

As Robert Hunter says in *O Seasons, O Castles:* "In nature, there is no such thing as a clash of colors. The more carefully you look, the deeper the subtleties of harmony. It is not so much that things flow into each other or around each other like perfect jigsaw pieces; rather it is that there is only One Thing out there. And, somehow, it is not really 'out there.' Somehow, it is 'in here' too. Inside. At the furthest wavelength of thought, the sea and the wind and the trees and sand are . . . me. It is a thought that blinks into the mind, like a giant laughing eye, and then is gone for a long, long time."

Kicking God Out of the Garden

Early human societies and modern land-based spiritual cultures such as the American Indians witnessed and worshiped Godhead, Atman, the Great Spirit in the natural world. Taoism, for example, is *based* on the notion that we stay in a sacred balance with the Tao—Indivisible Unity—by observing and following the ways of the natural world. "The highest good is like water," says Lao Tsu; "Water gives life to the ten thousand things and does not strive."

The *I Ching*, perhaps the oldest formalized spiritual doctrine in the world, is widely used today throughout China and also in the West. The sixty-four hexagrams of the *I Ching* derive from the combinations of the eight trigrams: Heaven, Earth, Water, Fire, Thunder, Mountain, Lake, and Wind. These trigrams are, in turn, derived from combinations of yin and yang, the primal duality that creates the physical world. Thus, through adopting the pat-

"I do not think that the measure of a civilization is how tall its buildings of concrete are, but rather how well its people have learned to relate to their environment and fellow man."

SUN BEAR OF THE CHIPPEWA TRIBE

terns of the natural world, spiritual scriptures were created that have inspired and assisted human society for thousands of years.

The American Indians, of course, teach us the same central lesson. "Our religion goes back 30,000 years, farther than that; it is ancient, before anything was written down," says Oglala Lakota elder, Noble Red Man. "The truth is not something you can write down and hold in your hand. The truth can only be held in your heart. Our grandparents tell us everything. We don't lie and make up new rules all the time. God is nature, nature is God. That is very simple. We have known it from before time."

However, some cultures—most notably, Western industrial culture, based upon a belief in the infallibility of the rational human mind—extracted God, sacredness, from the earth. Perhaps it was not humankind that was kicked out of the Garden by God, but rather God who was kicked out of the Garden by a human society. That society thought, arrogantly, that it could survive and prosper indefinitely, armed only with reason and ingenuity. Wendell Berry, a poet, essayist, and farmer, articulated the problem perfectly in *A Secular Pilgrimage:*

If God was not in the world, then obviously the world was a thing of inferior importance, or of no importance at all. Those who were disposed to exploit it were thus free to do so. And this split in public attitudes was inevitably mirrored in the lives of individuals: a man could aspire to Heaven with his mind and his heart while destroying the earth, and his fellow men, with his hands. . . . This contempt for the world or the hatred of it . . . has reached a terrifying climax in our own time. The rift between body and soul, the Creator and the Creation, has admitted the entrance into the world of machinery of the world's doom.

Thus we see that the ecological crisis is a spiritual crisis, and it is no small coincidence, therefore, that the modern-day environmental movement frequently resembles a religious movement. Obviously, for us to survive and grow as a species, as a society, or as individuals, our hands and our brains are not enough; we need to listen to our hearts and souls.

Findhorn and the Devas

In our modern world there are many instances of people returning to the garden as a source of spiritual work and inspiration. One of the best known is the Findhorn Community in northern Scotland. Eileen and Peter Caddy and Dorothy Maclean founded the community on the cold, seemingly desolate Findhorn Bay, whipped by the North Atlantic winds. Here, in the last place one might have selected as a garden site, the community has developed a miraculous bounty of fruits, vegetables, nuts, flowers, herbs, and even tropical trees.

They attribute their success to their willingness to listen to the "nature spirits"—to enter into a harmonious conspiracy with the spirit in living things. "It was the reality of the garden growth," says Dorothy Maclean, "that brought home to us the reality of the devas. Out of this grew a new way of gardening, and a deeper understanding of life as a whole. We were learning the importance of cooperation, not only with nature, but amongst ourselves as well."

Maclean says that in a meditation shortly after arriving at Findhorn Bay, she received a directive from within:

"If thy heart were right, then every creature would be a mirror of life and a book of holy doctrine. There is no creature so small and abject, but it reflects the goodness of God."

THOMAS À KEMPIS
Imitation of Christ

"The forces of Nature are something to be felt into, to be reached out to . . . sense the Nature forces such as the wind, to perceive its essence . . . be positive and harmonize with that essence. . . . You can cooperate in the garden. Begin by thinking about the nature spirits, the higher over-lighting nature spirits, and tune into them. That will be so unusual as to draw their interest here. They will be over-joyed to find some members of the human race eager for their help. . . . All forces are to be felt into, even the sun, the moon, the sea, the trees, the very grass. All are part of my life. All is one life."

The community has followed these meditative visions and the Findhorn garden has flourished. How similar Ma-clean's vision is to the vision received by Saint Hildegard of Bingen during the Middle Ages, when she heard the Holy Spirit say to her: "I am that supreme and fiery force that sends forth all the sparks of life. Death hath no part in me, yet do I allot it, wherefore I am girt about with wisdom as with wings. I am that living and fiery essence of the divine substance that flows in the beauty of the fields, I shine in the water, I burn in the sun and the moon and the stars. Mine is the mysterious force of the invisible wind. I sustain the breath of all living. I breathe in the verdure, and in the flowers, and when the waters flow like living things, it is I."

At Findhorn, the gardeners take care to leave one corner of the garden wild, a place where the natural spirit of things can live without human intervention. If we can recognize this spiritual force in wild nature, then, like the followers of Zarathustra, we can see that the garden is paradise, the place where the human spirit cooperates with the divine wild spirit of nature.

Natural Cultures

Another way to gain an appreciation for our spiritual connection to the whole earth is to investigate those cultures that have honored that connection. Most notably, the American Indians have based their entire culture, from education to government, on a respect for the natural world.

"If you have a respect for all of life," says Russell Means, "you've got it made. You have peace of mind. One

"The Buddhist scriptures tells us there are eight objections to living in a house: it is a lot of trouble to build; it must be kept in repair; some nobleman might seize it; too many people may want to live in or visit it; it makes the body tender; it provides concealment for committing evil deeds; it causes pride of ownership; and it harbors lice and bugs.

"There are ten advantages, on the other hand, in residing under a tree: it can be found with ease; it can be found in any locality; the sight of falling leaves is a reminder of the impermanence of life; a tree arouses no covetous thoughts; it affords no opportunity for evil deeds; it is not received from any person; it is inhabited by good spirits; it needs no fence; it promotes health; it does not involve worldly attachments."

PUJIMALIYA

only has to look at those really old people among the natural peoples of the world, the red people, Polynesians, Africans, the Samis of Norway, the Inuits of the frozen north.

"Only industrial society has put a value on time, and we realize that time is insignificant because our own lifetime in this world is but a blink of the eye. And when you have that knowledge, that life is beautiful and you can enjoy it rather than worry about it, then you can even accept death just as you accept birth as part of the total sacred loop of life."

The Indian cultures consciously patterned their lives on a recognition of the limits of nature. As Chief Fools Crow of the Oglala Lakota has said: "The Creator gave to us all the living things so that we would know how to act. The natural world is our Bible; by watching the chipmunk and the meadowlark and even the tiniest flower we learn the lessons that the Creator has put before us. Everything is sacred. This very land is our church."

Though throughout the world the simple, natural societies have suffered under the expansion of industrial societies, still there are land-based spiritual communities surviving that have an important lesson to teach. Author Vine Deloria, Jr. (*God is Red* and *We Talk, You Listen*) says it this way:

It is doubtful if American society can move very far or very significantly without a major revolution in theological concepts. . . . Within the traditions, beliefs and customs of the American Indian people are the guidelines for mankind's future.

There is a reason why shrines exist. . . . Mount Sinai, for example, has been a holy mountain for a considerable length of time, thus indicating that it has a religious existence over and above any temporary belief held by particular people. If this concept is true, then economics cannot and should not be the sole determinant of land use. Unless the sacred places are discovered and protected and used as religious places, there is no possibility of a nation ever coming to grips with the land itself. Without this basic relationship, national stability is impossible.

That a fundamental element of religion is an intimate relationship with the land on which the religion is practiced should be a major premise of future theological concern.

What Vine Deloria is saying is that our spiritual quest is not only enriched by a reverence for the earth, but that it is incomplete without it.

And, since we cannot have human culture or personal growth without a healthy planet, this notion leads us invariably to the realization that we have a political responsibility to the earth as support system for everything we do.

The Three Laws of Ecology

Ecology, it has been said, can be applied at the most minute, personal level of behavior, and at the most "cosmic." A good way to appreciate *all* of these is to keep in mind the Three Laws of Ecology, articulated in their contemporary form by Patrick Moore, the Canadian ecologist who was one of the founders of the Greenpeace movement—drawing on Bookchin, Hegel, et al.

The First Law of Ecology . . . states that all forms of life are interdependent. The prey is as dependent on the predator for the control of its population as the predator is on the prey for a supply of food.

The Second Law of Ecology . . . states that the stability (unity, security, harmony, togetherness) of ecosystems is dependent on their diversity (complexity). An ecosystem that contains 100 different species is more stable than an ecosystem that has only three species.

The Third Law of Ecology . . . states that all resources (food, water, air, minerals, energy) are finite and there are limits to the growth of all living systems. These limits are finally dictated by the finite size of the earth and the finite input of energy from the sun.

The New Aesthetics Ecological Planning

"Our spirits are enriched and constantly recharged by our functional and ritualistic connections to the natural world" writes Sim Van der Ryn in *Ecological Planning*. "The preindustrial aesthetic was always based on that kind of connection. Whether evidenced in the miniature garden found in each home in a dense Japanese neighborhood, or the simple Arab courtyard fountain, or the shade elms of New England commons, the whole picturesque "architecture without architects" of the earlier world adapted habitat to local materials, site, climate, and ecosystem.

"The importance of aesthetics is the kind of participation that it brings about with natural systems. It is from this relationship that the new aesthetics must be derived. For the most part, however, Americans have lost that intimate connection and an awareness of their place in the natural world. The "natural" aspect has been reduced to empty symbols, such as the tract house lawn, which started out as a sheep meadow—the lawn was there for sheep to crop. Ecosystems have become dim landscapes to be appreciated out of car windows—low-information media like TV screens.

"The task, then, of ecological design, is to begin to recreate the opportunities for people to derive meaning and satisfaction from their experience with natural cycles."

Mother of the Buddha

The Hopis believe it is their sacred duty and responsibility to care for the earth: Caring for the living earth is a natural extension of caring for oneself or one's family, or community. We are nature; to be responsible for ourselves is to be responsible for the whole thing.

On this subject, poet Gary Snyder wrote in the introduction of the *Journal For The Protection of All Beings:* "Now we must become warrior-lovers in the service of the Great Goddess Gaia, Mother of the Buddha. The stakes are all of organic evolution. Any childish thoughts of transcending nature or slipping off into Space must wait on this work—really, of learning finally who and where we are, acknowledging the beauty, walking in beauty."

Ecology has shattered the old politics. Accepting the earth itself, the whales, the trees, as a part of the ultimate political constituency, creates a new political theater. That there are limits to human expansion and growth tells us that some political questions are going to be decided in a somewhat higher court than parliaments or even the United Nations: some political realities are decided by the capacity of the earth to physically support certain activities.

"Be praised, my Lord, with all your creatures, especially master brother sun, who brings day, and you give us light by him . . .
"Be praised, my Lord, for sister moon and the stars, in heaven you have made them clear and precious and lovely.
"Be praised, my Lord, for brother wind and for the air, cloudy and fair and in all weathers—by which you give sustenance to your creatures.
"Be praised, my Lord, for sister water, who is very useful and humble and rare and chaste.
"Be praised, my Lord, for brother fire . . .
"Be praised, my Lord, for sister our mother earth . . ."

ST. FRANCIS OF ASSISI

The emerging color of politics is clearly *green*. This political awareness involves a sensitivity to the limits of any human enterprise, the actual voice of the natural world, the rights of trees and rivers to exist and perform their function, the right of coyote to howl, the liberation of the earth from any exclusively human vision.

A Bio-Ethical Approach

The tenets of an earth-based political consciousness include Hegel's "unity through diversity" and Russell Means' "respect for . . . every living thing." In an effort to sketch out possible social direction stemming from these tenets, Peter Faulkner, teaching a course in "bio-ethics" at Stanford University, wrote in 1979 an essay titled "Posterity Rights," which addressed our political responsibility to future generations.

Posterity rights should have been articulated years ago. But precisely what rights should be protected? How and by whom? To prevent what kinds of wrongs? For what period of time? Finally, once these rights are translated into specific duties, what effect will their discharge have on economic and political systems, on resource consumption rates and on prospects for disarmament and permanent peace? As a first step in exploring these issues, consider three basic rights for posterity.

Unborn generations have the right:

(1) to an intact genetic heritage and to freedom from contamination by carcinogenic and mutagenic processes and substances released today,

(2) to enjoy both plant and animal wildlife in the same variety and environment existing today, and,

(3) to a proportional share of the earth's resources.

The operative effect of our three propositions is to dilate the scope of rights to include all present living things and then project that circle forward into time to form a cylinder of protection enveloping future entities. Two generic tactics may be useful in reaching this objective: elevating the standard of care and shifting the burden of proof.

"Coming, going, the waterfowl
Leaves not a trace,
Nor does it need a guide."

DOGEN, ZEN HAIKU

The Gaia Hypothesis

One of the most stirring and beautiful ideas to have emerged in our time—the Gaia Hypothesis, described as a "wedding of the traditional intuitive wisdom to contemporary scientific insight"—was first put forward by James E. Lovelock in 1975, in the book *Gaia, A New Look At Life on Earth*. Lovelock rejects the popular notion of the planet we live on as an inert lump of rock. Instead, he suggests that "the entire range of living matter on Earth, from whales to bacteria and from oaks to algae, could be regarded as constituting a single living entity . . . endowed with faculties and powers far beyond those of its constituent parts."

In other words, the world is a giant living creature that sustains us in the way a body sustains bacteria. Lovelock gives this theoretical super-being the name Gaia (pronounced like "maya"), which is the name the ancient Greeks gave to the goddess Mother Earth.

Interestingly, we have a distinguished scientist telling us in the last half of the twentieth century that the ancient Greeks were right after all. The native Indians, too.

Three Books and a Guide on the Goddess

Drawing Down the Moon: Witches, Druids, Goddess-Worshippers, and Other Pagans in America Today (Beacon, 1981), by Margot Adler.

The standard and most readable overview, the result of much traveling and research, by a journalist and priestess in a Wicca coven.

The Politics of Woman's Spirituality, Essays on the Rise of Spiritual Power Within the Feminist Movement (Anchor, 1982), edited by Charlene Spretnak.

The editor is the author of *Lost Goddesses of Early Greece: A Collection of Pre-Hellenic Myths*. The essays are of high quality and suggest that "women, with their 'new' spirituality—which is the oldest on Earth—are leading humankind beyond the patriarchal politics of hierarchy and separation."

The Spiral Dance: A Rebirth of the Ancient Religion of The Great Goddess (Harper & Row, 1979), by Starhawk.

Starhawk, feminist, therapist, witch, is a prominent spokesperson for "The Craft."

Lovelock used the techniques of gas chromotography to measure and compare the atmospheres of Mars and Earth, and made the startling discovery that while Mars had been dead for millions of years, *something* had been manipulating Earth's atmosphere during all that time, maintaining a perfect temperature for life to thrive.

"This led us," Lovelock writes, "to the formation of the proposition that living matter, the air, the oceans, the land surface, were parts of a giant system which was able to control temperature, the composition of the air and sea, the pH of the soil and so on as to be optimum for survival of the biosphere."

"To see a world in a grain of sand
And heaven in a wild flower
Hold infinity in the palm of your hand
And eternity in an hour."

WILLIAM BLAKE

Pagan Earth Rites

In the last decade or so the rise of feminism and gay liberation has led to a much-needed reexamination of the alternatives to a patriarchal male-dominated spirituality. The Women's Movement, in particular, has inspired a renewed interest in the pre-Christian pagan earth religions, which place the figures of the Goddess, and the Great Mother, at their center.

"The image of the Goddess inspires women to see ourselves as divine," writes Starhawk in *The Spiral Dance,* "our bodies as sacred, the changing phases of our lives as holy, our aggression as healthy, our anger as purifying, and our power to nurture and create—but also to limit and destroy when necessary—as the very force that sustains life. Through the Goddess, we can discover our strength, enlighten our minds, own our bodies, and celebrate our emotions. We can move beyond narrow, constricting roles and become whole."

Lovelock carries his idea one step further. He suggests that the human race, collected together as a species, is Gaia's emerging nervous system and brain. We are the planet becoming aware of itself, awakening to some kind of incredible consciousness, greater than anything any individual human could ever hope to know.

Something of this special feeling that one, indeed, is probably part of an entity *like* Gaia (at the very least) is expressed by another scientist, John A. Livingston, in his 1953 study of humanity's fancied separation from non-human nature, titled *One Cosmic Instant, A Natural History of Human Arrogance:*

> Though I do not expect that I shall be reborn directly as a crocus, I know that one day my atoms will inhabit a bacterium here, a diatom there, a nematode or a flagellate— even a crayfish or a sea cucumber. I will be here, in myriad forms, for as long as there are forms of life on Earth. I have always been here, and with a certain effort of will, *I can sometimes remember.*

In his 1979 attempt to express the awareness that had evolved in the previous decade, Theodore Roszak, the historian, published a book titled *Person/Planet* in which he stated:

> The needs of the planet are the needs of the person. And, therefore, the rights of the person are the rights of the planet. If a proper reverence for the sanctity of the Earth and the diversity of its people is the secret of peace and survival, then the adventure of self-discovery stands before us as the most practical of pleasures.

Recommended Reading

The Gift of Good Land, Wendell Berry (North Point Press, San Francisco, 1981). This collection of essays from farmer, poet, writer Wendell Berry, brings together his environmental consciousness with his sense of family and community. He speaks *from* the earth; he does not just write about nature or to nature, but has, rather, completely integrated his verse and his prose with its content and with the content of his own life.

Earth Wisdom, Dolores LaChapelle (Guild of Tutors Press, Los Angeles, CA 1978). Dolores LaChapelle is both scholar and naturalist, but much more valuable to the reader is the fact that she is an extremely sensitive observer of natural rhythms. Her insights are priceless.

Man and Nature, Seyyed Hossein Nasr (Mandala Books, Unwin Paperbacks, London, 1968, 1976). The clearest and most readable outline of the history of a natural spiritual philosophy.

Black Elk Speaks, John C. Neihardt (Lincoln: University of Nebraska Press, 1979). The poetic autobiography of Black Elk, an Oglala Sioux medicine man. His visions reflect the spirit of his era, those years marked in history by the "Messiah movement," Little Big Horn, and the Massacre at Wounded Knee.

Resources

Organizations:

Buddhists Concerned for Animals, Brad Miller, President, 300 Page St., San Francisco, CA 94102, (415)485-1495. Started by Buddhists, but open to anyone, this organization keeps a close watch and reports on animal experimentation and abuse. Publishes a newsletter.

Farallones Institute, 15290 Coleman Valley Rd., Occidental, CA 95465, (707)874-3060. A center dedicated to organic horticulture.

Greenpeace, 2007 R. St., NW, Washington, D.C. 20009, (202)-462-1177 (U.S.A. headquarters). International environmental activism organization. Publishes a quarterly newsletter, *The Examiner,* reporting on their activities and other ecological news. Free to donor list.

Sierra Club, 730 Polk St., San Francisco, CA 94109, (415)981-8634. Environmental organization that publishes a bimonthly magazine $10/year and a *National News Report Newsletter,* reporting on recent congressional and court actions on environmental issues. $15/year for thirty issues.

Publications:

Nomadic Books, P.O. Box 454, Athens, GA 30603. A service and clearinghouse of cheap travel information.

A Pilgrim's Guide to Planet Earth (Spiritual Community Publications, 1981). Compiled by the people who put out the *Spiritual Community Guide,* this one includes sacred spots, places of pilgrimage, vegetarian restaurants and meditation and growth centers around the world.

Tranet, P.O. Box 567, Rangeley, ME 04920. $30/year, six issues. A transnational network of, by, and for people who are changing the world by changing their own life-styles. A compact newsletter is chock-full of networking news about groups worldwide involved in social transformation.

Whole Earth Review (formerly *CoEvolution Quarterly*), P.O. Box 38, Sausalito, CA 94966. $20/year, four issues. An offshoot of the *Whole Earth Catalogue,* provides good information and tools for living lightly on the earth.

13

Social Action

In opposition to the U.S. war with Mexico, Henry David Thoreau refused to pay his taxes, and for this act of civil disobedience the government put him in jail.

When his friend, Ralph Waldo Emerson, offered to pay the taxes for him, Thoreau refused to allow it. Frustrated, Emerson went to the prison to visit him. "Henry," he asked, "what are you doing in there?"

Thoreau replied: "What are you doing out there?"

Thoreau's politics were a reflection of his spiritual leanings. Like Emerson, he was one of the leaders of the early American Transcendentalist Movement inspired by the European theosophists, the Upanishads of ancient India, and their own meditative visions. These beliefs had lead him to the conclusion that war, unless waged clearly for self-defense, was as wrong as killing except under those same circumstances; he reasoned that to support an injustice with money was the same as performing the injustice itself.

But as Thoreau's story so clearly illustrates, belief is not enough; we must act. Religion without action is a poor refuge for the human heart. Gandhi once said that "those who think religion and politics are not connected don't know much about politics, nor about religion."

"What good is it," questioned Jesus (James 2:18), "if a man claims to have faith but has no deeds? Can such faith save him? Suppose a brother or sister is without clothes and daily food. If one of you says to him, 'Go, I wish you well; keep warm and well fed,' but does nothing about his

"Politicians wish to move great masses of people. We do not need to move great masses of anyone. We need to let the bitterness of the moves we have already accomplished die down."

STEPHEN GASKIN

physical needs, what good is it? In the same way, faith by itself, if it is not accompanied by action, is dead."

In our own time, social scientist Barbara Ward coined the rallying cry of modern peace activists: "Think globally, act locally." In other words, our philosophies, visions or spiritual beliefs may be in the realm of unity and global connectedness, but our actions must always be specific, focused, useful at a hands-on level.

A story from the life of Buddha offers a similar perspective. When the Vedic laity came to Buddha and asked him how they could enter the heavenly abode of Brahma he explained to them that the doorways to the realm of Brahma were right here on earth and that they were four in number: we enter the highest heavenly abodes, Buddha told the people, through loving kindness (*metta*), compassion (*karuna*), sharing joy (*muditha*), and equanimity (*upekkha*). It is through service in this world, not by abandoning this world, that we attain to heavenly realms or spiritual fulfillment.

The converse is also true. Not only does spirituality require action, as all traditions agree, but effective action in the social realm requires some measure of love, or spiritual development. How spiritually motivated social action differs from the traditional kind is a big question, and is the subject of this chapter. The distinction is critical if our social interactions are to keep pace with our spiritual development.

Where to Start

What difference can one person make in a world so beset with problems and injustices and where can we begin? Mother Teresa has an answer. "We may wonder: Whom can I love and serve? Where is the face of God to whom I can pray? The answer is simple: that hungry one, that naked one, that lonely one, that unwanted one, is my brother and my sister. If we have no peace, it is because we have forgotten that we belong to each other."

Mother Teresa, not only through her words, but through her example, teaches us that we start very simply by acknowledging the suffering in the world that is right before our eyes, and by working to alleviate it. We do not need to seek a position of "power" in order to help the world. Each of us is surrounded by opportunities to serve.

Gandhi said: "Almost anything you do will seem insignificant, but it is very important that you do it." Our actions in the world are the greatest test of our insights and growth. If we can apply our spiritual insights to helping the world around us, then perhaps we really are learning something. If not, our concepts, ideas, or personal growth are surely suspect.

Spiritual Social Action

Social action, as we are talking about it here, implies a challenge to society, to the status quo, and comes out of a deep desire to see change. Spiritual social action, then, can be seen as actions motivated by a desire for change that is itself motivated not solely by material interests, but also by moral or spiritual goals. "Man cannot eat by bread alone." In our age, both capitalism and Marxism can be

"Cultivate Virtue in your self,
and Virtue will be real.
Cultivate Virtue in the family,
and Virtue will flourish.
Cultivate Virtue in the village,
and Virtue will spread.
Cultivate Virtue in the nation,
and Virtue will be abundant.
Cultivate Virtue in the world
and Virtue will triumph
everywhere."

LAO TSU

"We were Lawless people, but we were on pretty good terms with the Great Spirit."

TATANGA MANI, WALKING BUFFALO

"Instead of hating the people you think are warmakers, hate the appetites and the disorder in your own soul, which are the causes of war."

THOMAS MERTON

said to suffer from overly material interpretations of the human condition, purging from politics the creative aspirations and transcendent visions of the individual. A spiritual sociology would incorporate, and indeed derive from, these incalculable mysteries of the human spirit and the living environment.

Emmanuel Mounier, one of the founders of the European Personalists movement, broke away from the Communist Party for what he saw as the very dangerous "spiritual imperialism of the collective man." Likewise, in the United States, Martin Luther King, Jr.'s challenge to democratic capitalism was not over mere racism, but over the spiritual bankruptcy and moral hypocrisy of the system. The Benedictine monk Brother David Steindl-Rast says: "We have to put the *values* of America back in front of the American people; when people see that their country's actions are not in keeping with its professed values, then they will begin to change their actions."

Theodore Roszak suggests in *Person/Planet* that there is a middle path between collectivism and individualism, which he calls "mystical anarchism." He writes: "Anarchists of this stripe manage to ally themselves with any number of religious traditions—though, invariably, within any tradition they profess, they find their way to a characteristic kind of mysticism, to a warm, intuitive trust in the essential goodness of God, nature, and human community. They have known the darkness, but never despair. Tolstoy's Russian Orthodoxy, Buber's Hassidism, Maurin's proletarian Catholicism, Gandhi's caste-destroying Hinduism, Gary Snyder's Buddhism—all of these share the same transcendent delight in the creative possibilities of human fellowship."

Spiritual social action is the material-world manifestation of the invisible realms of emotion, interconnectedness, intuition, truth, God, Dharma, the Tao. It can be spontaneous because it is grounded in perennial values; it can be forceful because it is serving; and it heals not only the served, but the server.

Good Visions, Good Works

Good works are the social gospel that derives from the individual witnessing of one's own spirituality, one's own truth. "The essence of the Epistles of Paul," said Martin Luther King, Jr., "is that Christians should rejoice at being deemed worthy to suffer for what they believe. The projection of a social gospel, in my opinion, is the true witness of a Christian life. This is the meaning of the true *ekklesia*—the inner, spiritual church.

> "The true gentleman does not preach what he practices till he has practised what he preaches."
>
> CONFUCIUS

Dorothy Day, for example, was a lay Christian in New York City in the 1930s when she decided to put her spiritual values to work; her efforts had great political reverberations in her time. Her first step was to open soup kitchens to feed the unemployed and hungry. Her "Houses of Hospitality" flourished into a network of social activity. Once, when questioned by the FBI on the suspicion of being a subversive, Dorothy Day told her interrogators: "All I do is feed people if they are hungry and give them a place to sleep."

In 1972 Dr. Larry Brilliant was one of thousands of disillusioned young westerners traveling in India looking for spiritual meaning. In northern India he met the spiritual teacher Maharaji who taught the path of meditation and service. Inspired by this teacher, Dr. Brilliant and his wife Girija decided to devote their lives to providing medical aid to those who were in need.

They began by joining the World Health Organization, and for five years they worked toward the eradication of smallpox. Then, in 1978, they founded SEVA (Sanskrit: "service") with the goal of eradicating preventable blindness worldwide. They started in Nepal. During their first five years, with low overhead and efficient techniques, they were able to perform thousands of simple four-minute cataract operations at a cost of less than $5 each. Their foundation, entirely financed by donations, was able to cure the average trachoma case for fifty cents worth of antibiotic ointment; $2 would provide sufficient vitamin A to protect a child from malnutrition through childhood. SEVA has not only helped millions of people directly, it has shown other world medical organizations by example how inexpensive medical treatment can be when motivated by love and service.

Diane August, 49, was attending a meeting of the Association for Humanistic Psychology in 1982 when the discussions of higher consciousness and world peace motivated her to do something that would implement these ideals. She made small blue lapel ribbons, which she handed out to people as a show of support for the United Nations session on disarmament in June of that year. Within weeks, orders were pouring in through the mail. She then saved $2,000 and invested it in rolls of blue ribbon and some office supplies. Diane began to provide the ribbons to peace groups who sold them for a dollar. Women's Strike for Peace raised $1300 in one day selling ribbons, and many other groups literally supported themselves on the proceeds from the ribbons. A small idea blossomed into a nationwide symbol of support for disarmament.

The Mahayana Buddhists take a vow to work for the liberation of all sentient beings from suffering. The Buddhists at the Zen Center in San Francisco took this vow seriously and formed the organization Buddhists Concerned For Animals. They have taken on the University of California at Berkeley laboratories, the U.S. military, and

"It is no use walking anywhere to preach unless our walking is our preaching."

ST. FRANCIS OF ASSISI

"My greatest weapon is mute prayer."

MAHATMA GANDHI

commercial industries for mistreatment of animals and fla-
grant disregard of animal rights legislation. They have fi-
nanced legal briefs, organized rallies, and sponsored
conferences all in an effort to bring their spiritual beliefs
into practice.

Molly Rush, a mother of six from suburban Pitts-
burgh, got involved with the antinuclear campaign when
she just couldn't ignore the facts anymore. "This nuclear
arms race is not way out there," she realized. "It will
certainly touch my children's lives if something isn't done
about it." She said that she got to the point where she
couldn't look her children in the eyes, knowing what she
knew.

Her decision to act came at a Catholic retreat in Cleve-
land led by Dan Berrigan. She took the message from the
Epistle of James (1:22) to heart: "Only be sure that you
act on the message and do not merely listen; for that would
be to mislead yourselves." She and seven others, including
Dan and Phil Berrigan, staged a protest at the General
Electric Weapons plant at King of Prussia, Pennsylvania.
The group, known as the Plowshare Eight, was taken to
court, and Rush spent two and a half months in prison.

Her spiritual beliefs helped her through the ordeal of
prison: "The more they took away from me," she reported,

"The greatest challenge of the day is: how to bring about a revolution of the heart, a revolution which has to start with each one of us."

DOROTHY DAY

"Progress must be quite gradual, and in order to obtain such progress in public opinion and in the mores of the people, it is necessary for the personality to acquire influence and weight. This comes about through careful and constant work on one's own moral development."

THE *I CHING*

"the more free I felt." The real prison, she suggests, is not physical confinement, but the self-imposed spiritual confinement of feeling hopeless and powerless. In taking personal responsibility, choosing her own course of action and following it, Rush found that this sense of despair has been replaced by a sense of peace and hope. "It's a very mysterious thing," she explained. "I don't feel optimistic. I don't think it's possible to be optimistic, looking at the hard realities. But hope is a refusal to despair in the face of a despairing situation. And I do feel hope."

Her message to those who find themselves in a despairing frame of mind is: "Free yourself. Let yourself do what you know is right, and it will be all right. . . . Don't think beyond the first step; just take that one, and maybe the next one will be a little easier. That's been my experience."

Creating the New Society

Societies are not fixed, complete, or static structurings of individuals; they are in constant flux. Those institutions that resist change eventually fall away like old skeletons. In a sense, people are continually creating a new society, and individuals, groups of individuals, and masses of individuals all participate in shaping the winding road through history that this creation makes.

Nevertheless, the social contract that we make with our neighbors, in exchange for the support and comfort of community, has terms, rules; we agree to behave in certain ways, and not in others. Changes within society are changes with this contract.

Social action, be it voting, protest, letter writing, or revolution, is a process of reshaping the terms of our social relationships. Spiritually motivated social action is no different in this; it seeks to inculcate certain values in a society where those values are seen to be lacking.

Here, of course, we enter difficult territory because our values necessarily differ. We cannot afford to be stymied by the fact that values differ from person to person or from culture to culture; rather, while honoring our differences we must look for those places where our values unite or are compatible. For this kind of social action implies certain elements that cut across all cultural barriers: vision, value judgments, discrimination—a stand for what one feels is safe, useful and nurturing in a society, and a stand against what one feels is dangerous and destructive of both the material world and the human spirit.

"The world of tomorrow," says Ali Mazrui, African researcher of world order, "can be tamed either through outside force or through shared values. The transmission of values and their internalization are more relevant for world reform than the establishment of formal institutions for external control."

In *New Age Politics* Mark Satin articulates some of the ethics and values that would likely form the platform of a new society in harmony with diverse spiritual beliefs. He sites four "New Age ethics" as (1) the self-development ethic, the right to pursue our spiritual growth; (2) the ecology ethic, finding a harmony between human society and all other forms of life; (3) the self-reliance/cooperation ethic that realizes both the need to be able to care for oneself as well as the natural interdependence that we share with others; and (4) the nonviolence ethic.

"If we could share this world
below,
If we could learn to love . . .
If we could share this world below,
We'd need no world above."

RAY FARADAY NELSON

"Nothing is more distinctive of the
Old Being than the separation of
man from man. Nothing is more
passionately demanded than social
healing. This is our ultimate
concern and should be the infinite
passion of every human being in
every age. To bring about the New
Creation and to do that now, with
ourselves first. This alone matters.
In comparison everything else—
religious, education, economics,
politics—matters very little—and
ultimately not at all."

PAUL TILLICH

Ends and Means

The manner in which spiritually motivated social action addresses change differs significantly from social action based on materialism and power. "Such tasks as disarmament or control of nuclear weapons are difficult to achieve through anger, hatred," advises the Dalai Lama. "The question of survival of mankind depends on kindness and love. These are the universal religion."

"Will you end wars by asking men to trust men who evidently cannot be trusted?" asked Benedictine monk Thomas Merton in his journal. "No. Teach them to love and trust God; then they will be able to love the men they cannot trust, and will dare to make peace with them, not trusting in them but in God. For only love—which means humility—can cast out the fear which is the root of all war."

Both the Dalai Lama and Thomas Merton teach that in healing our societies our end, our goal, our vision, does not justify our means. Rather, our means must be exemplary of our goal. "Live the revolution now," is the credo of the Quaker-inspired Movement For a New Society in Philadelphia. They set up alternative community services not provided by the government. They believe this is far more efficient than trying to lobby the government to do work that they can do themselves.

The utopian "tomorrow," which we so easily fall into waiting for, never comes. Life is a succession of todays, and it is the quality of our lives today, more than any particular strategy for reform, that determines what tomorrow will be like. People are beginning to realize that if we are going to create a new society, then we must do so with the same values and integrity that we want to see incorporated in that society.

The methods we use, the tactics, the way we form our organizations, the way we communicate—in short, our *means*—must carry the essence of our vision's end. Our work starts with ourselves, aligning our personal lives with our values, but it does not stop there. We must take care to continue keeping our actions faithful to our values as we move them out into society.

Aligning Ends and Means

The following list may give some examples of how we can begin to align our goals with our actions:

If we want to see:	*We must learn to:*
1. the world's abundance shared	1. live more simply
2. ecological harmony	2. become conservers rather than consumers
3. world peace	3. develop non-aggression
4. equal rights shared by all	4. overcome personal prejudices
5. a world family	5. put no restrictions on our openness and love

Shambhala

The idea of a society built on high ideals is hardly a new one. Most societies at least profess high ideals. In Tibet there is the story of Shambhala, the city of the great lost enlightened society. The tenets of Shambhala were the natural qualities of compassion, generosity, mindfulness, and wisdom that arise from minds at peace with their own passions and fears.

In our times, Tibetan Buddhist teacher Chogyam Trungpa Rinpoche has revived the idea of Shambhala, or the enlightened society, as not only an ancient myth, but as a living vision, an ideal toward which we can apply ourselves now.

This is not to say, however, that models of such societies do not already exist. The American Indian cultures, for example, all share the common trait of being built upon spiritual knowledge rather than social science, devoid of spirit. "We don't make any separation between religion and the rest of our life," says Oglala Lakota chief Matthew King. "There are special times of year when we have ceremonies or go into the hills to seek visions, but our real religion is living the right way every day. An Indian leader

"The best possible work has not yet been done. If I were twenty-one today I would elect to join the communicating network of those young people, the world over, who recognize the urgency of life-supporting change, knowledge joined to action: knowledge about what man has been and is, can protect the future.

"There is hope in seeing the human adventure as a whole and in the shared trust that knowledge about mankind, sought in reverence for life, can bring to life."

Margaret Mead

"Music attracts the angels in the universe."

BOB DYLAN

doesn't have special privilege like in America or in Europe; an Indian leader lives like the rest of the people. We teach our children how to walk in a sacred manner on this earth; then there is no room in the society for evil."

There are many modern examples of spiritual social action being applied to community development; one of the most strikingly successful is the *Shramadana* movement in Sri Lanka. In 1958 Buddhist high-school teacher A. T. Ariyaratna took a handful of his students and started community work camps in the poorest of outcaste villages. Based on the precept of generosity, the students and community members would give their labor for such projects as building roads and bridges, landscaping, digging irrigation ditches, or building schools. The movement spread to over 4000 towns and villages, and is now the largest nongovernmental organization in the country, offering a model of development that is self-reliant and culturally stabilizing. Ariyaratna named the movement *Sarvodaya Shramadana Sangamaya,* which means "Awakening the Community through sharing our energy."

In 1978 American social activist Joanna Macy traveled to Sri Lanka to learn firsthand about the movement. "People do wake up by giving," she explains. "I am convinced that the chief strength of the movement lies in the fact that it asks people what they can give, rather than what they want to get. This is empowering to people. Even if all you can give is a betel leaf or a matchbox of rice, you walk differently on the earth as a bestower."

The examples thus exist—in legend, history, in practice and in theory and vision—that point the way to Shambhala, to the enlightened society. We are not bound by the circumstances of our lives, by history, nor by some mythical "human nature" that precludes a healthy society where people live in peace. We are free to create that new society.

We are not powerless. When one person believes something, and acts on that belief, others of like mind will be found. When enough people believe and act on that belief, the vision begins to take form. "I refuse to accept the cynical notion," said Martin Luther King, Jr., "that nation after nation must spiral down a militaristic stairway into the hell of nuclear destruction. I believe that unarmed truth and unconditional love will have the final word in reality."

Recommended Reading

Social Action

On the Duty of Civil Disobedience, Henry David Thoreau (Peace News, 1963). This is the classic American essay on the citizen's responsibility to follow his or her spiritual ideals in the face of unjust laws. Deeds, not words, urges Thoreau.

New Age Politics: Healing Self & Society, Mark Satin (Dell, 1979). A survey of the modern union between self and society as a political force and a practical guide to a new political platform based upon new-age ethics.

New Genesis: Shaping A Global Spirituality, Robert Muller (Doubleday, 1982). An inspiring call to world peace built on spiritual principles by the Assistant Secretary-General of the United Nations and former French resistance fighter.

The Best Books on Nonviolence

Non-violence in Peace and War, Mohandas K. Gandhi (Garland Pub., Ahmedabad, India, 1948 and 1949). Gandhi's most complete treatment of the subject.

Leading Edge: A Bulletin of Social Change, Box 42050, 4717 N. Figueroa St., Los Angeles, CA 90042. An excellent guide to indicators of social transformation the world over.

A.F.S.C. (American Friends Service Committee, 1501 Cherry St., Philadelphia, PA 19102, (215)241-7000. A Quaker-based organization dedicated to social change. Publishes a newsletter, $10/year for eleven issues.

Interhelp, P.O. Box 331, Northampton, MA 01061, (413)586-6311. A network whose purpose is to provide people with the opportunity to experience and share their deepest responses to the dangers which threaten the planet. Sponsors workshops and trainings and publishes a newsletter. $10/year for ten issues.

Oxfam America, 115 Broadway, Boston, MA 02116, (617)482-1211. An international agency for self-help development and disaster relief in 30 poor countries. Newsletter, free to donors.

The Peace Project, 1770 King St., Santa Cruz, CA 95060, (408)-425-5061. Facilitates psychological and spiritual peace work. Materials on prayer and meditation and peace.

Plenty U.S.A., P.O. Box 90, Summertown, TN 38483 (615)964-3992. A nongovernmental organization dedicated to creative collaboration in the areas of community development, village-scale technology, and environmental protection, with a special concern for indigenous peoples.

Seva Foundation, Central office, 108 Springlake Dr., Chelsea, MI 48118 (313)475-1351; regional office, 1301 Henry Street, Berkeley, CA 94709. An international network to relieve suffering through health and service projects in India, Nepal, Guatemala, Mexico, the U.S., and elsewhere. Seva is sanskrit for "service." Publishes newsletter and gift catalog with its Canadian sister organization, *Seva Service Society,* P.O. Box 33807, Station D, Vancouver, B.C., V6J 4L6, Canada, (604)733-4284.

Resurgence, Worthyvale, Manor Farm, Camelford, Cornwall, PL 32 9 TT, United Kingdom, $20/year, $27.50 airmail, six issues. Inspired by E. F. Schumacher and now edited by Satish Kumar, an Indian peace activist, this magazine looks at peace, ecology and social action from a spiritual perspective.

14

Inner Guidance

In *The Three Pillars of Zen* Philip Kapleau recounts the following story about the Zen master Ikkyu:

One day a man of the people said to Zen Master Ikkyu: "Master, will you please write for me some maxims of the highest wisdom?"

Ikkyu immediately took his brush and wrote the word "Attention."

"Is that all?" asked the man. "Will you not add something more?"

Ikkyu then wrote twice running: "Attention. Attention."

"Well," remarked the man rather irritably, "I really don't see much depth or subtlety in what you have just written."

Then Ikkyu wrote the same word three times running: "Attention. Attention. Attention."

Half-angered, the man demanded: "What does that word 'Attention' mean anyway?"

And Ikkyu answered gently: "Attention means attention."

Paying attention may seem like a very simple thing, but when we look at how our minds actually work, it becomes apparent that, in fact, we pay attention much less than we might think. "For the ordinary man, whose mind is a checkerboard of crisscrossing reflections, opinions, and prejudices," comments Philip Kapleau, "bare attention is virtually impossible; his life is thus centered not on reality itself but in his ideas about it."

"Meditation is not a means to an end. It is both the means and the end."

J. KRISHNAMURTI

"We are sick with a fascination for the useful tools of names and numbers, of symbols, signs, conceptions and ideas. Meditation is therefore the art of suspending verbal and symbolic thinking for a time, somewhat as a courteous audience will stop talking when a concert is about to begin."

ALAN WATTS

"[There is a type of dancer who can] convert the body into a luminous fluidity, surrendering it to the inspiration of the soul. This . . . sort of dancer understands that the body, by force of the soul, can in fact be converted to a luminous fluid. The flesh becomes light and transparent, as shown through the X-ray—but with the difference that the human soul is lighter than these rays. When, in its divine power, it completely possesses the body, it converts that into a luminous moving cloud and thus can manifest itself in the whole of its divinity."

ISADORA DUNCAN

Nearly all spiritual practices are based on attention. In fact, whenever you think you have lost the path, or whenever you feel confused by esoteric terminology or technique, remember that all these techniques or teachings are various ways to help you learn to pay attention.

The highest wisdom, as Ikkyu insists, is based on attention—as are all forms of spiritual practices and exercises—from the simplest meditation to the most complex visualization.

Meditation, for example, is based on attention to the workings of the mind.

Prayer is based on attention to the presence of the sacred in life, and to the thoughts that express our longing for relationship with that presence.

The martial arts, Hatha Yoga, and spiritual dance are based on attention to spirit moving through the body.

And the disciplines of inner guidance are based on attention to the wisdom of the "still, small voice within."

Attention may seem at first like a very ordinary thing. But it is the cornerstone of the spiritual life. In fact, we could say that paying attention is the essence of true spirituality.

When we pay attention, whatever we are doing—whether it be cooking, cleaning or making love—is transformed and becomes a part of our spiritual path. We begin to notice details and textures that we never noticed before; everyday life becomes clearer, sharper, and at the same time more spacious.

Pray as You Are Used to Doing

There was once a Sheik who heard about a holy man who prayed constantly. This man lived on an island, and the Sheik decided to visit him. When he arrived he found a poor and simple fisherman. True, he moved his lips as if in constant prayer, but his manner of saying the prayers was all wrong.

The Sheik corrected the man, who listened patiently, and then repeated the words as the Sheik had explained them. Finally, he humbly thanked the Sheik, who boarded his boat to return to his town. The Sheik was just thinking to himself what a fine service he had done this ignorant fellow, when his disciples all turned toward the island with a look of astonishment. There, walking on water, he saw the fisherman approaching rapidly. When he got within hearing, the fisherman called out, "Excuse me, Sir, but I have forgotten some of the words. Could you please instruct me again?"

The Sheik could not believe his eyes. "No, no," he called out. "Forget what I taught you. Just go on praying as you are used to doing."

Bare Attention

Most of us have come to identify completely with our thoughts. Thus, becoming aware of our thoughts and emotions is the first step to learning how to truly pay attention.

In the practice of what might be called "basic meditation," especially as practiced by Buddhists, we train ourselves to pay attention to what is. This kind of attention is called *bare attention*—attention that sees clearly without indulging in distracting thoughts.

Concentrating on breathing is the most common method of focusing attention in meditation, but many other things can also be used as a focus. Some approaches, such as mantra meditation popularized by TM, use words and sound; others use images or visualizations; and still others use external objects to focus on, such as a candle flame, or a flower, or the moon at night. Sometimes the flow of

thoughts itself or the ever changing sensations of the body are used as the focus of attention.

Most meditation teachers recommend beginning by using some simple object as an aid, but the important thing to remember is that it is not the particular object or technique that matters. What's important is the process of bringing one's mind back to its object of focus when it wanders. It's important to do this gently and without judgment, by the way. Meditation takes effort, but it is not a war. It is a way of making friends with yourself.

Attention Is Its Own Reward

Meditation has many benefits, but if we practice meditation in order to attain a specific goal—even if that goal is as worthy as attaining a "higher" state—we are not truly meditating.

The purpose of meditation, paradoxically, is to learn to be without purpose. Since nearly everything we do in life is done with some goal in mind, most of our actions are only means towards an end, pointing us continually towards a future that does not yet exist. But meditation, when no goal disturbs it, allows us to discover the richness and profundity of the present moment. We begin to realize the miraculous power of our own lives—not as they will be, or as we might imagine they once were at some golden time in the past, but as they actually are. Meditation is one of the few things in life that is not about *doing* but about *being*.

In an essay called "The Practice of Meditation," Alan Watts echoes this thought: "The practice of meditation," he says, "is not what is ordinarily meant by practice, in the sense of repetitious preparation for some future performance. It may seem odd and illogical to say that meditation in the form of yoga, Dhyana, or zazen, as used by Hindus and Buddhists, is a practice without purpose—in some future time—because it is the art of being completely centered in the here and now. . . ."

Watts goes on to give basic instructions on meditation, commenting on the depth of this seemingly simple practice:

> Simply sit down, close your eyes, and listen to all sounds that may be going on—without trying to name or identify them. Listen as you would listen to music. If you find that verbal thinking will not drop away, don't attempt to stop it by force of willpower. Just keep your tongue relaxed, floating easily in the lower jaw, and listen to your thoughts as if they were birds chattering outside—mere noise in the skull—and they will eventually subside of themselves, as a turbulent and muddy pool will become calm and clear if left alone.
>
> Also, become aware of breathing and allow your lungs to work in whatever rhythm seems congenial to them. And for a while just sit listening and feeling breath. But, if pos-

"The mind which responds with conditioned automatic likes and dislikes is dominated by reactive pleasure and pain. With training, this conditioned reactivity is reduced, and the mind gradually becomes less reactive and more calm. As such, it becomes more easy to control and remains unperturbed in the face of an increasingly broad range of experience. Finally, it is said to be able to encompass all experiences and to allow 'the one thousand beatific and one thousand horrible visions' to pass before it without disturbance. Of such a mind it is said,

> Pleasure-pain
> praise and blame
> fame and shame
> loss and gain
> are all the same."

DR. ROGER WALSH

sible, don't *call* it that. Simply experience the nonverbal happening. You may object that this is not "spiritual" meditation but mere attention to the "physical" world, but it should be understood that the spiritual and the physical are only ideas, philosophical conceptions, and that the reality of which you are now aware is not an idea. Furthermore, there is no "you" aware of it. That was also just an idea. Can you hear yourself listening?

In the classic *Zen Mind, Beginner's Mind,* Shunryu Suzuki-Roshi, the late Zen master of the San Francisco Zen Center makes a series of similar observations:

When we practice zazen our mind always follows our breathing. When we inhale, the air comes into the inner world. When we exhale, the air goes out to the outer world. The inner world is limitless, and the outer world is also limitless. We say "inner world" or "outer world," but actually there is just one whole world. In this limitless world, our throat is like a swinging door. The air comes in and goes out like someone passing through a swinging door. If you think, "I breathe," the "I" is extra. There is no you to say "I." What we call "I" is just a swinging door which moves when we inhale and when we exhale. It just moves; that is all. When your mind is pure and calm enough to follow this movement, there is nothing: no "I," no world, no mind nor body, just a swinging door.

Retreats

In a spiritual practice, quantity sometimes means quality. After some experience with a contemplative practice, it is worthwhile to set aside time for a longer length of uninterrupted practice. Such a retreat might last one day—from sunrise to sunset, for example—a weekend, a week, or even longer. Zen centers and other contemplative centers often offer structured retreats lasting from one day to three months.

Retreats allow you to go more deeply into your practice. They also have a way of intensifying the mind, so that emotions and reactions, both positive and negative, have a way of becoming magnified. Remember this—and, as always, be gentle with yourself.

Awakened States

From one point of view, then, there is neither purpose nor meaning to spiritual discipline. Life is sufficient in itself and the practice of meditation or contemplation regardless of results is its own reward.

From another point of view, however, the purpose of "attention" is to produce "awareness" and thereby reach or uncover the "awakened" state of mind Watts and Suzuki describe. Many sages and teachers have spoken of this state as "mystical" consciousness. William James, in that classic of the perennial philosophy, *The Varieties of Religious Experience*, puts the matter this way:

> The further limits of our being plunge, it seems to me, into an altogether other dimension of existence from the sensible and merely "understandable" world. Name it the mystical region, or the supernatural region, whichever you choose. . . . We belong (to it) in a more intimate sense than that in which we belong to the visible world. . . . The unseen region in question is not merely ideal, for it produces effect in this world. When we commune with it, work is actually done upon our finite personality . . . and consequences in the way of conduct follow in the natural world upon our regenerative change. But that which produces effects within another reality must be termed a reality itself, so I feel as if we had no philosophic excuse for calling the unseen or mystical world unreal. . . . The whole drift of my education goes to persuade me that the world of our present consciousness is but one out of many worlds of consciousness that exist, and that those worlds must contain experiences which have a meaning for our life also; and that although in the main their experiences and those of this world keep discrete, yet the two become continuous at certain points, and higher energies filter in. . . . We can experience union with *something* larger than ourselves and in that union find our greatest peace.

This awakening, or mystical consciousness, whatever we might call it, leads paradoxically back to our own world, the world of everyday life, a world which we find to our surprise is at once different and the same.

"If the heart wanders or is distracted, bring it back to the point quite gently. . . . And even if you did nothing during the whole of your hour but bring your heart back, though it went away every time you brought it back, your hour would be very well employed."

ST. FRANCIS DE SALE

Where and When to Meditate

In many ways, meditation seems to go against the grain of our busy lives. Some meditators find it helpful to set aside a special place for practice—either a small room or a corner of your study or bedroom. It is best to keep your meditation place simple and clean: an uncluttered space inspires an uncluttered mind. Your space may be nothing more than a comfortable straightbacked chair, or meditation cushion (called a zafu in Japanese Zen), facing a blank wall, or it might include a small shrine or altar holding a candle, incense, or perhaps a representation of whatever figure inspires and connects you to the practice of meditation. An image of the Buddha, for example, or Jesus, or a teacher, can remind you of the journey you have set out on.

In most practices, meditation is done in a relaxed and upright sitting position, one which is neither too rigid nor too relaxed. As in all aspects of meditation practice, an attitude of alert relaxation is best. If the cross-legged position is uncomfortable, try a straight-backed chair or a meditation bench or pillow. In Zen meditation, sitting is interspersed with a walking meditation, in which one walks slowly, hands folded, and continues to focus on the out-breath or on walking itself. Lying down is generally not recommended because you might fall asleep.

It can be helpful to set aside a definite time for daily practice. It helps to start each day with a period of meditation, but twilight and evening, before retiring, are also good times to meditate as long as you are not too tired.

Regularity of practice matters more than when or how long you practice. There will always be times when it seems that you are too busy to sit down and do "nothing." At these times, try and sit anyhow, if only for five minutes. More often than not, you will find that the five minutes turns into ten or fifteen—and you will probably get more done than if you had skipped your daily practice.

What To Do After Meditation

When you meditate regularly, you will find that you bring the qualities of mind you develop in meditation into your everyday life. Zen Buddhists think of the daily activity after meditation as a kind of "moving meditation," and they practice bare attention during work and other activity. "By focusing the mind wholly on each object and every action," says Philip Kapleau, "zazen strips it of extraneous thoughts and allows us to enter into full rapport with life."

In *The Myth of Freedom,* Chogyam Trungpa Rinpoche says, "Sitting practice needs to be combined with an awareness practice in everyday life. In awareness practice you begin to feel the aftereffects of sitting meditation. Your simple relationship with breathing and your simple relationship with thoughts continues. And every situation of life becomes a simple relationship—a simple relationship with your car, a simple relationship with your father, mother, children."

Prayer: Attention to the Word

One thing we humans do very well is talk. We talk to our friends, our lovers, our business associates, our enemies. Much of the time we talk to ourselves, and sometimes we even talk to God—or however we think of the spiritual force in our lives.

"Prayer is a relationship flowing out of love, with another Person or Persons."

M. BASIL PENNINGTON

"You see, the whole world is praying all the time. The animals and even the leaves on the trees are praying. The way to receive light from God is through praying. The only difference is that some people pray unconsciously, some pray consciously, some pray super-consciously. You can walk into a restaurant and see a person who says, 'I'm so hungry. I need some soup.' Deep down his soul is praying to God, 'God, please give me life, I'm at the end.'"

SCHLOMO CARLBACH

Talking in this sense is called prayer. It need not be formal—in fact any verbal articulation or utterance that is spiritual in nature might be called prayer: a poem, a song, mantra, a cry from the depths, a spontaneous thanksgiving or blessing.

The essential and distinctive element of prayer, says M. Basil Pennington, a Trappist monk and leader of the Contemplative Reawakening in Christianity, is that prayer is "a relationship flowing out of love, with another Person or Persons." Prayer is thus a reaching out beyond ourselves—to God, the Presence, a helper like a saint, or Bodhisattva, or to something nameless, the universe at large.

Prayer is also a way of joining together with others in community, recognizing our common spiritual kinship. Prayer is praising as well as asking, praise of what is most High and Praiseworthy. ("Let everything that breathes praise the Lord!" sings the one-hundred-and-fiftieth Psalm.)

Prayer is finally not separate from our deepest being. "You are prayer," says Father Edward Hays, a young American who has done much to bring contemplative prayer back to life. "You are a special and sacred word of God made flesh. To pronounce your own unique word is to pray the most beautiful—if not the holiest—of prayers."

Four Ways of Centering

Contributed by Hazel Henderson

I have four basic ways that I use to center myself.

1. The first is to be in my garden. It's my very secret, spiritual place. It's not that large, but it's very beautiful. I find that being in the garden gets me in touch with my basic spiritual yearning, which is to feel at one with the planet and the universe. Lying in the sun, planting trees, just generally being in the garden gets me right out of the everyday world into one of the spirit.

2. The next thing I find nourishing is hanging out on my back porch with friends I really care about, sharing poetry. I love the English romantics like Shelley and Keats, but my very, very first friend in the poetry world was Omar Khayyam, the eleventh-century Persian tentmaker. His book, *The Rubaiyat of Omar Khayyam*, is

a gem of distilled wisdom. That old man has talked to me across the centuries as long as I can remember.

3. Then there is dancing. I find I have to dance almost every day; I basically just fling myself around. I like to dance to reggae music outside in the sun in the early mornings with the birds singing. I learned this from Jean Houston. I always have danced, but I used to feel slightly odd about it—having to push back all of the chairs in the living room when we lived in a cold climate. But Jean said, "Gosh, no. All of this nonlinear body movement is really very good for you. The whirling dervishes really knew what they were doing."

4. The other thing that is wonderful for me is something I just learned ten years ago—splashing paint on canvases. Like most people, I was acculturated to be a consumer of other people's art. And I would save up my money and buy "approved" art at little print shops. One day I went to a shop to buy some approved sort of print when I walked past piles of squishy tubes of acrylic paint and different size canvases. Instead of spending the money on the print, I bought an armful of tubes of acrylic paint and a canvas and went home and had a go. I have never stopped doing that since. I have no technique, of course. It's just the primary delight of playing with color and texture. I had no idea what fun it would be to throw paint around. I become totally absorbed, completely quiet, and utterly joyous.

Ms. Henderson is a futurist and the author of *Creating Alternative Futures: The End of Economics*.

Dreams as Inner Guidance

"Since ancient times, dreams have been honored as a source of wisdom and guidance in life," says Frances Vaughan in *Awakening Intuition*. "Messages from the gods, later translated as messages from the unconscious, have come through dreams in all cultures." By consciously working with our dreams we can gain access to self-knowledge that is there for the asking.

Dreams can also be used to work out unconscious fears and life challenges. Lucid dreams are ones in which you are conscious that you are dreaming. "When you have a lucid dream," says Vaughan, "you can change it and shape it in any way you wish. Learning to control your dreams takes time and requires patience, but the rewards make it worthwhile. For example, you can decide to confront a threatening figure in a dream instead of running away, and see what happens. The effects of working consciously in your dreams are not limited to changing your dream reality. When you change your dreams, your waking-consciousness also changes. Conversely, if you make changes in your waking life and consciousness, your dreams will change because dreams and waking life reflect each other."

Societies that consciously bring their dream world into active interplay with the waking world display a remarkable absence of social aggression.

In 1935 psychologist Kilton Stewart met an isolated jungle tribe in Malaya known as the Senoi. These people had been practicing dream control techniques and social dream therapy for many generations with the result that their culture had virtually eradicated hostile behavior.

From childhood, the Senoi learn to interpret their dreams, express their dreams socially, and use the dreams to balance social anxieties and needs.

The Senoi claimed that there had not been a violent crime or intercommunal conflict in their society for three hundred years. The visionary novel, *The Kin of Ata Are Waiting For You* by Dorothy Bryant, based on such a society, is a description of life where the spiritual path, daily life, and the dream world meet.

Inner Guidance

Silence is one of the most important qualities of the spiritual life, for only when we are silent can we begin to hear the voice that is truly our own—what the Quakers call "the still small voice within." This is the sound one mystic has referred to as "the Spirit of Life that is always speaking to our souls."

The source of this voice—which may be without sound, and yet is heard—is called by many different names: the inner guide, guardian angel, spirit guide, the collective unconscious, or just plain intuition. Actually all of us hear the whisperings of this inner voice every single day of our lives, but many ignore it.

According to Carl Jung, intuition is one of our four basic psychological functions, along with thinking, feeling, and sensing. It might seem, as Francis Vaughan says in her book *Awakening Intuition,* that some people have more intuition than others, but as Vaughan says, "it is potentially available to everyone. Some people choose to develop it, others do not."

The best way to develop your ability to contact the inner guide is through practice, says Robbie Gass, a psychotherapist and musician who teaches workshops on how to get in touch with your inner wisdom. "Like an ability or muscle," he says, "hearing your inner wisdom is strengthened by doing it. The key to this practice is to act upon what you hear. It is the repeated experience of acting on inner guidance and seeing the positive impact, that builds this connection and your trust in it."

Gass has developed a simple four-step process to use for developing your ability to receive inner guidance:

Centering

In order to gain access to your inner wisdom you have to be quiet. "Your inner knowing is like a mirrorlike pool of water," says Gass. "The unquiet mind is like ripples on the surface of the pool. This distorts any image you may receive." Any process of quieting your mind and relaxing will work for this first step. If you are especially angry or anxious, centering will probably take a longer time; take the time to do it. There is really no point in going on to the next step until you do.

Asking

Now, ask a simple direct question, he suggests. "Use questions that could be answered in one or two simple phrases." The more precise you are about what it is you want to know, the more likely you are to get a clear answer. Fuzzy questions or loaded questions like "Why is everyone unfair to me?" produce fuzzy answers.

Receiving

Then simply listen for an answer to come. Listening is not quite the right word, for information comes in many different forms, says Gass. "Some people hear words, others see symbols or graphic pictures. Some people actually see printed words, others feel body sensations, feelings or energy, or simply hard-to-describe experiences of just knowing."

The first information you receive is usually the clearest, he says. "The information you are asking for already exists; you are not figuring it out, but rather just connecting to it. When the answer seems to come instantaneously, as if it just pops out, this is usually a good indication that it is clear information." It's important at this point to pay very close attention. "Record the information or experience faithfully either in your mind or by writing it down, making sure you don't alter or interpret what you receive."

Application

Now you have to decide how you are going to apply this information in your life. Once your rational mind jumps back into the ring, the inner message is open to all manner of misinterpretation. Says Gass: "After we receive

"You know, when you have no money and you really need a cup of coffee, you pray, 'God, please give me a quarter for a cup of coffee. I'm really at the end.' But when you have a thousand dollars you don't remember to pray for a quarter. What's so special is when you have the money and you still remember to ask God to give. There was a holy rabbi who even when the food was on the table in front of him, before he'd eat it he'd pray, 'Please, God, feed me.'"

SCHLOMO CARLBACH

inner wisdom, other parts of the mind typically try to interpret or make sense out of it. This is a major source of distortion. For example, imagine asking for guidance about a relationship . . . and you see an image of the two of you stepping back from each other. Now your mind steps in and says, 'Oh, we're not supposed to be together. I knew it! My inner guidance is telling me not to see this person again!' That particular interpretation is not necessarily indicated by the inner message. The image may equally have been suggesting that more space is needed in the context of being *in* the relationship. Inner images are often symbolic, representing inner states rather than prescriptions for a particular action. Recording the message just after you receive it helps differentiate between the guidance and interpretation."

How to Tell the Good From the Bad

The biggest conflict people face in trying to use their inner wisdom is how to evaluate the quality of the messages they receive—how can you tell the clear information from the amalgam of projections of fears and desires within you? To help learn the difference, Frances Vaughan suggests keeping a record of your hunches in a journal. "In this way you can check up on yourself, to see how often your hunches turn out to be accurate."

There is another and more subtle sense in which we can determine the validity of our inner wisdom. Says Gass: "To me, inner knowing feels different from our projections, desires, fears and fantasies. When the inner voice stops and interpretation begins, there is a noticeable shift in the tone and quality of the mental processes." In their book *Higher Creativity*, Willis Harman and Howard Rheingold call this state "that feeling of being true though not demonstrable."

William James terms this state "noetic" truth—a feeling of absolute inner certainty that something is true in the absence of concrete proof. Harman and Rheingold say that "some rare states involve a kind of 'knowing' which although it might not be verifiable by objective means, carries such a strength of conviction that the person who experiences such a state is, and remains, convinced of the validity of that knowledge."

Dance

In India Shiva is also called Nataraja, the King of Dancers, and is said to have danced the world into creation. Perhaps more than any other art form, we can say that dance joins us to creation. When we dance in a circle (one of the most widely danced forms), we dance with the earth around the sun. We dance for joy, to reenact myths, to welcome the God in our bodies, to worship, to woo, to gather power and courage for the hunt.

The famous dances of the Mevlevi (Whirling Dervishes) are a highly disciplined form of meditation. "I can teach you how to turn in three months," said one sheik, "but it can take the rest of one's life to learn the Turn." (For an introduction to the Whirling Dervishes read: *The Whirling Dervishes* by Ira Friedlander.)

The Sufi-inspired Dances of Universal Peace (generally known as Sufi Dancing) were designed by the late Murshid Samuel Lewis (affectionately called "Sufi Sam") to bring the dances of the Sufi Whirling Dervishes to a larger public. According to Khalif Saadi Klotz, dance instructor at San Francisco's Center of the Study of Spiritual Dance and Walk, "One of the fundamentals of dance as a spiritual or esoteric practice rests in the idea of breaking down of the ego or thought of self—that the small self can be lost in a grand movement or ecstasy as well as in complete repose or meditation. The other fundamental lies in the quality of devotion or repetition of a sacred phrase (preferably with mantric value)—whether that phrase be Allah, Ram, Sita, or another."

The Dances of Universal Peace are drawn from traditional Sufi dancing as well as other traditions, such as Shaker dancing. Says Saadi Klotz, "As Murshid Samuel Lewis envisioned, the practice of the Dances would not only benefit the dancers themselves by helping them find God within—through experience—but would also spread magnetism and blessings to all beings."

Attention: A Final Word

Whether the focus of our spiritual practice is prayer, meditation, listening to inner guidance, or some combination of the three, all of us fall prey to the same mistake—trying too hard. The following Zen story, "Try Softer," offers sage advice on achieving that delicate balance between letting go and disciplining ourselves:

A young boy traveled across Japan to the school of a famous martial artist. When he arrived at the dojo he was given an audience by the sensei.

"What do you wish from me?" the master asked.

"I wish to be your student and become the finest karateka in the land," the boy replied. "How long must I study?"

"Ten years at least," the master answered.

"Ten years is a long time," said the boy. "What if I studied twice as hard as all your other students?"

"Twenty years," replied the master.

"Twenty years! What if I practice day and night with all my effort?"

"Thirty years," was the master's reply.

"How is it that each time I say I will work harder, you tell me that it will take longer?" the boy asked.

"The answer is clear. When one eye is fixed upon your destination, there is only one eye left with which to find the way."

Recommended Reading

Zen Mind, Beginner's Mind, Suzuki-roshi (Weatherhill, 1970). A beginningless and endless book to be kept at the bedside of both beginners and old hands. The all-time classic.

Meditation in Action, Chogyam Trungpa (Shambhala, 1969). The first and most direct book by a contemporary Tibetan meditation master. This is meditation "concerned with seeing what *is*." Nothing mystical or hidden here.

How To Meditate, Lawrence LeShan (Little, Brown, 1974). The best of the survey guides on meditation. LeShan is experienced, practical, to-the-point, and not easily fooled. A good introduction.

Classics of Christian Contemplation

The Little Flowers of St. Francis, translated by Raphael Brown (Doubleday, 1958). Legends and sayings of the saint who sang the praises of "Brother Sun, Sister Moon, and Our Lady Poverty," and talked to men, animals, and God in the same voice.

Meister Eckhart, translated by Raymond Blakeney (Harper & Row, 1941). Meister Eckhart, a mystic's mystic, lived in the Rhineland during the thirteenth and fourteenth centuries. He wields paradox like a Zen master. Perhaps his most famous utterance, "the eye with which I see God is the same eye with which God sees me," has sometimes been used as a subject for meditation.

The Wisdom of the Desert, translated by Thomas Merton (New Directions, 1960). Sayings and stories of the hermits and monks who lived in the Egyptian desert during the fourth century, A.D. "If we were to seek their like in twentieth-century America," says Merton, "we would have to look in strange, out-of-the-way places."

Resources

Journey of Awakening, A Meditator's Guidebook, Ram Dass (Bantam, 1978). More practical advice from the author of *Be Here Now.* An excellent directory of meditation groups and retreat centers makes up almost half the book.

The New Consciousness Sourcebook, Spiritual Community Publications, Box 1067, Berkeley, CA 94701, (415)644-3229. A guide to meditation and spiritual groups in North America.

15

Perils of the Path

Some years ago there was a Japanese Zen master who decided to modernize one of the old koans so that his students could more easily relate their spiritual practice to contemporary life. The old koan went something like this: "How can you stop a galloping horse while sitting still?" In place of the galloping horse, the roshi used the image of the Tokyo Express, so that the koan now went: "How can you stop the Tokyo Express while sitting still?"

Koans sometimes drive people to very intense grapplings with the paradoxical nature of reality, and one of the master's students in particular found himself engaged in a life-and-death struggle with the Tokyo Express koan. No matter how hard he tried, or didn't try (for he tried that, too), the master would simply ring his little bell and dismiss the student.

Finally, at the end of his rope, the student left the monastery early one morning, made his way to the tracks that carried the speeding commuter trains to Tokyo every morning, and sat down on the tracks, legs crossed in the proper full-lotus position, lowered his eyes just so, and began to sit *zazen*—right in the path of the 7:05.

He never knew what hit him, and if he did get the answer to the koan, he never got the chance to tell anybody.

In Japan, where people have some experience with such things, there was no scandal, though some people shook their heads. He had acted correctly by throwing

"O you followers of Truth! If you wish to obtain an orthodox understanding of Zen, do not be deceived by others. Inwardly or outwardly, if you encounter any obstacles kill them right away. If you encounter the Buddha, kill him; if you encounter the Patriarch, kill him; . . . kill them all without hesitation, for this is the only way to deliverance. Do not get yourselves entangled with any object, but stand above, pass on, and be free!"

Lin-chi

himself one-hundred percent into his koan. But he had made one mistake, and a fatal one at that: he had taken the teacher's words literally, and in doing so he had missed the point.

The spiritual path is perilous and slippery with paradox. Having to make a distinction between following instructions and taking those same instructions too literally is just one of the many distinctions that we must make on the path. And, given the influx of new religious practices and groups, it is not so surprising that many people have become sitting ducks for self-styled teachers, charlatans, quick-change-your-life-in-one-weekend artists, and hosts of other con men and women.

There are also the ever-present dangers of spiritual materialism, spiritual pride, and becoming blissed- or spaced-out. Every level, every step on the path seems to have its corresponding stumbling block. It is no wonder that the Upanishads, one of the oldest sacred texts in the world, describes the spiritual journey as walking on the razor's edge.

Merely finding a competent teacher or relevant tradition out of the many that seem to be available is, itself, a challenge. How can we choose wisely among all the possibilities? And having chosen, how can we balance surrender and trust in a teacher with an open mind and healthy skepticism? What about the frightening tales of authoritarianism and spiritual fascism from former cult members? What relation, if any, do such things have to do with the notion of true spiritual obedience as expressed, say, by St. Benedict in his monastic rule?

There are no easy answers to any of these questions, and the final authority—since any spiritual path must be freely chosen—is one's own best judgment. But there are certain guidelines—some from great masters and others from psychologists and other outside observers—that can help you hone your intelligence and keep your balance. For, while there are many reasons to take care, there is no reason to turn back, even if that were possible. The pitfalls and perils, the stumbling blocks and obstacles, are an essential part of the journey. Indeed, *how* we respond to their challenge is the way we make the journey our own.

"Beware of false prophets, which come to you in sheep's clothing, but inwardly they are ravening wolves."

MATTHEW 7:15

Spiritual Materialism and the Eight Great Perils

Spiritual materialism is probably the most basic and pervasive peril of the spiritual path. It is a term coined—as far as we can discover—by Tibetan meditation master Chogyam Trungpa, in his classic, *Cutting Through Spiritual Materialism.*

"The problem," Trungpa says, "is that ego can convert anything to its own use, even spirituality. Ego is constantly attempting to acquire and apply the teachings of spirituality for its own benefit. . . . It is important to see that the main point of any spiritual practice is to step out of the bureaucracy of ego. This means stepping out of ego's constant desire for a higher, more spiritual, more transcendental version of knowledge, religion, virtue, judgment, comfort, or whatever it is that the particular ego is seeking."

Thomas Merton agrees, writing in *New Seeds of Contemplation:*

"Sometimes contemplatives think that the whole end and essence of their lives is to be found in recollection and interior peace and the sense of the presence of God. They become attached to these things. But recollection is just as much a creature as an automobile. The sense of interior peace is no less created than a bottle of wine. The experimental 'awareness' of the presence of God is just as truly a created thing as a glass of beer. The only difference is that recollection and interior peace and the sense of the presence of God are spiritual pleasures and the others are material. Attachment to spiritual things is, therefore, just as much an attachment as inordinate love of anything else."

Attachment to "enlightenment" isn't the only pitfall of the spiritual path. There are many others which travelers have noted over the years. Here are eight of the most common ones:

The Stink of Zen. This expression refers to the odor of people who make a big deal of *their* having undergone particularly powerful, ego-shattering spiritual experiences—with the emphasis definitely on the fact that such a thing has happened to them.

Being in a Hurry. The spiritual journey is a lifelong journey at the very least. North Americans in particular

"Nevertheless the flowers fall with our attachment
And the weeds spring up with our aversion."

DOGEN

"Monks and scholars should accept my word not out of respect, but upon analyzing it as a goldsmith analyzes gold, through cutting, melting, scraping and rubbing it."

BUDDHA

expect, even demand, instant results. This may work for breakfast foods, but it is not the way the spiritual path works. "Patience" is an important quality in every spiritual tradition.

Guru-Chasing in the Spiritual Supermarket. The spiritual supermarket is well-stocked these days. At the beginning of the search it is necessary to sample a bit to know what's out there, but this can all too easily become "spiritual window-shopping"—a substitute for getting down to the real living of a spiritual life. A teacher can show you the way, be an example, but a teacher cannot do it for you. Window-shopping is nice, but at some point it is necessary to sit down and eat.

Getting High. There are lots of different states of mind that we may experience during spiritual practices. Some of them feel very good, indeed. High or "blissed-out" states may come about through prolonged meditation, fasting, diet, the use of drugs, or sleep deprivation. While these practices can be instructive under certain conditions, they can also become a distraction; they are not the aim of spiritual practice—merely a stage along the way.

Everything is Maya. Or illusion. True, perhaps, on one level (the absolute) and not so true on another (the relative), where most of us live most of the time. A variant of this is thinking that spirituality exempts you from the laws of the phenomenal world. It doesn't. No matter how deep your understanding or how wide your love and compassion, you still have to pay the bills, stop at red lights, take out the garbage, and do the dishes. As Ram Dass once put it, you have to remember your zip code even in the throes of intergalactic bliss.

Everything is Karma. Or destiny or fate. This belief is the source of the infamous "spiritual passivity" syndrome. In fact, the word *karma* is simply the sanskrit word for "action,"—and the teaching of karma refers to nothing more mysterious than the law of action and reaction, otherwise known as cause and effect. What you do today results, to some extent, in what happens tomorrow. Therefore pay attention to your actions in the present. Don't blame or focus on the past.

Putting too great a stock in miracles. The Buddha, it is said, met a yogi who bragged that he could walk across a stream, on top of the water, and that therefore his spiritual powers were greater than the Buddha's. The yogi demonstrated, and he could, in fact, walk on water. He told the Buddha that it had taken him twenty-five years or so of hard spiritual training to obtain this power. The Buddha scratched his head and asked why he had bothered, since for a mere five rupees the yogi could have taken the ferry.

Getting sidetracked by the Occult. "Occult" means hidden. This is the realm of secret teachings, magic, visitations from beyond. At their best, the occult teachings are what's left of an esoteric tradition (or science) that was mostly destroyed by the Church. (Check out Manly Palmer's *Secret Teachings of the Ages* for an overview.) At its worst it degenerates into "black magic"; magic that is for power. Paying more attention to signs and portents, rather than to the here-and-now, is a symptom that you have lost your way in this admittedly fascinating realm.

Favorite Buddhist Hindrances

Contributed by Jack Kornfield

DESIRE:
"When I have to choose between two evils, I always try to pick the one I haven't tried yet."

—Mae West

ANGER:
"You mean could one be 'just angry,' with nothing extra—like a thunderstorm that comes and goes? Gosh, I wish I could do that!"

—Zen Master Suzuki Roshi

PRIDE:
"If one is to do good one must do it in the minute particulars. General good is the plea of the hypocrite, the flatterer and the scoundrel.

—William Blake

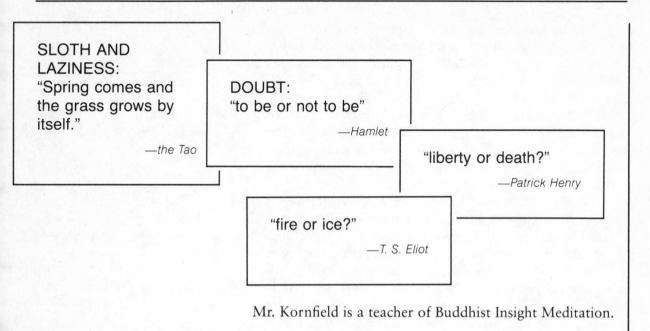

SLOTH AND
LAZINESS:
"Spring comes and
the grass grows by
itself."

—the Tao

DOUBT:
"to be or not to be"

—Hamlet

"liberty or death?"

—Patrick Henry

"fire or ice?"

—T. S. Eliot

Mr. Kornfield is a teacher of Buddhist Insight Meditation.

The Little Known Perils of Meditation

Prolonged or very intensive meditation practice can have a powerful effect when certain techniques, such as special breathing exercises, are used. At this level of meditation, the energy that may be awakened can seem anything but relaxing. People may find themselves having involuntary bodily movements, such as shaking, trembling, violent twitching, and muscular spasms. Painful headaches and visual aberrations are other possible effects. According to some writers, these effects may be due to the awakening of a powerful force called "kundalini," which is said to lie, coiled like a serpent, at the base of the spine. According to Gopi Krishna, author of *Kundalini: The Evolutionary Energy in Man,* kundalini "is the real cause of all genuine spiritual and psychic phenomena, the biological basis of evolution and development of personality, the secret origin of all esoteric and occult doctrines. . . ."

Be that as it may, the awakening of kundalini—or any powerful psychic energy during meditation—can result in serious physical and psychological difficulties.

*"It is not for us to question why, on certain
mornings, the master is silent."*

In his book *Kundalini: Psychosis or Transcendence?*
psychiatrist Lee Sanella gives us the following dramatic
analogy:

> Tissues are torn, blood vessels severed, blood spilled, much
> fluid is lost; the heart races and the blood pressure soars.
> There is moaning, crying and screaming. A severe injury?
> No, only a relatively normal human birth. The description
> sounds pathological because the symptoms were not under-
> stood in relation to the outcome: a new human being.

In a darkened room a man sits alone. His body is swept by muscular spasms. Indescribable sensations and sharp pains run from his feet up his legs and over his back and neck. His skull feels as if it will burst. Inside his head he hears roaring sounds and high-pitched whistling. Then suddenly a sunburst floods his inner being. His hands burn. He feels his body tearing within. Then he laughs and is overcome with bliss.

A psychotic episode? No, this is a psycho-physiological transformation, a rebirth process as natural as physical birth. It seems pathological only because the symptoms are not understood in relation to the outcome: an enlightened human being.

When allowed to progress to completion, this process culminates in deep psychological balance, strength, and maturity. Its initial stages, however, often share the violence, helplessness, and imbalance that attend the start of human infancy.

The awakening of kundalini is just one of the spiritual emergencies that people have reported. Others stem from experiences of unusual or heightened states of consciousness—the despair of *The Dark Night of the Soul*, described by St. John of the Cross, the ecstasy of visionary experiences, the fear felt during the "melting" of individual boundaries. Even the most positive experience, if it is sudden and unprepared for, can leave people frightened and disoriented.

Many people experiencing difficulty with meditation seek help from traditional medical facilities and doctors. But since these psychiatrists and physicians usually have no familiarity with meditation or kundalini, they almost inevitably misdiagnose and/or mistreat these symptoms, often doing more harm than good. In the past few years, many health practitioners with spiritual orientations have recognized the need to educate both the medical profession and the public about the existence of genuine spiritual emergencies.

A list of qualified doctors and helpers for "the increasing number of people who are having unusual experiences and are seeking understanding assistance and support" can be obtained from the Center for Spiritual Emergencies at Esalen Institute in Big Sur, California.

"As people seek in various ways to know and to grow, some naively think that higher consciousness can result from forcefully practicing certain disciplines in mechanical fashion. This sort of sophisticated 'power trip' is warned against by spiritual masters in the kundalini tradition. *Don't* meditate to awaken kundalini, they say, because you will probably harm yourself. Forcing it prematurely is possible, but extremely dangerous. Rather, seek to grow in love and understanding. Seek to refine your character and cultivate your mind through selfless service, discriminating studies, and dedicated spiritual training. Do that, and kundalini will awaken gently, automatically, and without the unhealthy effects that are being seen more and more frequently. *Desiring* something—even such a noble goal as the awakening of kundalini—is misguided."

JOHN WHITE

Kundalini First-Aid

In *Stalking the Wild Pendulum*, scientist-mystic Itzak Bentov, who has developed the first psychophysiological model for understanding this process, calls kundalini "the ultimate stress-releasing mechanism." According to Bentov:

> Helping the person to understand and accept what is happening to him or to her may be the best that we can do. Usually the process, left to itself, will find its own natural pace and balance. But if it has already become too rapid and violent, our experience suggests it may be advisable to take steps such as heavier diet, suspension of meditations, and vigorous physical activity, to moderate its course.

The Main Danger Is Spiritual Passivity

Kabir was a fifteenth-century Sufi and Hindu master and poet. In *The Kabir Book,* Robert Bly has given us astonishingly vivid English versions of Kabir's ecstatic poems. Bly writes in his introduction: "To Kabir, the main danger is spiritual passivity. Kabir is opposed to repeating any truth from another teacher, whether of English literature or Buddhism, that you yourself have not experienced."

Here are some words from Kabir:

> Suppose you scrub your ethical skin until it shines,
> but inside there is no music,
> then what?
>
> ....
>
> Mohammed's son pores over words, and points of this
> and that,
> but if his chest is not soaked dark with love,
> then what?
>
> ....
>
> The Yogi comes along in his famous orange.
> But if inside he is colorless, then what?
>
> ....
>
> Kabir will tell you the truth: go wherever you like,
>   to Calcutta or Tibet;
> if you can't find where your soul is hidden,
> for you the world will never be real!

The Best Advice: Following the Middle Way

Bentov's advice of moderation is echoed by all of the great traditions. In Buddhism, the path itself is called the Middle Way. The Buddha cautioned against falling into the trap of extreme behavior or views. The follower of the Middle Way does not go to extremes of asceticism or indulgence, in terms of behavior; or to externalism or nihilism, in terms of view.

Walking the Middle Way does not necessarily mean doing everything in "moderation," however, at least if we think of moderation as a lukewarm state of mind. The path demands intensity and even passion at times. The person on the Middle Way is not swayed by or attached to opinions, biases, or even a particular point of view. Far from being a path of compromise, the Middle Way is uncompromising in its commitment to the logic of the spiritual journey.

On the Peril of Having and Not Having a Teacher

There is a Tibetan proverb which puts the case rather neatly: A guru is like a fire. If you get too close, you get burned. If you stay too far away, you don't get enough heat. A sensible moderation is recommended.

In our society the idea of a spiritual teacher, instructor, guru, preceptor, is conspicuous by its absence. We think of teachers as imparting the contents of some subject as if we are empty vessels to be filled. A spiritual teacher on the other hand works on a very different level. A spiritual teacher may act as a mirror or guide, preventing you from falling into the trap of self-delusion and enabling you to see yourself as you really are.

In *New Seeds of Contemplation*, Thomas Merton speaks of the importance of having a teacher:

> The most dangerous man in the world is the contemplative who is guided by nobody. He trusts his own visions. He obeys the attractions of an interior voice, but will not listen to other men. He identifies the will of God with anything that makes him feel, within his own heart, a big, warm, sweet interior glow. The sweeter and the warmer the feeling, the more he is convinced of his own infallibility. And if the sheer force of his own self-confidence communicates

itself to other people and gives them the impression that he is really a saint, such a man can wreck a whole city or a religious order or even a nation. The world is covered with scars that have been left in its flesh by visionaries like these.

Michael Murphy agrees with the importance of having a teacher, but in a *New Age* interview he tries to cast some light on why the authority of teachers gets blown out of proportion in our culture:

> We do need teachers, and there is such a thing as true authority—a person who really knows something. But the trouble is what they used to call in psychology "the halo-effect": a person's authority is overextended, and you get people going to, say, Einstein for political opinions—or to a guru for an opinion on every matter.
>
> Independent judgment is a fairly rare quality among human beings. Part of being alive and growing and the whole art of living is to refine that independent judgment—to learn a kind of courage to stand up for one's inner voice and to be able to say when the emperor has no clothes.

Ram Dass agrees. We are bound to make mistakes in choosing teachers, but dealing with those choices is a learning in itself. In *Journey of Awakening, a Meditator's Guidebook* he has this to say:

> Some people fear becoming involved with a teacher. They fear the possible impurities in the teacher, fear being exploited, used, or entrapped. In truth, we are only ever entrapped by our own desires and clingings. If you want only liberation, then all teachers will be useful vehicles for you. They cannot hurt you at all. If, on the other hand, you want power, a teacher may come along who talks about liberation but subtly attracts you by your desire for power. If you get caught and become a disciple of such a teacher, you may feel angry when this teacher turns out to be on a power trip, not leading you to enlightenment. But remember: at some level inside yourself, you already knew. Your attraction to this teacher was your desire for power. Your anger is nothing more than your anger toward yourself.

"The problem with introducing Oriental spirituality into America today is that the cultural barrier which the light from the East must pass through functions as a thick prism. The prism consists of American consumer culture and psychological individualism. Robbed by the prism of its color and sharpness, the now-refracted Oriental light serves as one more support for the structure its original teachers had most hoped it would undermine: the isolated, Western competitive ego."

HARVEY COX

The idea of true spiritual authority—and the proper relationship to it on the part of the student—brings us to the question of "obedience" on the spiritual path. The very idea of "obedience," spiritual or otherwise, is suspect, or at least controversial in America, but it is an important aspect of spiritual training in many spiritual traditions. True obedience, as Thomas Merton tells us in the following quotation, is much more than merely a matter of following orders or giving up one's will—rather it implies taking full responsibility for the conduct of our lives.

No one can become a saint or a contemplative merely by abandoning himself unintelligently to an oversimplified concept of obedience. Both in the subject and in the one commanding him, obedience presupposes a large element of prudence and prudence means responsibility. Obedience is not the abdication of freedom but its *prudent use* under certain well-defined conditions. This does nothing to make obedience easier and it is by no means an escape from subjection to authority. On the contrary, obedience of this

kind implies a mature mind able to make difficult decisions and to correctly understand difficult commands, carrying them out fully with a fidelity that can be, at times, genuinely heroic. Such obedience is impossible without deep resources of mature spiritual love.

The great teachers often sum up the issue the most succinctly. The Buddha offers this advice on belief:

> Do not believe in anything simply because you have heard it. Do not believe in traditions because they have been handed down for many generations. Do not believe in anything because it is spoken and rumored by many. Do not believe in anything simply because it is found written in your religious books. Do not believe in anything merely on the authority of your teachers and elders. But after observation and analysis, when you find that anything agrees with reason, and is conducive to the good and benefit of one and all, then accept it and live up to it.

On Cults and Organizations

Dealing with a spiritual teacher is often challenging enough, but dealing with the organization that may surround that teacher or set of teachings can be even more confusing and challenging. During the seventies, the popularity of groups with tightly structured, highly "authoritarian" organizations, gave rise to what some sociologists called "The Great American Cult Scare." Most of us wouldn't want to be associated with some of the more controversial, "authoritarian" religious groups whose followers appear to be mere "followers," but Harvey Cox, a noted theologian at the Harvard Divinity School, cautions us against being too harsh in our critique.

In the introduction to *Strange Gods, The Great American Cult Scare* he writes: "The basic issue is still that of religious freedom. As bizarre as some of the new religious movements may seem to us (and some of them appear bizarre indeed), it is hard for people to see that oddness or distastefulness has nothing to do with a religious movement's claim to religious freedom. It is precisely *un*popular movements that most need due process of law, the supposition of innocence until proven otherwise, and the protection guaranteed by the Constitution."

Still, we shouldn't confuse the principle of freedom of religion with a lack of discernment on the part of the individual seeker. If anything, the protections afforded by the First Amendment require that we must sharpen our criteria for involvement with a spiritual group. There is no Better Business Bureau of Spirituality (Jim Jones's People's Temple was affiliated with the very respectable National Council of Churches)—and the peril is further complicated by the way in which taste, needs and levels of understanding differ from person to person.

In *The Observing Self,* an eminently reasonable book about psychotherapy and mysticism, Dr. Arthur Deikman writes:

> It is important to recognize that cults and religious organizations of various kinds do perform important functions for their members. They satisfy members' needs for acceptance and protection, and often provide members with a disciplined, healthy routine of balanced living, good diet, and exercise. By also providing security, firm direction, and a controlled community life, they can have a psychotherapeutic effect, reducing anxiety and teaching more adaptive behavior. The group's dogma can provide a framework of meaning and hope absent in the lives of many of its members prior to joining. At the least, such groups provide distraction, entertainment, and social opportunities. The worst offer group and parental security at the price of destructive regression.

There are, however, certain criteria we can use as guidelines while investigating the wares in the "spiritual supermarket." Daniel Goleman, human behavior editor of the *New York Times* and the author of *Varieties of Meditative Experience,* suggests we should "be wary" of:

> *Taboo Topics:* questions that can't be asked, doubts that can't be shared, misgivings that can't be voiced. For example, "Where does all the money go?" or "Does Yogi sleep with his secretary?"
>
> *Secrets:* the suppression of information, usually tightly guarded by an inner circle. For example, the answers "Swiss bank accounts," or "Yes, he does—and that's why she had an abortion."

"I say beware of all enterprises that require new clothes, and not rather a new wearer of clothes. If there is not a new man, how can the new clothes be made to fit? If you have a new enterprise before you, try it in your old clothes."

HENRY DAVID THOREAU

Spiritual Clones: in its minor form, stereotypic behavior, such as people who walk, talk, smoke, eat and dress just like their leader; in its more sinister form, psychological stereotyping, such as an entire group of people who manifest only a narrow range of feeling in any and all situations: always happy, or pious, or reduce everything to a single explanation, or sardonic, etc.

Groupthink: a party line that over-rides how people actually feel. Typically the cognitive glue that binds the group; e.g., "You're fallen, and Christ is the answer" or "You're lost in *samsara,* and Buddha is the answer" or "You're impure, and Shiva is the answer."

The Elect: a shared delusion of grandeur that there is no Way but this one. The corollary: you're lost if you leave the group.

No Graduates: members are never weaned from the group. Often accompanies the corollary above.

Assembly Lines: everyone is treated identically, no matter what their differences; e.g., mantras assigned by dictates of a demographical checklist.

Loyalty Tests: members are asked to prove loyalty to the group by doing something that violates their personal ethics; for example, set up an organization that has a hidden agenda of recruiting others into the group, but publicly represents itself as a public service outfit.

Duplicity: the group's public face misrepresents its true nature, as in the example just given.

Unifocal Understanding: a single world-view is used to explain anything and everything; alternate explanations are verboten. For example, if you have diarrhea it's "Guru's Grace." If it stops, it's also Guru's Grace. And if you get constipated, it's still Guru's Grace.

Humorlessness: no irreverence allowed. Laughing at sacred cows is good for your health. Take, for example, Gurdjieff's one-liner, "If you want to lose your faith, make friends with a priest."

A Final Story

As God and Satan were walking down the street one day, the Lord bent down and picked something up. He gazed at it glowing radiantly in His hand. Satan, curious, asked, "What's that?" "This," answered the Lord, "is Truth." "Here," replied Satan as he reached for it, "let me have that—I'll organize it for you."

Blinding Yourself to the Negative

Josh Baran uses the expression "the shadow" to refer to those unconscious parts of ourselves—and of groups—that we would rather not see. "People are afraid to own their shadows, their confusion," he says, "and the same is true of groups. In 99 percent of groups the teacher is treated as infallible. In reality, teachers may be very clear and wise in some areas and very unconscious in others. But the game is set up so that either the path is perfect or it's worthless.

"Often a teacher's mistakes or personality quirks are interpreted as deliberate teaching methods." Baran encourages people to trust their own unfiltered perception. "I tell them to consider the possibility that things are just what they seem. If the teacher is drunk, for example, he's simply drunk. If he's violent, he's just violent.

"Students don't want to throw away all the good," he cautions, "so they try to blind themselves to anything negative."

And a Final Word of Caution

People who have just been introduced to the spiritual path, and people who have had some kind of big experience of the "emptiness" or illusory nature of this world, are most prone to this one last peril. No matter what "truth" you have seen—or think you have seen—it is always important to remember that on the relative level, which is where we all live most of the time, the law of cause and effect (karma) is always operative. No one is freed from the simple teachings of ethical responsibility.

In *Taking the Path of Zen* Robert Aitken makes this point very clearly:

> I have heard some people say that since Zen says we must be grounded in the place where there is no right and wrong, it follows that Zen has no ethical application. But if there were no application of our experience of the unity and the

"I see the best and approve it, then I follow the worst."

OVID

individuality of all beings, then Zen would be only a stale exercise in seclusion, the way of death. Yamada Roshi says, "the purpose of Zen is the perfection of character." It is a way to realize self-nature—and its application lies in the practice of harmony in the everyday world. At the training center, all conditions of the world are present. If you can cope there socially, you are doing very well.

I am reminded of the story about "Bird's Nest Roshi." He was a teacher who lived in the T'ang period and did *zazen* in a tree. The governor of his province, Po Chu-i, heard about Bird's Nest Roshi and went to see him. This Po Chu-i was no ordinary politician. He was one of China's greatest poets, well-known for his expression of Zen Buddhism.

Po Chu-i found Bird's Nest Roshi sitting in his trees, doing *zazen*. He called to him, saying, "Oh, Bird's Nest, you look very insecure up there. Tell me, what is it that all the Buddhas taught?" Bird's Nest Roshi replied by quoting from the *Dhammapada:*

"Qui veut faire l'ange fait la bete. (Whoever tries to act like an angel makes a beast of himself.)"

PASCAL

Always do good;
Never do evil;
Keep your mind pure—
Thus all the buddhas taught.

So Po Chu-i said, "Always do good; never do evil; keep your mind pure—I knew that when I was three years old."

"Yes," said Bird's Nest Roshi, "a three-year-old child may know it, but even an eighty-year-old man cannot put it into practice."

Recommended Reading

Five Books to Read Before You Leap

Turning East, The Promise and Peril of the New Orientalism, by Harvey Cox (Simon and Schuster, 1977). Harvey Cox, professor at Harvard Divinity School, investigates the new orientalism in his front yard, which he calls Benares-on-the-Charles.

Krishnamurti, The Years of Awakening, by Mary Lutyens (Farrar, Straus, Giroux, 1975). A finely etched biography by a woman who knew Krishnaji as a child (her mother was his close friend). The true story of what happened when a spiritually gifted young boy is picked by Theosophists Ledbetter and Besant to become the next World Teacher, and of the spiritual crisis that led him to denounce his title and dissolve the Order that had grown up around him. Must reading for all would-be Avatars.

Let My Children Go, by Ted Patrick and Tom Dulack (Ballentine, 1970). Ted Patrick is the crusading Big Daddy of Deprogramming. "They're all crooks," he says. "You name 'em. I've taken 'em all on." Along the way he did his best to destroy the First Amendment—to say nothing of individual rights. A good case of the cure being worse than the disease.

The New Religions, by Jacob Needleman (Doubleday, 1970). One of the first—and still one of the best—books on the subject. Needleman is the man behind the Center for the Study of New Religious Movements, and combines scholarship and sympathy in an exemplary way.

The Romance of American Communism, by Vivian Gornick (Basic Books, 1978). Josh Baran of *Sorting It Out* recommends this as the best book on the subject of belonging, heart and soul, to a group.

Resources

The Spiritual Emergence Network

The Spiritual Emergence Network is an attempt to build a network of qualified doctors and helpers for "the increasing number of people who are having unusual experiences and are seeking understanding, assistance and support."

Write: Spiritual Emergence Network, 250 Oak Grove Ave., Menlo Park, CA 94025, or call 415/327-2776.

Afterword

If I Had My Life to Live Over Again

You don't, or won't—but since you're still living this life, there's no better closing advice for this book than the following poem written by an 81-year-old woman in Louisville, Kentucky. It has been fairly widely reprinted, and it demonstrates that the voice of experience is innocent, after all:

If I Had My Life to Live Over

I'd like to make more mistakes next time. I'd relax, I would limber up. I would be sillier than I have been this trip. I would take fewer things seriously. I would take more chances. I would climb more mountains and swim more rivers. I would eat more ice cream and less beans. I would perhaps have more actual troubles, but I'd have fewer imaginary ones.

You see, I'm one of those people who live sensibly and sanely hour after hour, day after day. Oh, I've had my moments, and if I had it to do over again, I'd have more of them. In fact, I'd try to have nothing else. Just moments, one after another, instead of living so many years ahead of each day. I've been one of those persons who never goes anywhere without a thermometer, a hot water bottle, a raincoat, and a parachute. If I had to do it again, I would travel lighter than I have.

If I had my life to live over, I would start barefoot earlier in the spring and stay that way later in the fall. I would go to more dances. I would ride more merry-go-rounds. I would pick more daisies.

NADINE STAIR